the exploratorium

Smithsonian Institution Press   Washington and London

the exploratorium

The Museum as Laboratory

Hilde Hein

Foreword by Philip Morrison

Editor: Lorraine L. Atherton
Production Editor: Duke Johns
Designer: Alan Carter

"The Sun Artist," by Muriel Rukeyser, reprinted on p. 156 by permission of International Creative Management, Inc. Copyright © 1976 by Muriel Rukeyser.

"A Rationale for a Science Museum," by Frank Oppenheimer, reprinted on p. 217 with permission from *Curator* 11/3. Copyright © The American Museum of Natural History, 1968.

Library of Congress Cataloging-in-Publication Data

Hein, Hilde S., 1932–
The exploratorium : the museum as laboratory / Hilde Hein.
p.   cm.
Includes bibliographical references.
ISBN 0–87474–466–0 (alk. paper).—
ISBN 0–87474–369–9 (pbk. alk. paper)
 1. Exploratorium (Organization)   2. Museums—California—San Francisco.
I. Title.
Q105.U52S264   1990
507.4'794'6—dc20   89–600348

British Library Cataloguing-in-Publication Data is available
Manufactured in the United States of America
97 96 95 94 93 92 91 90   5 4 3 2 1

♾ The paper used in this publication meets the minimum requirements of the American National Standard for Permanence of Paper for Printed Library Materials Z39.48–1984

Contents

Foreword

A strange, dim, and lofty arc draws the visitor in, to wander from one exhibit to the next, hundreds of them set within the acres of floor spanned by this celestial attic. When it first began to grow, it was already a delight; today the Exploratorium has grown to what must be the most original museum of science in the world. For me, it is also the most brilliant. Of course that judgment is subjective, the opinion of one physicist. The museum is itself openly subjective, for it is styled "a museum of science, art, and perception."

Curiously enough, a great many scientists who have visited the place share my pleasure in it. The fact argues for a community of opinion; the subjectivity of one scientist is widely shared. What is even more exciting is that a million visitors, as various in their interests as visitors to a beach, largely agree. The researcher, the teenager, and the little family group alike enjoy what they perceive here. The crux is perception; here learning is direct, experiential. Indeed, no one can convince you by words alone that the random-dot pattern displays a three-dimensional form. You must see it—or perhaps miss it—for yourself. It is that feeling of shared experience that dominates the subjectivity of the research worker and the serious student of science, and here it is offered over and over again to everyone who will try.

There is not much of a collection of famous artifacts here, not many models of imposing works, nor mementos of the great. Most of what is here was made right in the building, drawing on the richness of a contemporary world city. The collection rests on a set of ideas, ideas that have been made concrete by artist and artisan, with eye, hand, and tool animated by and interacting with purpose and concept. The machine shop is wide open, right by the door. Every visitor can see there both the necessities and the freedom to employ them.

The working of wood, metal, glass, even light and air, is what produces the artful systems on display. The spectrum is as real as the mirrors, and the vortex as tangible as the steel beams. There is even a dance of symbols on the computer screen where simple rules of manipulation play out their complex consequences. The place of the artist here is secure, too. For art and science deal alike in minute particulars, with the thing itself, the phenomenon behind the function unfailingly in place. These artists in residence have worked in the same shops using the same tools as the experiment designers, but they have bent the phenomena to present something beautiful of their own. The unity of art and science is achieved through perception, an experience necessarily mediated by the senses and sensibilities of the onlooker, who is an essential participant in the work.

This important book, the first fully reflective account of the Exploratorium and its history, gives the reader an inner view of the origins, operations, and implications of the Exploratorium, at a time when novel institutions for informal education are rising in social importance. Professor Hein is well prepared for the task; she is a philosopher of science who was a sympathetic and curious dweller among the people who made the place during the years of its swiftest growth.

There are challenges still unmet. If art and science are manifest in the concrete, through direct participation by the visitor, how can abstractions, the concepts of science that go beyond mere perception, be conveyed? The issue is given sharp expression in the fact that the electronics shop, a place of major importance in this milieu, is not open to the visitor. Indeed, there is not much to be seen there, as Hein's analysis makes clear. Consider how much more the uninitiated but interested observer can learn from opening the case of a ticking clock than by staring at the chips of a digital timepiece. That is parallel to the distinction between watching a machinist and a circuit-builder at work. The challenge is evident.

The electrical exhibits make the point again. Here perception is itself gained only through instruments. Sensing has become a process that is once removed. The Exploratorium, like most scientists, needs to work by inference and analogy. But are not our eyes and ears themselves but inborn instruments? Their proper use and interpretation, like that of a microammeter, had once to be learned by test and retest, sometimes reasoned, more often only implicit. If that view is at all correct, there will one day open a broad public way into energy and charge and gene frequency and exponential change through elaborated experience, beginning with but going beyond what we call common sense. The Exploratorium is well on the road. The journey will not be a short one.

The hope behind this display of friendly marvels is the unity of human beings. a unity that lies below all their differences, that rests in their common ability to share in reason and delight. That egalitarian hope is not new in science. Perhaps it rises in all times of transition, as it appeared in the days of the tireless traveler Alexander von Humboldt, who took his thermometer and his search for unity to the cold current off Peru. He was a democrat in the service of kings, a man between two eras; he journeyed romantically afar, but he always took along with his instruments the critical spirit of the Enlightenment.

There is at work here a fundamental but playful healing. Its subtle prescriptions are not covert but wide open, open as the book that follows.

Frank and Jackie Oppenheimer founded the museum almost twenty years ago. Jackie died years back; now Frank Oppenheimer has followed. I cannot avoid a personal note to close this foreword, for that couple were close friends of mine for fifty years. I write not simply in memorial but in deep appreciation.

Within the appealing and ingenious work of that small, shifting community of people who gathered around them, the Oppenheimers clearly offered a lead in ideas, insights, and enthusiasms, held as part of a set of values. Theirs were values passionately held, unstingingly expressed in deed, and wholeheartedly articulated. Hilde Hein, herself an old friend, has sought to bring those values eloquently into view. The center of the vision was "that human understanding will cease to be an instrument of power . . . for the benefit of a few, and will instead become a source of empowerment and pleasure to all."

Ours, too, is a time of transition. Everyday firsthand experience seems less varied, commonplace, while images far from commonplace are in profusion. Science and technology are steadily pressed to the service of wealth and power as never before. The unceasing rise of abstract concepts that are all the same filled with practical power bids to partition modern society into the few who are knowing and the many who watch change without insight.

We thirst for remedies, and the Oppenheimers found one way. It is to bring into public life—as open to all, in Frank's own customary comparison, as an ocean beach—the tense and subtle unities between play and purpose, between science and art, between hand and mind. It was that effort that formed the Exploratorium, and that informs it still, even now that the originators are only a vivid memory.

The strengths of the place are those that thrive amid human diversity, and so they transcend the personal. They shine there now, and they will shine there for a long time across the wide and busy floor, as on a bright day you might see the dazzling beam and grand rainbow of the "Sun Painting" itself.

Philip Morrison

Acknowledgments

This book has been ten years in the making, and a great many people have, wittingly or unwittingly, been a part of it. Next to Frank Oppenheimer himself, whose complex presence has been a goad and a guide throughout, the person who has been most sustaining is Norman Mainwaring. Without his help and unwavering faith, I doubt that I would have stuck with the task. Others on the Exploratorium board, on the staff, and in various capacities related to the museum gave me their time and their insight. I am also grateful to the many people who answered my questions over the telephone and in person, and especially to those inside and outside the museum who read parts of the manuscript and gave me their reactions. They include Aaron Bernstein, Charles Carlson, Dorothy DeCoster, Eleanor Duckworth, Nancy Garrity, Harvey Gold, Sheila Grinell, Evelyn Fox-Keller, Tom Tompkins, and Howard and Roslyn Zinn.

Portions of the chapter on the vision section and of the "Mutual Enrichment of Art and Science" chapter have been presented at museum symposia and professional meetings, and I am grateful to the audiences and commentators whose interest helped me to shape and sharpen my ideas. A condensed version of the vision section discussion appeared as an article in the *Mu-*

seum Studies Journal, Spring 1987. Special thanks are due, too, to Esther Kutnick of the Exploratorium graphics staff. Her intelligent and sympathetic help in the selection and production of pictures to illustrate the book was invaluable.

My thanks also go to Ann Pax, who acted as an editor and touchstone, representing the reaction of people I wanted to reach; Barbara Letourneau, typist and friend; and several unknown reviewers and one whose identity became known. And to my constant friends in the Bay area, who put me up and put up with me on my frequent visits, who listened to my sagas and included me sporadically in their lives, my heartfelt thanks.

Over the years that I have been working on the manuscript I have had grant support through the Exploratorium from the National Endowment for the Humanities, the Alfred P. Sloan Foundation, and the Philip Stern Foundation, as well as individual assistance from the American Philosophical Society, the American Council of Learned Societies, and generous grants from the College of the Holy Cross. I am grateful for their help.

Introduction

On January 29, 1986, just days short of the first anniversary of Frank Oppenheimer's death, a show called "Seeing the Light" opened at the IBM Gallery of Science and Art in New York City. The show, commissioned by IBM, consisted of more than eighty replicas of some of the most popular exhibits on light, color, and human perception produced at the Exploratorium, the museum of science and art that Oppenheimer founded in San Francisco in 1969. The New York show was a triumph for Oppenheimer in the city where he was born and spent his childhood, and he would have loved to see the New Yorkers thronging to enjoy such phenomena as the bending of light, reflections, shadows, and the spectacular color displays caused by gas discharges. The show was the fruition of Oppenheimer's dream and of his long struggle to create a first-class science museum.

The Exploratorium has become a model for museums and science centers throughout the world. This book tells the story of the Exploratorium from its beginning and of the ideas that it embodies. It is in part a historical account of the campaign that Oppenheimer and a few associates waged to win support and recognition for a new type of museum that bewildered as many people as it delighted. Now widely regarded as among the world's greatest museums of science, it has altered the standing of museums as educational institutions and has radically affected the teaching of science. Although well-endowed institutions such as the Lawrence Hall of Science in Berkeley and the Ontario Science Centre in Toronto were being built concurrently,[1] Oppenheimer had no public funds and had to convince people privately that the Exploratorium was an idea whose time had come. The story of how that was done reveals his deep commitment and that of others who worked with him. It also shows the elasticity of a cultural and bureaucratic system that resists innovation and yet is capable of absorbing it.

Since Frank Oppenheimer was the prime mover of the Exploratorium and its director until his death, my account of the museum concentrates on his opinions and activities. Oppenheimer remained the final authority at the Exploratorium, running it, according to some, as a benevolent despot. A charismatic personality, he was able to gather about himself an assortment of scientists, artists, students, businessmen, labor leaders, politicians, and counterculturists, all of whom identified something they believed in within his aspiration and made some contribution to its realization.

By now even art museums have adopted the principle of interactivity, which is the heart of the Exploratorium's exhibit philosophy, and Oppenheimer is regarded as a pioneer of the participatory museum movement. In the sixties, however, although he had established credibility among scientists and in educational circles, his ideas for a museum still seemed revolutionary. The Exploratorium had a radically new component, a message of empowerment, which is now embedded in the exhibits at the museum, both in their conception and in their execution. Visitors can enjoy the exhibits and even learn from them without stopping to reflect on them philosophically, but in this book I mean to call attention to those philosophical implications and the features of the museum that express its commitment to self-liberation.

The political consequences of that doctrine of self-liberation have not been fully realized. One can only imagine what they might be, for the museum that Oppenheimer tried to create is more fundamentally democratic and has more faith in the capacity of humans for self-realization than cultural institutions ordinarily do. A measure of his success, however, can be taken from the new class of users who have been brought into museums and who now approach the institutions confidently and with entirely new expectations.

Museums usually house static displays to be admired from a respectful distance. Even natural history collections, the primary content of science museums, tend to require only a passive and reverential appreciation of the odd and various specimens someone has painstakingly assembled. Such exhibits can instill wonder at the rich diversity of the universe, but they tend also to encourage awe for the brilliance of those few scholars who have been able to unravel its complexity. Science museums often glorify scientists more than they teach museumgoers the practice of science. Visitors are invited to admire the accomplishments of others, but not to think that they might go and do likewise.

The proposal that Oppenheimer brought to wealthy San Francisco society was for a museum in which people would directly experience and manipulate things, instead of being told about them. The public was to interact with objects as an experimental scientist does in the natural world or in a laboratory. The museum was to teach that the subject matter of science is all around us and that its comprehension is accessible to all. It was to remove science from the exclusive domain of the experts, to demystify it, and to restore it to the common sphere. It was to convince people that doing science can be interesting and fun for everyone.

At first glance, the atmosphere of the museum seems to reinforce the myth of science as magic. As visitors leave the bright California sunlight to enter the darkness of the Exploratorium, they are overwhelmed by the spectacle of flashing lights and weird sounds. Some people are intimidated at first, but most soon recover their bearings and feel at ease with the exhibits, often becoming absorbed in a single one and oblivious to the surrounding pandemonium.

The exhibits are the museum's principal educational device. They have been carefully designed and tested to attract and hold the attention of visitors so that people will want to figure them out and make them work. The philosophy that imbues the exhibits is clearly expressed in a statement by Oppenheimer: "The whole point of the Exploratorium is to make it possible for people to believe they can understand the world around them. I think a lot of people have given up trying to comprehend things, and when they give up with the physical world, they give up with the social and political world as well. If we give up trying to understand things, I think we'll all be sunk." Perhaps we are sunk. People do seem overwhelmed by the complexity of the world and content to leave the decision-making to the experts, even if the experts are not always reliable. Some people have given up on rationality altogether and cast their lot with mysticism or escapist substances. Those are reactions of despair, and the Exploratorium offers a more optimistic alternative. It begins with the conviction that the universe is intelligible to ordinary human beings and that they can have an effect on it. I will show how that philosophy shaped every feature of the museum, how it influenced the selection of its content, and what indirect effects it has had on other museums and supportive agencies.

In addition to affirming the human capacity to understand the natural world, the museum recognizes that human curiosity and a playful sense of inquiry are virtues, not to be stifled or mistrusted but to be cultivated as spiritually liberating. The Exploratorium pronounces the free play of imagination the root of science and technology, and the museum is unambiguous in its celebration of human fabrication. That position has not gone unchallenged, even by the museum's devotees. On occasion, staff members have called on the museum to denounce some of the aggressive and exploitative uses of technology. At a time when technology threatens to destroy all life on earth, its uninhibited endorsement may seem contradictory. Nevertheless, under Oppenheimer's direction the Exploratorium maintained its positive view of technology, while acknowledging possible subversion and disaster, and neither condemned human invention as such nor denounced technology as driven by an inherent logic of destruction. It considered technology and the products of art and science natural expressions of human capacities continuous with matter and life. The things that humans make are themselves natural phenomena and, like other phenomena, can be studied and used. They can be used well or badly, and like other forms of expression, they can be defective or pathological, and their consequences may be injurious. They remain no less human for that. Oppenheimer's view prevailed, as it often did at the Exploratorium, and human production, as a form of human behavior, was represented as a significant part of the whole of nature.

Human productions include science and works of art, and their integration is another theme that is central to the Exploratorium's exhibit philosophy. Again deviating from conventional museum practice, Oppenheimer rejected the dualism of the two cultures and stoutly affirmed that art and science are united in the human quest for understanding. Our experience of the natural world is mediated through both the expressions of art and the findings of science. Neither has a monopoly on truth or a fix on reality, but both are sources of insight that help shape our concept of reality. On Oppenheimer's insistence works by artists are distributed throughout the museum among exhibits from experimental science, and both types of exhibit are offered as revelatory probes of the natural world. Audiences quickly accepted that conjunction, and artists and scientists benefited from their association. It took a good deal longer for the agencies that normally fund either art or science to cast their lot together. The Exploratorium's eventual success in making such collaboration possible worked to the advantage of other institutions and launched the careers of several young artists.

The thesis that science has an aesthetic dimension and art a cognitive one is implicit in the experiential concentration and perceptual focus of the museum. Oppenheimer stated it explicitly in a document that he circulated in the beginning to potential supporters. It is most convincingly expressed in the exhibit style of the museum, which strives to engage people through their senses in the study of their perceptual processes and reactions. The participatory, or hands-on, exhibit experience has since then become routine among museums, thanks in large part to the Exploratorium's influence.

In the Exploratorium, if visitors are willing to play, they are drawn into dialogue with the exhibits, and one exhibit leads to the next with an expressible logic. No account of the Exploratorium could be complete without emphasizing the educational process, and I will stress the manner in which it is manifested in all of the museum's undertakings. Oppenheimer maintained that education was the museum's fundamental mission, although museums were not then recognized as serious teaching institutions for the general public. Thanks to the perseverance of the museum's supporters, museums are no longer confined to being repositories for scholarly research on the one hand and centers for tourist entertainment on the other. Their emphasis is much less on collecting rare and unusual objects than on fostering an appreciation for the things that form our common world. The Exploratorium has shown a way to make perceptible what is normally unperceived and to make ordinary experience a topic of educational interest. It has also helped to shape the manner in which education is disseminated. It has the potential to do even more, for its interactive pedagogic technique contains a key to empowerment that could transform education on a broad scale and make it an avenue of general self-determination.

The self-initiated and mutual education that the museum promotes is eminently suited to a museum environment, but it is not impossible elsewhere. In refining an ideal of nonhierarchical teaching and learning, in which visitors help themselves and each other to learn, the Exploratorium has become a promising model for democratic educational institutions in general. The interactive techniques of the Exploratorium and its principles are adaptable to classrooms and learning situations at every pedagogic level. As the demand for education swells beyond conventional age limits and institutions, there may be more to learn from the programs devised by such unconventional sources as the Exploratorium. I will discuss the ways in which some of them emerged in response to specific contextual needs.

Museums have advantages and disadvantages relative to more traditional teaching institutions. Museums attract occasional and heterogeneous audiences that are often motivated by widely differing interests, and so they address their visitors by means of immediate, self-contained experiences. Because museums often rely on material resources and direct sensory appeal to evoke an experience, they can speak to audiences with limited and diverse verbal capacities. On the other hand, the experiential emphasis restricts the effect the museum can have to those who are able to undergo it physically. The effort of recruitment and outreach is therefore more necessary to a museum's public program than it is to schools.

Where direct personal interaction with exhibits is a necessity, as it is at the Exploratorium, there are inherent limits on the numbers of people that can be reached. When crowds get too large visitors interfere with each other and problems of space and exhibit maintenance become unmanageable. The ambition to teach must therefore be balanced against physical constraints. Furthermore, however ingeniously exhibits are constructed, they require conceptual and often mathematical supplementation to be explanatory. Museums cannot be substitutes for research laboratories and libraries, but they can initiate interest in the work that is done there. Ideally they may serve as an introduction that will propel the museum visitor to study and investigation. Obviously, the resources for further study should also be made available.

In the course of its history the Exploratorium developed its own verbal and visual materials to enhance its teaching program. They were disseminated through schools and workshops in and outside the museum. As the museum became more widely known, it produced additional resources for the benefit of other museums and institutions that wished to emulate its programs. I will discuss the Exploratorium's effort to satisfy the growing demand for indirect outreach without sacrificing its experiential orientation. Although this book is not a product of the museum, it is an example of the second-order discourse that the museum called into being.

I am writing about the Exploratorium because I believe in the philosophical and political ideas that it embodies. As a teacher and philosopher and a feminist committed to political emancipation, I am hopeful that the museum experience can open new roads to understanding. The Exploratorium, in its imaginative approach to science education, serves as a case study and a model. My aim is to learn lessons from the story of the Exploratorium that might be applied to other situations. I do not offer a blueprint for designers of other institutions, although I hope that some of what I have to say may be helpful to other people with projects of their own. I hope that by concentrating on a single case study, I can suggest how certain ideals might be propagated within existing social conditions in ways that are innovative but not beyond the pale. Since so many of our institutions, and especially the educational ones, appear to be falling short even of their stated goals, the search for feasible alternatives seems particularly urgent. The Exploratorium is a validated alternative. Beginning with no support and with little credibility, it bent the system to make room for it and quickly spawned a generation of emulators. Perhaps my account will inspire someone to be similarly imaginative.

I venture to set down my own conception of what the Exploratorium is in keeping with the spirit of empowerment that the museum fosters. I have concentrated on the things that are to be found in the museum, especially the physical exhibits, and have read them as the text that reveals its exploratory mission. I have also looked at the museum shops where the exhibits are created, and reflected on how the work is done. I describe programs and publications as they articulate the museum's mission and as they are expressed in museum practice and policy. My presentation of the Exploratorium story is therefore less a chronicle of events than a declaration of a thesis. I have extracted that thesis from Oppenheimer's written and spoken words, as well as those of other museum staff members, but above all from my own experience and observations of the Exploratorium. I have spent many hours on the museum floor, playing with exhibits and watching visitors interact with them, and over the course of a year, I took part in almost all phases of museum life. I have enriched those experiences through comparative study of other museums, through other reading, and through conversation with many people who were associated with the Exploratorium in a variety of ways. I have come to know the Exploratorium staff as friends and collaborators, and many of them have helped me in my work.

My involvement with the Exploratorium goes back to its origins. Long before founding the museum, Oppenheimer talked to me about his idea of a museum devoted to perception. The notion took shape in his mind gradually. Once expressed, it seemed to me so entirely natural that I marveled that no one had done it before. Although I am not a practicing scientist, or an explorer or gadgeteer, as he was, I was invariably attracted by Frank Oppenheimer's view of science, and especially by his concern to teach fundamental ideas. Partaking of his enthusiasm and sometimes seeing with his eyes has made the world a richer place for me. I have learned to see and appreciate more and have come to believe, as he did, that the ability to see and appreciate is dormant in everyone and can be reawakened. I also share his hope that by making the effort to do so we might help the world to survive with sanity.

Many versions of the Exploratorium story might be written. Mine reflects my philosophical preoccupations. It recounts some of the early opposition that the Oppenheimers and their friends met with in trying to establish the museum. Many more personal anecdotes might be told, for the museum was a carnival of colorful figures. But I have given ideas priority over people and described trends rather than specific controversies in the belief that they are more likely to be of lasting interest and use. Because I was repeatedly asked by outsiders how the Exploratorium was supported, I decided to write a chapter on funding. Researching it turned out to be illuminating; it helped me clarify just how dynamic the interaction is between funding agencies and their beneficiaries. Far from being a passive supplicant, the museum educated the agencies and helped to shape their future guidelines. Surely that is an important lesson.

Another surprise had to do with the growth of the museum as an institution. The most interesting developments occurred early in the museum's history. Later refinements followed the predictable bureaucratic pattern of large institutions, becoming increasingly fragmented and specialized and therefore preoccupied with problems of management, communication, and organization. Some members of the staff, especially the veterans of early struggles, have expressed concern about the worldly success of the museum, finding in it evidence of compromised integrity. I think their alarm is exaggerated but not unfounded. There is a risk that Oppenheimer's simple message, so clearly expressed in the makeshift exhibits with which the museum began, will be obscured in the external elegance that the museum can now afford.

The IBM show provides an illustration: The exhibits that it includes are beautifully crafted, the product of years of experimentation and observation of public use of exhibits on the museum floor. Veteran members of the San Francisco staff who came to oversee the New York installation were bemused by its glamour as much as by the delight with which sophisticated New Yorkers responded to it. Would the visitors have reacted as well to the rickety-looking San Francisco exhibits, to their lack of uniformity, to the disorderly environment with its noise and confusion? Could the spirit of the Exploratorium survive among carpeted floors, designer-approved furnishings, and audiences disciplined to wait in line and respectfully follow instructions? The exhibits that went to New York were engineered for permanence and conveyed a sense of present perfection that its San Francisco ancestor had expressly avoided. Are those superficial differences, or did the original Exploratorium have a special, irretrievable transience? Did the New York show reflect the abandonment of its inquisitive spontaneity, or was it a triumphant celebration of the museum's coming of age?

In my view the past and future success of the Exploratorium depend on its fallibility and incompleteness. Exhibits are never finished, because someone may always come along with a better idea, or there may be a more interesting way of saying the same thing. New people bring new questions as well as new answers. One lesson that can be learned from the Exploratorium is that change, uncertainty, and even disorder are not intolerable. Instead of giving up in despair, we can try to understand what is happening, relying on the best possible means available to us while knowing that they are imperfect and that we may be mistaken. To me that seems preferable to pursuing certainty at the price of self-destruction.

At a time when the meaning of rationality is in doubt, the Exploratorium continues to endorse a rather old-fashioned, commonsensical view of reason. A human faculty that is both a source of pleasure and a means to understanding, it is not reducible to the mechanics of problem solving, nor should it be accorded inflated value as the ultimate power base or the only desirable human faculty. Oppenheimer did not underestimate the importance of irrational factors in human life, but he believed that on the whole, reason is a force for good and can be used to better our lives.

Finally, the glimpse of science that the Exploratorium gives us may affect our perceptions of and attitudes toward that discipline. When the museum was founded there was less mistrust and more hope in the future of science than there is today. Since then, despite great progress in such fields as computer science and molecular biology, the concern has grown not only that science is an instrument of power that can be misused but also that the will to domination is inherent in the foundations of science. Some feminists, environmentalists, and social critics have made that argument, while others are primarily interested in the political control of science. The Exploratorium proposes that science is a means to empowerment, that it enables people to choose and act for themselves rather than subjecting them to the authority of others. At least the museum offers an opportunity on a small scale for people to begin to figure things out.

Chapter 1

Roots and Soil of the Exploratorium

At the foot of the Golden Gate Bridge stands the San Francisco Palace of Fine Arts. A relic of a by-gone era, it is the improbable site of the Exploratorium, a world-famous museum of science and art. Tourists drawn by the dreamy lagoon with its swans and fountains, the sweeping colonnade, and the majestic rotunda, are stunned, once inside the building, to find themselves in a darkened space full of flashing lights and buzzing sounds. As their eyes and ears adjust, they begin to discern a panorama of apparatus, much of it surrounded by men, women, and children at play. Since its founding in 1969 the Exploratorium has introduced millions of people to the pleasure of science, and its style has transformed museums throughout the world.

The museum fulfilled the personal vision of Frank and Jackie Oppenheimer and was founded by them without public support. Frank, a physicist and the brother of J. Robert Oppenheimer, director of the first U.S. atomic bomb project, believed that science is a fundamentally humanistic discipline, beneficial to humankind. Like most of the American scientists of his age, Frank had been swept up by the political events of World War II and diverted from scientific research to its practical application. Neither the world nor the practice of science was ever to be

the same again, but Frank Oppenheimer retained his love of the subject and wanted to share his understanding of science with his fellow
human beings. He conceived the museum as a means of introducing
others to the delight of discovering nature. The Oppenheimers
wanted to dispel the myths that had been fostered about the nature
of science and the fears that people harbored of its evil and magical
power. They hoped to restore the sense of wonder and love of the
natural universe that had given birth to science in the first place, and
they wanted to renew people's optimism and confidence in their capacity to understand the world. The Oppenheimers were dismayed
at the despair that seemed to follow from the widespread belief that
the universe is an obscure and inaccessible mystery, impenetrable to
all but a gifted few. They deplored the apparent willingness of people to abdicate their own judgment and to place blind faith in occult
powers and oppressive authority. Acknowledging certain misuses of
science and the horrors that followed from them, the Oppenheimers
nevertheless continued to believe in reason and science as forces for
human liberation, and they felt compelled to spread that message.

The Exploratorium was not the first science museum, even in the
United States,[1] but it did break with the tradition of such museums,
which tend to represent science as a set of accomplishments that have
already been achieved. The new museum was to affirm the continuity of the past with the present and thereby empower people to
choose their own future. It was not to be a warehouse where ideas
are stored but a factory, like nature, a source of raw materials for
the production of ideas. A better model of the planned museum was
a teaching laboratory. The Oppenheimers meant to create an environment where people could become familiar with the details and
the procedures of science and technology by exploring the apparatus
used in their pursuit. In such an atmosphere people might overcome
their estrangement from science and begin to see its unfamiliar
equipment simply as devices that allow us to go beyond the limits
of our unaided senses. Revealing the laboratory as an object of observation as well as an instrument of inquiry might help to reintegrate
the scientific results found there with the observations and discoveries that people make in their daily lives. The Oppenheimers
were inspired by what they had learned from other museums, but
they hoped to improve upon them with new ideas and methods of
teaching.

Museums have always reflected the ideals and intentions of their
originators, but they have typically changed to conform to the

changing values of their society. The first museums were private family or state storehouses where spoils of war and accumulations of wealth were housed and displayed. Those collections represented the power of their owners and were preserved and passed on as symbols of that glory. They came to be prized as a collective cultural heritage, although only a privileged few could aspire to possess such treasures. But in the late seventeenth century museums began to receive public support and to become educational institutions instead of merely repositories of beautiful and curious objects.[2] Conservation and private research continued to be important museum functions, but as museums admitted more of the public, collections were arranged to benefit larger audiences with the new social needs and interests engendered by urbanization, industrialization, and the emergence of political states. Where private collections had mirrored the taste and wealth of their patrons and benefactors, publicly supported museums were designed to instill new values in their audiences. The public museums helped spread the fruits of learning, opening new domains for human understanding and conquest. The rise of science in the seventeenth century was closely related to the new museum movement, for the museums enabled scholars to examine and compare the objects that had been assembled as a result of their investigations. Scholars were excited not only by their new knowledge but also by their new-found faith in the perfectibility of man. The discovery of the laws of nature, together with their application in technology, represented the high point of human achievement and the hope of human progress. The triumph of human knowledge displaced military conquest as the mark of man's superiority over nature, and the discoveries of science became the treasures that were celebrated in public expositions. Often collected at universities and centers of scientific research, natural history specimens and artifacts and technical inventions from all over the world were housed in cities throughout western Europe.[3] Built to entertain as well as to edify, museums were temples to human achievement, erected to glorify human genius and intelligence.

In nineteenth-century Europe, especially in Britain and Germany, museums began to play a part in advancing the industrial revolution. Manufacturers wanted workmen to receive practical technical training so they could make industrial products. Formal academic education continued to be available exclusively to the wealthy few, but museums could complement academic teaching with programs designed to teach skills to the many. No longer confined to glorifying past achievements, museums now offered concrete vocational preparation. They taught manual arts, design, and draftsmanship—all skills demanded by a growing industrial society. They featured popular lectures and interpretive programs that illuminated their collections for the public. With the changing political climate, museums also acquired a more democratic image as centers of useful education rather than storehouses of useless treasures.

American museums have always emphasized public education, using their collections as the basis of experiential learning. They provided educational and cultural programs for local communities, often collaborating with public schools. Some illustrated the techniques of local industry, and others taught their application, as well as the principles of pure science and research. Many universities established museums as adjuncts, along with laboratories and libraries. Eventually American museums assumed preeminence in educational programming. The most celebrated teaching museums, however, have been not in America but in Europe.[4]

Of the European museums, three particularly impressed Frank and Jackie Oppenheimer. The Palais de la Découverte, in the Grand Palais of Paris, was built with public funds for the International Exposition of 1837. It was attached to the University of Paris and governed and supported by the French Ministry of Education. Designed for the use of students, it did not feature collections. (They were maintained elsewhere by the Conservatoire National des Arts et Métiers in what is now the Musée National des Techniques.) The exhibits in the Palais de la Découverte used models to demonstrate concepts in the fields of physics, chemistry, biology, medicine, mathematics, and astronomy. The emphasis on models that teach rather than collections that illustrate or exemplify drew the Oppenheimers' interest, as did the employment of students to display the exhibits and show the public how they operate. The high school explainer program, which became one of the Exploratorium's most important commitments, was directly inspired by the Oppenheimers' visit to the Palais de la Découverte.

The second important influence, the South Kensington Museum of Science and Art, was also the offshoot of an international exhibition, the popular Crystal Palace. Like the French museum, it had government support and an educational purpose. Enthusiastically endorsed by Queen Victoria and Prince Albert, the 1851 exhibition was to compare industrial progress among nations, glorifying that of Great Britain in particular. The assets of that highly successful exhibition and the collections assembled for it became the basis of the museum that opened on the same site in 1857. Still the most frequented museum in Britain, the South Kensington Museum remains one of the great educational centers of science and technology. The Oppenheimers visited it frequently during a fellowship year in London in 1965.

Perhaps the most famous of the European science museums is the Deutsches Museum in Munich. Unlike the French and British institutions, it was founded by a single individual, Oskar von Miller, a Bavarian engineer. He was well supported, however, by the Bavarian and German national governments and encouraged by private industrialists, scientists, engineers, and scientific organizations. In 1911 the city of Munich donated an island in the River Isar as a site for the museum and financed its construction with help from the Bavarian state and the German Empire. Material, labor, and transportation costs were all donated, but since World War I delayed construction, the museum was not completed until 1925.

The museum was, above all, a glorification of outstanding German and world scientists, but it also pioneered the modern movement to demonstrate scientific laws and show their application to technology and industry. Among its historical exhibits it displayed original experimental equipment and replicas and scale models of inventions and discoveries. Period settings included an alchemist's laboratory and a reconstruction of Galileo's study, as well as dioramas of industrial environments, but the focus was on scientific ideas rather than the coincidence of their discovery. Techniques for displaying modern technology emphasized the application of scientific principles rather than their historic importance. Museumgoers could activate some of the exhibits and even the scale models with pushbuttons and cranks. The exhibit techniques of the Deutsches Museum have influenced other museums throughout the world, and the interactive approach in particular made a lasting impression on the Oppenheimers.

By the middle of the twentieth century, quite a few major American cities—Chicago, Boston, Philadelphia, Portland, and Seattle—had science museums, some with private and some with public support, and each to varying degrees applauded the achievements of modern science and industry.[5] New York, where Frank Oppenheimer was raised, had a Museum of Science and Industry in the basement of the RCA building from 1936 to 1949. Even earlier there had been a small science museum on Fifth Avenue and Twenty-fifth

Street that Oppenheimer remembered visiting as a boy.[6] Although many of today's scientists and engineers recall those museums fondly and evidently learned a good deal in them, they were, for the most part, not primarily teaching institutions—at least they were not perceived as such at the time. Science was taught in certified schools and universities, and museums at best contained research collections of interest to specialists or were merely popularizers of science.

That was the prevailing situation when Frank and Jackie Oppenheimer returned to the United States from Europe in 1965. Stimulated by what they had found there, they began agitating for a science museum in America that would rival the best of the European museums and would have additional features all its own. They envisioned a museum that would not glorify science and scientists or praise the fruits of science but instead would testify to the excitement of the activity of science and teach people to take part in it. Unlike many teaching institutions, this museum was to display natural phenomena and real effects rather than simulated models. It was to reveal nature as observed by artists as well as by scientists, even that nature thought to be inaccessible, and it was to help people discover nature for themselves, trusting their own perceptual and interpretive capacities. The museum would facilitate experiential learning. Expensive laboratory equipment would be available to the general public. With the help of such instruments, the world of the infinitely large, the microscopically small, and the inconceivably remote can be drawn into the domain of possible experience. Ordinarily, only scientists experience those dimensions, but that is because only they have the means to do so, not because others lack the capacity. The new museum was to provide the means for people to discover hidden phenomena for themselves and to delight in their discovery, much as one takes pleasure in identifying a planet in the sky or in finding a wildflower on a walk in the woods. Oppenheimer frequently drew on the image of a walk in the woods to describe the museum. It was to be a place where people could come, alone or in groups, to find out about the natural world and to share their discoveries with their companions. But what we see in the woods is limited by our senses, aided perhaps by a hand lens. In the museum, special instruments extend the realm of human observation to reveal a world that is normally concealed from us.

Even more important, the museum was to refamiliarize people with those features of everyday phenomena that most of us have ceased to notice. The exhibits that Oppenheimer had in mind isolated and simplified events so that the visitor could concentrate on the ripple of waves in a pool or the pull of a car swerving around a corner and know them in a new way. Putting such ephemera on regular display in a museum would not be easy, but neither is the design of a scientific experiment. Both enterprises are, like a poem, meant to seize a fleeting moment of reality and fix it indelibly in human consciousness.

The whole of Oppenheimer's early life had been an apprenticeship to the self-appointed task of teaching science. Frank was born in 1912 in New York City to a German-Jewish family in comfortable circumstances. His father was a gentle and cultivated businessman and his mother a painter. His brother, Robert, eight years his senior, was a guide and mentor to Frank, and because Frank was so much younger, he was indulged almost as an only child. Of the ideals that Oppenheimer absorbed in his childhood, many were later realized in the innovative character of the Exploratorium. Among them was the prominence given to the aesthetic. Frank grew up with the arts, creating, loving, and collecting things that are beautiful. His parents gave Frank the sense that art, like science, is a way of perceiving the world and finding order in it, and they encouraged him to create and perform, as well as to merely enjoy the various art forms.

One exhibit idea that grew out of Oppenheimer's experience of the process of art was to reveal how an artist achieves a personal style. The objective was to show a concrete sequence of decisions made by an artist. Stylistic evolution cannot be discerned from only a single work, and so the Oppenheimers hoped to show how style develops by having artists work in the museum, using it as a studio. As they found, however, the subtle transformations in an artist's work come to be recognized as style shifts only comparatively and retrospectively. Like the cumulative process of scientific growth, artistic developments are individually imperceptible. Furthermore, most artists do not change their style as rapidly or as dramatically as, for instance, Picasso did, and so the exhibit project was soon abandoned.

Frank and his brother were very close. As young men, they sometimes vacationed in the Sangre de Cristo Mountains of New Mexico, a part of the country that Robert had come to know and love on a trip with a teacher. In 1928 the two brothers picked out a parcel of land with a cabin on it in the Pecos Valley, and their father leased it for them. They called it Perro Caliente (Spanish for "Hot Dog").

The beauty and isolation of those mountains was to have a powerful influence on both their lives. For many years, Frank and Robert returned to the Pecos Valley with colleagues and students, sharing with them the grandeur, repose, and fellowship of the mountains. But in the end, the remoteness that had made the valley a haven of peace and solitude recommended it to Robert as the site for the assemblage of a diabolical instrument of war. Robert's choice made nearby Los Alamos notorious throughout the world as the testing ground of the atomic bomb.

Both Oppenheimer brothers became interested in science at an early age. They went to the private schools run by the Ethical Culture Society in New York, and after traveling for a year, Robert attended Harvard College, winning his A.B. degree (officially as a chemist) in 1925. He went on to England and Germany to do graduate research, sending wonderfully informative letters home to friends and colleagues, including some to Frank, full of brotherly counsel and provocative information about life, art, and the latest discoveries of science.[7] Frank, in the meantime, had set up a small science library in his high school in memory of a teacher he had admired. He also paid occasional visits to the science museum on Fifth Avenue, and even then was beginning to think about how to make science interesting to the public. The news that Robert sent home about physics was thrilling. Spectacular advances were being made in the young area of quantum mechanics, especially in Europe, and Robert Oppenheimer was one of the principal agents who transmitted the new ideas to America. The letters from his years as a student, graduate student, and postdoctoral researcher fairly sparkle with the excitement of constant discovery. Perhaps that was why Frank chose not to heed Robert's advice to take up the study of biology. Instead, he followed his older brother's footsteps into physics.[8]

Frank became captivated by physics at Johns Hopkins University and, in his senior year there, concentrated on the problems of theoretical physics that were dear to Robert. Graduating in 1933 with a B.S. degree, he also followed his brother's path to the University of Cambridge, England, to begin graduate study. He worked at the Cavendish, the famous laboratory of Sir Ernest Rutherford, on atomic spectroscopy, and he spent a year and a half there developing techniques for measuring the spectra and intensity of radiation emitted from naturally occurring radioactive nuclei. In England, he accepted an invitation to spend an additional semester in Italy to work on nuclear particle counters in the physics department at the University of Florence. In 1935 he finally returned to the United States to pursue a doctoral degree.

Robert Oppenheimer, in the meantime, had been appointed to a joint teaching position at the University of California in Berkeley and the California Institute of Technology in Pasadena, and so each spring and summer he and a group of his graduate students would migrate back and forth between the two locations. On returning to the United States, Frank decided to join his brother's circle at Cal Tech. He began his doctoral research on artificially induced radioactivity under the direction of Professor Charles Lauritsen and quickly became a member of the international community of physicists who circulated among the various academic and research centers of the world. Though widely dispersed, the scientists maintained close and frequent communication, and news of their flourishing research was most effectively imparted through informal, personal exchanges that also cemented lifelong friendships. Those connections would sustain both Oppenheimers through the troubled years ahead; they were also the chief moral and scientific resource that Frank drew on when he founded the Exploratorium.

As a graduate student, Frank met and subsequently married Jacquenette Quann, then a student of economics at Berkeley. Jackie came of French Canadian working-class origins. She was scrappy and tough and had strong opinions and an acerbic sense of humor. As Frank was later to describe it, her influence was nowhere more evident than in the straightforward and unpretentious style that marked the Exploratorium.

As political activists, Frank and Jackie Oppenheimer were alarmed by the social and economic events of the mid-thirties. The Depression had brought about nationwide unemployment, miserable conditions for local migrant workers, and a struggling union movement. Fascism was rising in Europe, its triumph tragically heralded by Franco's defeat of the Loyalists in the Spanish Civil War. Like many of their idealistic young friends, Frank and Jackie studied Marxist solutions to the world's problems and looked hopefully to the new Communist experiment in the Soviet Union. In 1937 they joined the Communist Party and worked in it to organize teachers' unions in California and to aid the Loyalists in Spain. They left the party in 1940, having become disenchanted with the rigidity of its political bureaucracy and the unresponsiveness of democratic centralism, but that short-lived affiliation was to haunt them in the postwar period and for the remainder of their lives.

After Frank completed his Ph.D. at Cal Tech, the Oppenheimers moved to Palo Alto, where Frank obtained a teaching and research position at Stanford and where their children, Judy and Michael, were born. But before they left Pasadena, the physics community was galvanized by the news that the German chemists Otto Hahn and Fritz Strassmann had demonstrated, in December 1938, that the nucleus of the uranium atom could be split by neutron bombardment. The announcement reached American scientists in January 1939, and those familiar with nuclear reactions at once saw that a powerful energy-releasing chain reaction would be produced by the bombardment. The military implication was inescapable, and many scientists, including the Oppenheimers, who had until then refused to take part in war-related research, now believed they had no other choice.

The story of the mobilization of the American scientific establishment is now well known. Almost the entire community of American physicists was drawn into the enterprise. Robert Oppenheimer was appointed director of the weapon assembly project at Los Alamos in the fall of 1942, and Frank Oppenheimer worked on several uranium isotope separation projects at the Berkeley Radiation Laboratory and at the Westinghouse Corporation. After spending a few months at Oak Ridge, Tennessee, where all the American production of fissionable uranium was concentrated, Frank was called to Los Alamos to work on testing the implosion device. On July 16, 1945, in a protected bunker, the Oppenheimer brothers lay side by side, watching as the world's first plutonium bomb was detonated, creating a flash that was "brighter than a thousand suns"[9] and destined to change the world.

Soon afterward, two atomic bombs were dropped on Japan, putting an end to the war. Their task completed, the scientists returned to what most of them considered the true business of science. Many went back to teaching or research. Frank Oppenheimer returned to California to join Luis Alvarez and Wolfgang Panofsky in developing the first proton linear accelerator. Then, rejecting several opportunities to do commercial research on the use of nuclear energy for aircraft propulsion, Oppenheimer accepted a tenure-track position at the University of Minnesota, where he could teach and do research on the nature and origin of cosmic rays. But his research, which pointed to interesting astronomical implications, was abruptly halted by a turn of political events that was to cut Oppenheimer off from the scientific world for the next ten years.

The American alliance with the Soviet Union came to an end with the onset of peace. The two nations faced each other in a state of cold war, and anyone with a history of sympathy toward communist causes was viewed as suspect in the United States. No sooner had the Oppenheimers arrived in Minneapolis than they were placed under federal surveillance. FBI agents watched them and questioned their neighbors about their habits and visitors. In 1947, a late-night caller warned Oppenheimer that he was about to be denounced as a Communist Party member in the *Minneapolis Times-Herald*. Oppenheimer angrily denied the newspaper's allegation and denied it again when university authorities demanded a statement. He did not then admit his earlier affiliation but continued teaching at Minnesota and researching cosmic rays. Two years later the Oppenheimers were summoned to testify before the House Un-American Activities Committee. There they admitted their own party membership but refused to discuss the activities of any other persons. As a result, Oppenheimer was immediately fired from his position at the University of Minnesota, although he had been approved for tenure. Because of his refusal to implicate others, he was blacklisted and continually harassed by FBI inquisitions. No academic research or teaching positions anywhere in the country were open to him. And so Frank and Jackie Oppenheimer and their children withdrew to a ranch that they had recently purchased in the Blanco Basin of southern Colorado. They had intended it as a summer retreat, but they spent the next ten years there as cattle ranchers.

In Colorado their time was occupied with learning the skills of ranching. They irrigated meadows, put up hay, built fences, fed and doctored cattle, and learned to work cooperatively with their neighbors. Oppenheimer served as chairman of the Archuleta County Soil Conservation Board and was elected to represent the Archuleta County Cattlemen's Association as a delegate to the U.S. Senate agriculture subcommittee hearings. The children went to the local one-room schoolhouse, and Oppenheimer taught a course on electricity to the local 4-H chapter. He also helped students prepare entries for state science fairs and ran for election to the regional school board. When the science teacher of the Pagosa Springs High School moved away, Oppenheimer was invited to take his place, and so he began teaching general science, biology, and chemistry, as well as his own field of physics.

The teaching style that Oppenheimer developed at Pagosa Springs High School laid the foundation of the experiential approach to science that later became the hallmark of the Exploratorium. He used the resources of the local environment to teach basic concepts of science. The class went on field trips and scavenging missions to such exotic places as the town dump, where they collected old automobile parts and used them to study principles of mechanics, heat, and electricity, as well as to repair cars. They also learned biology empirically by studying local species of plants and animals and nursing back to health the sick and injured creatures that students often brought into class. The Pagosa Springs experience excited Oppenheimer's interest in teaching science at different levels and exposed him to a new learning audience. In 1959 he accepted an invitation to run a summer training program for high school science teachers in Boulder, Colorado. By that time, he had begun to attract some attention as a science teacher, and the world outside had changed once again.

Americans had suddenly developed a passion for the study of science, sparked by the launching of the Russian satellite *Sputnik*. That Soviet space triumph provoked the American competitive spirit. Technological superiority was proclaimed the only security in the cold war and necessary to win the space race. It became patriotic to study science. The brightest students were steered into science and engineering, but their teachers were not always equipped to instruct them. The quality of precollege science teaching became a matter of public concern in the United States. Scientists were besought to do something about it, and some of them found the prospect challenging. During the war years and immediately afterward, university science teaching had become highly professional. Research scientists held themselves largely aloof from general science teaching, which was perceived by teachers and students as rigid and dull. But now Americans, from President Eisenhower on down, were demanding more access to scientific information, and the image of the scientist as hero began to gain popularity. A few scientists from major universities and some imaginative outsiders were enlisted in the effort to develop curricular materials for schools and to train elementary and high school teachers.

One of the first and most influential science teaching programs was designed by Oppenheimer's good friend at the Massachusetts Institute of Technology, Gerald Zacharias. Zacharias's Physical Science Study Curriculum (PSSC) and several alternative model programs brought scientists and educators together to reform science teaching in schools throughout the country. While the programs were being tested in the schools, teachers flocked to regional centers to learn how to implement the programs and to improve their own background in science. Most of them were ill-prepared and frightened. They looked to the experts to help them satisfy the new demand. Oppenheimer became one of the chief collaborators in the development of PSSC and its descendant, the Elementary Science Study (ESS), another Boston-area education program. For several years Oppenheimer experimented with the various curricular materials that were being promoted by science educators, and in the process he devised some physical models and exhibits that later became part of the Exploratorium. More important than the actual exhibits, perhaps, were the conclusions that members of the ESS community reached about science and about children from their observation of both. Their ideas on learning by direct interaction were to have a small but significant effect not only on the content of classroom teaching but also on the style and integration of its delivery, the training of teachers, and even the design of classroom space.[10]

ESS, along with several comparable educational organizations, carried out research while promoting its results through regional in-service teacher training programs that also provided classroom materials and follow-up aids. Oppenheimer taught some of those units in Colorado and continued to work with students and teachers of every age and educational level. Having reentered the academic world at its elementary level, he was convinced that the pedagogy that worked there was equally applicable at the adult and university level. When, in 1959, he was finally invited to join the physics department at the University of Colorado, in Boulder, Oppenheimer brought that conviction with him.

He found that the climate of academic physics had greatly altered during his exile. Previously, he had felt he was working in a community of fellow enthusiasts to advance the understanding of the physical world. Now it seemed harder to do research of basic significance, and there was less excitement. Students were no longer active participants in a process of inquiry but instead were "preparing" for a career in physics. They were bent on accumulating the information and skills necessary for success, but they lacked spontaneous enthusiasm for learning, and it was not easy to generate that kind of interest among them. Physics was no longer the frontier field of science. The sense of vocation that had animated Frank and Robert Oppenheimer's pursuit of physics was now a rarity and would hardly have been understood. Science had become a means to practical achievement. Only a few devotees still perceived it as a liberal art and an enterprise of consuming intellectual interest. Public recognition of the need for scientists had transformed the conception of what science was. Even in the eyes of many of its practitioners, science had become a lucrative profession and had ceased to be a form of humanistic learning. To the scientifically illiterate public, scientists were the masters of an arcane discipline to be regarded with awe, if also with some mistrust.

Furthermore, the forefront of science had shifted from nuclear physics to molecular biology and the neurosciences. James Watson and Francis Crick's discovery of the structure of DNA stimulated a new style of biological inquiry and a new generation of researchers, some of them drawn from the ranks of physics.[11] Scientists and a believing public were buoyed by the discovery of the secret of life and were confident that only the minutia of its analysis remained to be done. As a result, science as a whole became less speculative and more sharply segregated into domains of specialized expertise.

Frank Oppenheimer's priorities had also changed. Though still committed to science as a vocation, he was involved less in fundamental research and discovery than in the stimulation of inquiry through teaching. At Colorado he resumed his early work in ultraviolet spectroscopy and organized a group that studied bubble chamber pictures, but he continued to lead teacher workshops, trying hard to break the pattern of robotlike transmission of information by an instructor to passive receivers. His writings from that period include educationally oriented articles, some for popular publications, in which he defended the spiritual and intellectual features of science over its purely utilitarian consequences.[12] A grant from the National Science Foundation enabled Oppenheimer to design a new way of teaching the standard college introductory physics course. He constructed nearly a hundred classical experiments, embodied in physical models, to be coordinated with course assignments. His Library of Experiments was housed in the attic of a campus building, where students could browse among the models and use them to elucidate assignments. The library undoubtedly was the prototype of the Exploratorium. It attracted considerable attention among Oppenheimer's colleagues and was copied and embellished at universities throughout the country.[13]

By 1965 Oppenheimer was thinking about other unconventional ways of disseminating science. He received a Guggenheim Fellowship to study the history of certain aspects of twentieth-century physics and to do bubble chamber research at University College,

London. It was during that sojourn in Europe that the Oppenheimers visited the major science museums there. And on returning home, they decided that the United States needed museums of similar quality that could teach good science to the general population.

An outspoken critic of the neglect of popular science teaching in the United States, Frank Oppenheimer suggested that museums try to fill the gap. As a consequence, he was invited to participate in a conference on museums and education, jointly sponsored by the Smithsonian Institution and the Office of Education, in Burlington, Vermont, in the summer of 1966. Its organizer, Charles Blitzer of the Smithsonian, later said that Oppenheimer "stole the show" from the museum professionals. Fifteen years later, Oppenheimer too commented about the meeting: "The result of attending the conference and of writing the paper[14] [on the educational role of science museums] was that I had unintentionally committed myself to pursuing the field."[15]

Not long after the conference, Blitzer invited Oppenheimer to help plan a new Smithsonian project in Hot Springs, Arkansas. It was to be a Mid-America Center sponsored by Governor Winthrop Rockefeller and Senator William Fulbright. By that time, however, the museum idea had taken root in Oppenheimer's mind, and he was determined to start a science museum of his own.

The first decision was where to build such an institution. Frank was inclined toward New York, but Jackie preferred the West Coast. San Francisco was an attractive site. The Oppenheimers knew the Bay area well and had good friends there. The city offered an unusually receptive and tolerant environment. It had absorbed wave after wave of colorful immigrant groups, including the latest surge of hippies and drop-outs, whose exuberant style proclaimed the bold experimentalism for which San Francisco had become famous. The city exuded a youthful spirit, and although an established social hierarchy did exist and did control the cultural institutions such as museums, it was not wholly impenetrable.

The possibility of creating an adventurous new learning center there seemed worth investigating, and so, in the summer of 1967 the Oppenheimers came to San Francisco to reconnoiter. One of their first visits was to an old friend, the *San Francisco Chronicle* columnist Herb Caen, who responded to their proposed science museum with a skeptical "What's that?" Nonetheless, he printed a quip about the proposal that elicited some significant attention.[16]

San Franciscans did not feel the need for a science museum. The city already had several art museums, an aquarium, a planetarium, a new maritime museum, and a museum of anthropology and natural history. Nearby was the recently opened Oakland Museum, which included some technology as well as exhibits on California ecology. There were several museums associated with regional educational institutions, most notably the Lawrence Hall of Science, which was just being established at the University of California. Although it soon began to attract general patronage, the Lawrence Hall was not meant to be a public museum. It was a teaching institution primarily concerned with the development of curriculum materials and teacher training aids for schools. Its staff was made up mostly of members of the university's physics department and a handful of people from the School of Education. Testing the atmosphere of the Bay area for his museum project, Oppenheimer met with the directors and staffs of all those institutions and found them friendly to his idea; at least they did not view the science museum as a competitor to their own institutions.[17] Despite the general public's lack of interest, the museum professionals offered support and encouragement. One group of physicians who had been lobbying for a local health museum decided to back Oppenheimer's more inclusive plan instead. Some people, of course, had prior cultural commitments and were wary of a proliferation of resources. A few resented the intrusion by newcomers or were suspicious of the Oppenheimers' political background.

Oppenheimer wrote a prospectus of the museum to help gain endorsements.[18] In it he described the museum's perceptual orientation and his plan to equip it with laboratory apparatus that could be manipulated by the public. No name had yet been selected for the new museum. At one point it was called "MOSAIC,"[19] an acronym for Museum of Science, Art, Industry, and Craft, but even in that earliest proposal he referred to the museum generically as "an exploratorium."[20] No one thought much of that name at first, but gradually it stuck.

Oppenheimer hoped to make the museum appeal to a broad public and to draw on the many skills and talents of that same public to help build the museum. He looked for support from local research institutes and universities, and also from small businesses and individuals. He sought help from industries and artists, and he planned, following the model of the Palais de la Découverte, to employ high school and college students to construct and demonstrate the exhibits. But first he needed a site for the museum, and so he began calling on city officials, corporate board members, school board officials, and high school principals. He visited members of the chamber of commerce, importuned local relatives and acquaintances, and even tried some East Coast funding agencies and national foundations. He set out to mobilize people armed only with his written proposal and a few sample exhibits that he had made. Mostly he relied on his own enthusiasm and energy and that of his friends.

Oppenheimer's old friends did not abandon him. Many of his wartime associates had become prominently placed and illustrious scientists. They counseled and encouraged him, made important introductions, and gave substantive assistance. Among his former colleagues at the Stanford Linear Accelerator Center, Wolfgang Panofsky had become its director and Luis Alvarez was a Nobel prize-winning scientist teaching at the University of California. Both men joined the museum's first board of trustees. Another friend was Edward U. Condon, former head of the U.S. Bureau of Standards and a colleague of Oppenheimer's in the physics department at Boulder. The Oppenheimers' long-standing friendship with Louis Goldblatt, executive secretary of the International Longshoreman's Union, also deepened through his association with the founding of the Exploratorium. Goldblatt was a distinguished figure in Bay-area labor arbitration. His history of negotiation with the city made him well-known in San Francisco social and political circles and an excellent source of introductions. One of the most valuable was to William Coblentz, an attorney and member of the board of regents of the University of California. Another was to Esther Pike (later Fuller), wife of the Episcopalian bishop and a leading member of San Francisco society. She became Oppenheimer's administrative assistant and smoothed his way with some of the city's philanthropic agencies. Oppenheimer's friendship with Edwin McMillan, the director of the Berkeley Radiation Laboratory, and his own earlier association with that organization gave him access to the University of California physics workshops, where he was able to build his early prototype exhibits.

Endorsements came from some of the most illustrious and highly placed scientific and cultural personages in the country.[21] Thomas Hoving, director of the Metropolitan Museum of Art in New York; Frederick Seitz, chairman of the National Academy of Sciences; Gerald Piel and Dennis Flannagan, publisher and editor, respectively, of *Scientific American;* and other figures of national reputation agreed to serve on an advisory committee for the museum. Hard work and attendance at countless meetings also won Oppenheimer local endorsements by the San Francisco Board of Education and by the chamber of commerce. There were offers of help from individual members of prominent San Francisco families and, finally, an important grant of $50,000 from the San Francisco Foundation. The award from that prestigious federation of private family funds was a public acknowledgment of local recognition of the Oppenheimers' project. It signified support and an economic base sufficient to get the museum started.

Frank Oppenheimer did not get an official endorsement from the *San Francisco Chronicle,* the city's most prominent newspaper. Its editor had rival commitments and was slow to give even reportorial coverage to the museum. But thanks to his friendship with Herb Caen, Oppenheimer made an informal connection with Scott Newhall, the *Chronicle*'s executive editor and a member of California's wealthy, landholding aristocracy. Newhall's wife, Ruth, herself a newspaperwoman and also a descendant of one of California's oldest families, turned out to be the critical link with the museum's future home in the San Francisco Palace of Fine Arts building. A perceptive and intelligent woman, she had studied science and mathematics at the University of California, and she took an immediate interest in Oppenheimer's proposal. Well-connected, competent, and full of energy, Newhall was ideally suited to get the museum project under way. She made it her business to introduce Oppenheimer to the people who were at that moment deciding the fate of the San Francisco Palace of Fine Arts.[22]

Newhall had just completed a book, *San Francisco's Enchanted Palace,*[23] in which she told the story of the Palace of Fine Arts building. The monumental structure was built in 1915 by the architect Bernard Maybeck for San Francisco's celebration of the Panama-Pacific Exposition on the occasion of the opening of the Panama Canal. In writing the book, Newhall had worked closely with a group of San Francisco citizens, incorporated as the Palace of Fine Arts League, who had taken a special interest in the preservation of the building, and they had been awarded the responsibility of settling on its future disposition. The site had been chartered as a cultural center, and Newhall saw in Oppenheimer's museum plan the perfect realization of the building's potential. She arranged for meetings between Oppenheimer and the citizens' group and helped him to formulate his proposal in a manner that meshed with their cultural interests.

Much beloved by San Franciscans, the Palace of Fine Arts and its grounds evoke an atmosphere of sentimental nostalgia. Maybeck intended that the building would fall into picturesque decay and be reclaimed by the earth and encroaching redwood trees. Like all the buildings for the exposition, it was slated for immediate demolition. But citizens intervened and repeatedly found new uses for the structure, including the housing of limousines for the first United Nations convention in 1945. As the building's condition worsened, the California legislature declared it a historic site and leased it to the city of San Francisco, which thereby became responsible for its upkeep. A bond issue, with matching funds from state and city, was floated in 1957, and with the help of a philanthropic grant from Walter S. Johnson, president of Frieden Calculators and the founder-owner of American Forest Products, sufficient money was raised to reconstruct the building in solid concrete.

The external reconstruction of the Palace was already complete in the summer of 1967, when the Oppenheimers made their first exploratory visit to San Francisco. Hans U. Gerson, heir to Bernard Maybeck's architectural firm and also an active member of the Palace of Fine Arts League, had supervised the reconstruction and was charged with planning the interior. Having noticed Herb Caen's column mentioning the Oppenheimer project, he found the idea of a science museum interesting and was responsive when Ruth Newhall suggested a meeting with the Oppenheimers after they came to settle in San Francisco in the summer of 1968.

The Palace of Fine Arts League was going to consider the disposition of the structure in the fall of 1968, just when the Oppenheimers appeared on the scene. Newhall and Gerson worked with Oppenheimer, helping him to shape a proposal and accommodating it to the design for the building that was to be presented to the league and to the city. Newhall arranged a series of meetings for Oppenheimer, culminating in a luncheon at the Palace attended by the city's newly elected mayor Joseph Alioto, state senator George Moscone, city supervisor Roger Boas, Walter Johnson and several other members of the Palace of Fine Arts League, and some San Francisco socialites. Oppenheimer made his presentation at that meeting and displayed the plans that Gerson had drawn for the interior of the building. There were some opponents and some political conflicts, but the principal figures at the meeting were sufficiently impressed by the project to warrant the Oppenheimers' taking an immediate leave of absence from the University of Colorado and selling their house in Boulder. In July 1968 they returned to San Francisco to devote themselves to the fulfillment of their project.

With a prospective home lined up for the museum, the Oppenheimers turned to the task of its creation. In December 1968 they formed a nonprofit organization, with a board of trustees whose first chairman was Donald McLaughlin, a geologist and president of the Homestake Mining Company. As a former regent of the University of California, he had also been one of the founders of the Lawrence Hall of Science. The trustees were a rich mix of civic and labor leaders, businessmen and Nobel laureates, media people, artists, and physicians.[24] The Palace of Fine Arts League gave its official approval to the museum in February 1969, and Mayor Alioto wrote a letter of endorsement to the San Francisco Parks and Recreation Commission, which had the final authority to lease city facilities. The museum was incorporated under the name "The Palace of Arts and Science Foundation," and that remained its official title until 1971,[25] when the term that Oppenheimer had coined in his 1967 proposal displaced the more cumbersome title. The museum filed for authorization to do business as the Exploratorium and began using that name on its letterhead and logo. Although the visual symbol was redesigned several times over the next few years, the name became permanent and has produced a trail of descendant neologisms adopted by other museums. It was at last mounted in wooden letters over the portico at the north entrance of the Palace.

In July 1969, just after the first agreement between the city and the Palace of Arts and Science Foundation was signed, the Oppenheimers moved a large borrowed trailer into the huge empty space of the Palace building. There they set up the first museum office. The next few weeks were taken up in a frantic effort to scavenge materials, build exhibits, and clean and scrub everything. Most of that work was done by Jackie Oppenheimer, with the help of a few friends and volunteers and their son, Michael. A certified electrician and mechanic, Michael became the Exploratorium's first curator of exhibits. The building had inadequate power and light, and the only sources of heat were four enormous fireplaces, but the Oppenheimers decided not to delay opening the museum for the sake of capital improvements, which in any event they could not afford. The construction of exhibits would take place before the eyes of the public and with its active participation. Only a small staff was needed to operate the museum: a secretary, a janitor, an assistant to help maintain exhibits, and a single explainer to greet visitors and interpret exhibits.

On August 20, 1969, with no fanfare whatsoever, the giant doors of the Palace of Fine Arts were opened and the public was allowed to wander in. Visitors arrived almost immediately. Tourists and curiosity seekers who were enjoying the park discovered the museum largely by accident and went in to see what was going on. There were almost no exhibits inside, only a small band of people industriously at work and a sign that read: "Here is being created the Exploratorium, a community museum dedicated to awareness."

Chapter 2

Creating the Museum: Design and Serendipity Meet

Thanks to good fortune and the Palace of Fine Arts League, the Oppenheimers had a site for the museum. The first year nonetheless was a hectic period of construction and settling in. To turn the Palace into a museum they needed to finish the interior, fill it with exhibits, and let the world know about the Exploratorium. To do that they needed money and every kind of support. Since each task seemed to presuppose all of the others, they decided they had no option but to pursue them all simultaneously.

Moving in meant emptying the Palace of its temporary residents and the debris that they had left behind. Birds and mice and occasional vagrants had made their home in it, and the Knights of Columbus habitually used the floor for their annual Christmas tree sale, which also attracted holiday revelers. Although solidly built, the Palace was filthy and needed repair and refurbishment. That was the first order of business, and it was combined with the task of making allies out of the skeptical neighbors in the wealthy Marina district. The Oppenheimers reasoned that little would be gained by building in secrecy, and since their aim was to win support for the museum, they invited the neighbors in to help. People did drop in, drawn by curiosity and by rumors of the projected museum,

23

and some stayed to volunteer their labor and material assistance.

At the same time, Frank Oppenheimer was struggling to find financial support for the museum and to win recognition of its aims. The proposal he had written in 1967 had been circulated within the scientific and museum communities as well as in the local San Francisco region. It came to the attention of Albert Parr, former director of the American Museum of Natural History in New York, who invited Oppenheimer to publish a portion of it in a national museum journal, *Curator*. "A Rationale for a Science Museum" appeared in November 1968. In it, Oppenheimer began with the observation that although the phenomena of basic science and the fruits of technology are increasingly important in shaping society and our daily lives, remarkably few persons understand or feel comfortable with them. Thus, he went on, there is "a growing need for an environment in which people can become familiar with the details of science and technology and begin to gain some understanding by controlling and watching the behavior of laboratory apparatus and machinery."[1] (See Appendix 1.) He affirmed the need for "an exploratorium," to bridge the gaps between traditional art museums, science centers, and museums of industry and technology. The new institution would supplement and be a resource for schools and adult education centers and would have the advantage over books, television, and other traditional learning resources in that it would contain physical props that "people can see and handle and which display phenomena which people can turn on and off and vary at will."[2] Its emphasis, in other words, was to be interactive—directed to people as thinkers, creators, and users rather than as passive consumers.

In the rationale, Oppenheimer imagined a museum that would introduce the several areas of science and technology by means of exhibit sections displaying the psychology of perception and the artistry associated with each of the senses. He suggested that the museum be laid out in "five main sections based respectively on hearing, on vision, on taste and smell, on the tactile sensations (including perception of hot and cold), and on proprio-sensitive controls which form the basis of balance, locomotion and manipulation."[3] Each section would be announced by exhibits having to do with aesthetic experiences appropriate to that sense. The hearing section, for example, might begin with a collection of musical instruments, vision might start with painting and the idea of perspective, taste and smell could be represented by food and perfume, touch by clothing and housing, and the section on proprio-sensitivity might include exhibits on dance and athletics. From that aesthetic beginning, visitors would next be invited to explore exhibits on the psychology and physiology of each of the senses; the physics of sound, light, and heat; the chemistry of olfaction and food assimilation; and the mathematics of feedback mechanisms. Those exhibits would be reinforced by related exhibits having to do with the technology of each of the senses—industrial techniques of sound reproduction and devices for listening; techniques for the manufacture of pigments, lighting devices, and optical instruments; food processing and cosmetics; the fabrication of textiles and housing materials; and the sophisticated technology of electronic control mechanisms.

The plan was elaborate and ambitious, but the museum was not to be coercive. Visitors to this "exploration center" would be free to follow whatever pattern of exhibit sequence appealed to them or to wander among the exhibits at random. The open and undivided space of the Palace was ideal for letting people make their own connections without constraint. The sole concern of the museum must be to stimulate genuine interest and so convey "the understanding that science and technology have a role which is deeply rooted in human values and aspirations."[4] Oppenheimer believed that people learn by interacting with the world and with each other, and the museum was to be a place in which they could be comfortable doing both. To be interactive the exhibits must be cognitively engaging, not merely physically manipulable. They must invite visitors' questions and then be clearly responsive to the questions put to them. They must be genuinely explorable. Designing such exhibits was a challenge, since they would certainly have to withstand a great deal of misguided and occasionally abusive treatment. It would require creative artistry, scientific knowledge, and craftsmanship to design exhibits that were sensitive yet not fragile, precise without being obscure, and clear in purpose without precluding alternative uses.

He had no illusions that such exhibits could be constructed rapidly, but rather than wait for them to be designed and completed, he settled for some temporary compromises to promote the idea of the museum and generate the needed support. Among the interim exhibits that he suggested were student science-fair projects, apparatus used in science demonstrations for educational TV, equipment used in schools and college laboratories, and machinery used for industrial production and scientific research. Such objects are often beautiful in themselves, apart from any practical or pedagogic function they may serve. They also made for interesting displays because, although they were not entirely unfamiliar to the public, they were not readily accessible either. People are often intimidated by complex apparatus and afraid to touch it. If they could have real physical access to it and could simply play with it in the museum without risk, they might overcome their fear of the instruments. In the world of school and work there are often too many other considerations that interfere with the sheer joy of exploring and understanding, but in Oppenheimer's ideal museum it would be fun to think about things and to observe the effects of manipulating them.

In setting priorities, the Oppenheimers decided that the restoration and renovation of the building and the fabrication of new exhibits would serve to demonstrate their intention, to let people know what the museum was to be. The building of the museum itself would be the first exhibit, and the public was invited to take part in creating it. In the meantime, an appropriate selection of borrowed exhibits could be displayed, and the endless task of building a network of supporters must proceed.

Happily, the Oppenheimers' circle of friends in the Bay area had grown. Many were attracted by the new museum's educational potential, and quite a few just wanted to be part of the adventure. The trustees that Oppenheimer had picked saw their role as essentially supportive of him. They left policymaking and the museum's day-to-day operations in his hands, but they contributed in a variety of ways to its functioning. Wolfgang Panofsky continued to be a confidant and a technical adviser. He loaned Oppenheimer one of his administrative assistants to help coordinate the museum's community management and outreach program. Thanks also to Panofsky the museum was able to obtain the loan of a portion of the Stanford linear accelerator as one of the major opening exhibits. Lou Goldblatt helped negotiate with city agencies regarding the use of the Palace of Fine Arts building. Walter Johnson agreed to serve as honorary chairman of the museum board. He continued to demonstrate his affection for the Palace by donating the remainder owed on the city of San Francisco's bond commitment to build the theater at the south end of the building.

Other trustees helped locate and create exhibits. Edward Condon revealed himself as an ingenious solicitor. His experience as head of the Bureau of Standards had given him intimate knowledge of the material holdings of the federal government, and he tirelessly badgered U.S. and private corporate agencies for contributions to the museum. Arthur Jampolsky, director of the Smith-Kettlewell Institute of Visual Sciences, obtained supplies of lenses, magnifiers, and other optical instruments to be used as exhibit components. He was also a liaison with academic researchers and persuaded other scientists and technicians to help with the construction of exhibits. Edwin McMillan, Oppenheimer's former colleague and now head of the Lawrence Radiation Laboratory, dispatched his assistant Cyril Orly to arrange for the transfer of tools and machinery to the museum so that the exhibits could be built right there in full view of the public.

In addition to the permanent board of trustees, temporary advisory committees were organized to oversee the development of various functions of the museum. An art committee was headed by Lorenz Eitner, chairman of the art department of Stanford University and also a trustee of the Exploratorium. It actually played a perfunctory part, for the aesthetic coherence and layout of exhibits fell ultimately to Jackie Oppenheimer and the staff, who contended with the daily challenges of the museum's yawning emptiness. Since word of the new museum and its interests spread rapidly through the local arts community, artists volunteered their work. The art committee helped in the selection of appropriate pieces, considering not only artistic merit but also relevance to the didactic aims of the museum. When an artist-in-residence program was funded, a panel of selectors made up of staff and civic arts representatives displaced the art committee.[5] A committee with more active responsibilities was assembled by Jampolsky to plan the development of the first coherent exhibit section, devoted to the subject of vision. The committee was composed of distinguished vision scientists from the University of California, Stanford, Stanford Research Institute, and the Smith-Kettlewell Institute. They proposed a series of exhibits that would represent the current understanding of the process of vision, and they consulted with the staff on the quality of the exhibits constructed.[6] When the museum contemplated new exhibit sections, it followed a similar procedure. Advisory committees of academic and research specialists were invited to brainstorm with the staff and to suggest exhibits that would reflect the current state of the art. The committees were also consulted on the evaluation of existing exhibits. Sometimes committee members became so absorbed in the exhibit process that they began actually constructing exhibits.[7]

The bulk of the work of the museum was not done by the board or the advisory committees, however, but by the small staff that the Oppenheimers were able to attract even though there was almost no money for salaries. One person who had experience organizing health fairs was hired to arrange for the loan of temporary exhibits.[8] A secretary ran the office and dealt with personnel and also scheduled school and community group visits to the museum. A janitor and a maintenance person cleaned the building and kept the exhibits repaired. Michael Oppenheimer worked on the design and development of new exhibits and maintained an inventory of spare parts to keep them in running order. He also took charge of museum security. A couple of high school students known as explainers were hired to demonstrate and explain the exhibits to the public. They opened and closed the museum during public hours and were the only floor staff to protect the exhibits against vandalism. When they were not busy with their public duties, they also did some maintenance and repair work and lettered signs.

The explainers' work was overseen by Sheila Grinell, a former graduate student from the University of California. In December 1969 Grinell was one of the first of many bright young people who, out of curiosity, came to investigate the new museum and then remained to become a part of it. She supervised and taught the explainers, designed some exhibits, taught the first school-related course, and created the museum's first catalog. She quickly became the museum's co-director of exhibits and programs, which involved her in all the museum's activities relating to the public. She trained new people to take over the projects that she had initiated, and many of the staff were as profoundly influenced by her view of the Exploratorium as by Oppenheimer's.

Esther Pike, Oppenheimer's administrative assistant, made an altogether different contribution. She had little to do with exhibits or with the physical maintenance of the museum, but her philanthropic experience and knowledge of San Francisco society made her invaluable. She was an intermediary between the museum and local foundations and fund-raising sources, as well as a competent adviser on financial affairs and management policy. She was also a hostess for social events and a key contact for community resources and special projects. She played a delicately diplomatic role as an interface between the young crowd of exuberant experimenters that the museum attracted and the more solid citizens on whose support the Exploratorium depended. Esther Pike was fond of the Oppenheimers but not altogether favorable toward the museum's philosophy or the social causes it fostered. Nonetheless, she introduced her future husband, Parmer Fuller III, regional vice president of the Pittsburgh

Plate and Glass Company, to the museum, and he served for seven years as chairman of its board of trustees.

Undoubtedly the most valuable person to the museum, next to Frank himself, was Jackie Oppenheimer. She shaped the Exploratorium indirectly through him and directly through her own efforts. She, as much as he, judged and learned from the other museums they visited in Europe and the United States, and she edited every statement that he published about the museum. All of the explanatory signs that accompanied the early exhibits had to pass her scrutiny. She decided where exhibits should be placed, cleaned and repaired them, scavenged materials, moved furniture, painted walls and screens, and generally maintained order. Jackie did whatever needed doing and filled in for whoever was absent. She arranged concerts and planned community events. She worked sensitively with volunteers and staff, always aware when discord and frustration threatened. She ran the museum store, ordering and maintaining its inventory of books, toys, and scientific instruments. Later, she took over and reorganized the graphics department and standardized its procedure for labeling exhibits. The Exploratorium catalogs and other publications produced under her guidance were nationally recognized for their excellence.[9]

Volunteers were essential too. Like most museums, the Exploratorium depended on donated labor, with all its attendant pressures and irregularities. In the early days, just about everyone who worked there began as a volunteer until a staff position could be invented to pay for that person's work. Volunteers staffed the information booth and guided morning school group tours. They worked in the machine shop and the office. Some taught as docents on the evenings that the museum was open. Some brought or made exhibits, and some, like the Oppenheimers' good friends Philip and Phyllis Morrison, spent weeks or months in the museum designing and trying out exhibit ideas. Not all the exhibit suggestions that people volunteered were acceptable (more than a few were the fantasies of crackpots), but the many clever ideas that proved fruitful have given the Exploratorium its own pluralistic flavor.

Many exhibits were in-kind donations offered because someone thought them appropriate to the museum. Oppenheimer retained final authority over the selections that were made, sometimes engendering considerable frustration among the staff. Insisting on authenticity, he refused to consider some of the experiments at the edges of science that were then in vogue. Proposals for exhibits on unidentified flying objects or extrasensory perception or telekinesis were blandly dismissed. No one could dispute Oppenheimer's integrity on those matters, but his blunt resistance to parascience and the occult sometimes evoked hard feelings and undoubtedly drove away some potential supporters. It also set a tone for the museum, marking it as a center open to innovation and experiment but never as a haven for the varieties of irrationalism and consciousness-expanding exploration that were popular in San Francisco at the time. Zany as it may have appeared to some of its visitors, the Exploratorium was from the beginning well within the intellectual mainstream. Never intended to be all things to all people, it reflected Oppenheimer's assessment of good and bad science and of his value system.

As dictated by Oppenheimer, the museum followed a temporary two-pronged strategy of exhibit building and exhibit borrowing. While exhibits were being designed to accord with the program outlined in the rationale, loaned exhibits that could be reconciled with that program were used provisionally, to fill the space.[10] Some of the exhibits that originated in the museum were simple and could be easily produced. Some were modifications or replicas of demonstrations that Oppenheimer had devised for his earlier curriculum work. Others were adaptations from textbook illustrations, academic research apparatus, and classroom models used in physics courses. A few were commercially available objects that happened to possess interesting perceptual qualities. Ingenious staff members found usable exhibit material everywhere—on street corners, in junk stores, at yard sales. Using everyday objects and drawing inspiration from the world of ordinary phenomena, they sought to bring home the point that the wonders of the world are everywhere, directly under our noses but often unnoticed.

When Edward Condon asked federal agencies, corporations, and major industries to donate exhibits, he made it clear that exhibits were not to aggrandize a particular industry or promote a product.[11] He took pains to explain to each agency or business how some part of its manufacturing or research concern revealed a principle or natural process that might relate to the Exploratorium's objectives. His requests for exhibit materials were also carefully couched to exclude weaponry or trade-fair exhibits. Condon's efforts began to bear fruit, drawing attention to the museum at the same time that they attracted loaned and donated exhibits that bore directly on the museum's perceptual motif. The Lockheed Corporation, for example, rather than offering commercial exhibits on aeronautical topics, as might be expected, donated an elegant optical exhibit on imaging. The exhibit, named "Touch the Spring" by the Exploratorium, invites the visitor to reach for an elusive virtual image. It has been one of the museum's most popular exhibits and is widely and variously imitated by museums throughout the world. Similarly, Bell Laboratories, universally associated with telecommunication technology, contributed a series of exhibits on pattern recognition. The discernment of patterns is a critical element of all forms of communication and Bell is a major research center in the area. Most people, however, know the company only through its commercial products, and they are what is commonly displayed in museum exhibits.

Nonpromotional exhibits that relate to the basic research supported by a corporation are not often found in museums of industry, but by revealing the connection between science and technology, they make both more comprehensible. One of the Bell exhibits, for example, illustrates how easily a familiar image, such as a portrait of Abraham Lincoln, is reconstructed from minimal clues. This simple exhibit suggests that a significant message, or ordered pattern, can be transmitted in reduced form and its complexity reconstituted by a receiving mechanism. In the Exploratorium the exhibit is situated alongside other exhibits on cognitive selection, visual perception, photographic resolution, and the placement of bits of pigment in the art of Georges Seurat. Making such connections is the essence of the Exploratorium philosophy.

Oppenheimer described the exhibit strategy that the Exploratorium followed as "opportunistic." Using that term as evolutionary biologists do, in a nonderogatory sense, he meant to refer to the adaptive behavior of organisms that utilize their environment to satisfy their needs as they are simultaneously shaped by it. The Exploratorium, like an organism, drew nourishment from the resources that surrounded it and transformed them into its own substance. The museum's opportunism was a positive and imaginative exploitation of the world. The biological metaphor also suggests the manner in which exhibits were mutually generative. One exhibit suggested another, or an existing exhibit was seen in a new light or improved on as a result of the introduction of a new exhibit. Exhibits were thus begotten from other exhibits by fission, by fusion, and occasionally by hybridization. The exhibits proliferated, along with a spirit of spontaneity and openness to innovation. Kept within bounds by Oppenheimer's rationale, the museum's fertility was astonishing, but it was not allowed to degenerate into a hodgepodge of unrelated exhibits.

One early exhibit might seem to stretch the museum's declared rationale. It was a collection of materials assembled and contributed by NASA, commemorating the August 1969 lunar landing of the *Apollo 11* mission, which coincided with the museum's opening. Space travel is not one of the museum's explicit themes, but it is obliquely related to perception at a distance, and several exhibits have explored the topic of aerial navigation. They were often the result of fortuitous loans or chance discoveries. One was a loaned exhibit of models of primitive flying machines conceived and sketched by Leonardo da Vinci. Another was a model of the Montgomery glider, an aircraft of local, technical, and historic interest. The glider was a rebuilt 1911 model of an engineless airplane that a Californian, John J. Montgomery, had flown in 1883, well before the famous Wright Brothers' flight in 1906. Montgomery was a blacksmith by vocation as well as a mechanic and physicist, and like Leonardo, he was inspired by the wing structure of birds. The Exploratorium model of his aircraft was reconstructed from a wing segment found at the nearby University of Santa Clara, where Montgomery had taught physics. The glider was reconstructed at the Lockheed Corporation, and a retired Air Force general who happened to have connections there arranged for its display at the museum. Although the glider was originally loaned for only three months, it was so popular that it stayed on at the museum for ten years and was returned to Santa Clara only when the Exploratorium was closed for renovations in 1979.

The space exhibits convey the power of human perception to stretch to the vast and distant. Another loaned exhibit revealed how technology extends perception to penetrate the infinitely small. Wolfgang Panofsky arranged for the Exploratorium to display a forty-foot segment of the Stanford linear accelerator. The instrument may be thought of as a giant microscope that allows observers to study the structure of an atom's nucleus by interfering with its behavior. The accelerator propels particles to great speeds; when they bombard the nucleus, it fragments in characteristic fashion on collision. Humans cannot directly perceive the results of such interventions, but recording instruments such as cloud chambers and bubble chambers can track them for us, and we can draw inferences from the recorded information. The Stanford accelerator segment came accompanied by its own spark chamber, which differentiates the particles and detects their passage. A visual model of the system was displayed along with the accelerator, and a console with a tape recording explained its operation to the public. It was impressive for its beauty as well as for its awesome utility, and it was hailed by *San Francisco Chronicle* art critic Thomas Albright as "the most impressive sculptural structure . . . less a product of human creativity than of discovery and appreciation."[12] The accelerator section was returned to Stanford after a few weeks, but some of its accessories and parts, including the spark chamber, remained behind to become permanent Exploratorium exhibits. After a few years, those instruments, plus a cloud chamber donated by NASA, were incorporated into a new historical exhibit section that was to depict the state of the art of physics at the time of Einstein's articulation of relativity theory.[13]

The museum space was rapidly filled with built and borrowed exhibits, but although they drew the public and won critical attention, they did not really convey the museum's professed purpose. Few people would have discerned the theme of perception as a common preoccupation of the displays, which occurred in seemingly haphazard succession. The museum needed a galvanizing, dramatic event to pull it into a coherent whole, and fortuitously, one materialized.

By chance, Oppenheimer learned about the British exhibit "Cybernetic Serendipity," which seemed to embody and harmonize everything the Exploratorium was trying to express. The discovery resulted from a routine request for help that Oppenheimer sent to the Smithsonian Institution. A research assistant at the Smithsonian was intrigued by the new museum project and offered to scout for interesting exhibit materials. When she saw "Cybernetic Serendipity" at the Corcoran Gallery Annex in Washington, D.C., she recognized it as Exploratorium material and recommended it to Oppenheimer. He flew to Washington at once to see it and arranged to have the entire collection delivered to San Francisco after its Washington tour. Its arrival was a turning point for the museum. "Cybernetic Serendipity" fit the overall program of the Exploratorium so well that the staff decided to celebrate the exhibit's opening as the official Exploratorium opening.

That event took place on October 11, 1969, just two months after the Oppenheimers had moved their trailer into the empty gallery of the Palace and set to work. This time the public was invited with fanfare, and people turned out in numbers to see what was going on in the Palace and how the newly reconstructed building was being used. The critics were delighted with what they found,[14] and the Palace of Fine Arts League also expressed its approval that the Palace of Arts and Science Foundation was perpetuating the spirit of the 1915 Panama-Pacific International Exposition.

"Cybernetic Serendipity" had been organized by Jasia Reichardt of the London Institute of Contemporary Arts and had been a great success in London in 1967. It examined the relationship between technology and creativity and explored the use of computers in the arts. Not all of the exhibit objects were computers, but there were several rooms full of machines and cybernetic devices: computers, robots, and mechanical feedback systems. They were supposed "to show some of the creative forms engendered by technology"[15] and to display some of the links between the random systems employed by artists and the goal-oriented systems devised by engineers. The machines were sufficiently proportioned to human size that they were not intimidating or alienating. Indeed, they were meant to elicit a friendly and playful interaction between human beings and machines. Some of the machines went through their mechanical and electronic paces in dumbly programmed order, but others insisted on interaction and functioned only by means of an exchange with visitors. The observer became a constituent of the work as art. Without that participation, the apparatus remained merely a machine. The show consisted of works by engineers, mathematicians, and architects as well as more-traditional artists, poets, and composers, but without reading all the notes relating to the works, a visitor would not have been able to trace the disciplinary backgrounds of their producers. The general impression of the machines in action was one of vibrating space filled with amplified sound, beeps and clicks, and flickering images on television screens.

Although the show was imported to the United States by the Smithsonian traveling exhibit service, it had been displayed only once, at the Corcoran Annex, because its complex technology was so unfamiliar to art museums that they were put off by the prospect and cost of assembling it. The Exploratorium staff was undaunted by the technology, but even they had to struggle to put the whole show together. It traveled across the country by truck, and the journey was hazardous to the exhibits. The show arrived in San Francisco in such a dilapidated state that the truck driver from the Corcoran stayed on and helped the staff assemble the exhibits. It took them nearly a month to get the show ready for the public. Once on view, however, "Cybernetic Serendipity" was a hit, and it launched the

Exploratorium on its way to becoming a museum of international reputation and influence. The show stayed at the museum long after the expiration of its original six-week contract. Finally most of it was packed up and returned to England in October 1971, but some individual pieces remained behind to become part of the Exploratorium's permanent collection.

"Cybernetic Serendipity" was of more than historic significance to the Exploratorium, for it also helped to conceptualize and give substance to the ideas that the museum was meant to express. Though assembled for display at an art institute, the show was a celebration of mechanical invention. It included pieces originally intended for utilitarian functions, many of them designed by engineers. Furthermore, its attitude toward machines was closer to the conventional view of science than of art. It presented the machine as an agreeable collaborator rather than a mere tool or a menacing enemy. The machine was, above all, an extension of human capability and a complement to natural intelligence.

The depiction of machines in modern art is not unusual. Since the turn of the century machines have often been used to symbolize power, speed, and violence, as well as order, rationality, or impersonality and alienation. In works where they actually operate, as in kinetic art, motors and mechanical devices are usually disguised or hidden behind the scenes. Their function is to activate the work of art, but they are not a part of it aesthetically. When we do enjoy machines as objects of aesthetic pleasure, we tend to appreciate their craftsmanship and adjustment of form to function rather than those features that distinguish a work as art. But "Cybernetic Serendipity" did display the machines as art, not as cleverly designed utilitarian instruments, and it did not disguise them or subordinate them to so-called higher artistic values. Neither did the show present machines as dehumanizing and unfriendly. It did not displace the concrete reality of the machines with abstractions and metaphorical associations. On the contrary, the machines noisily attracted attention to themselves. Some were humanoid in appearance, but most were unpretentiously machines. They were meant to affirm their own existence, although they also testified to the human creativity and resourcefulness that had invented them. Like traditional works of art, the objects displayed in "Cybernetic Serendipity" tended to sharpen aesthetic attention and to direct it toward the environment. For most urban dwellers, if not for everyone, that environment consists more of man-made artifacts than of untouched nature.

The phenomena revealed in "Cybernetic Serendipity"—such as magnetism, wave interference, electricity, and the polarization of light—were exactly the phenomena that the Exploratorium hoped to illuminate. The machines were playful counterparts of the laboratory apparatus used in scientific research, and as such they were perfectly suited to the Exploratorium proposal to familiarize the public with the equipment of science and to bring those phenomena into the realm of normal experience.

"Cybernetic Serendipity" shared another characteristic with Exploratorium exhibits. The machines were constructed of standardized parts, routinely available from manufacturers and retail outlets. That was why it was possible for the Exploratorium staff to repair, rewire, and sometimes even improve on the design of the exhibits that had arrived from Washington in such deplorable condition. Rather than treating the exhibit pieces as works of art, which must be restored as precisely as possible to their original condition, the Exploratorium viewed them as generic scientific apparatus. No matter how ingenious the design of a machine may be, once made it is repeatable and improvable. The only restraints on the reproduction of a machine are legal protections of patent and property claims, and there is considerable incentive to improve on its design.[16] Some of the exhibits were so idiosyncratic that the Exploratorium staff had to locate their makers to obtain wiring diagrams and electronic specifications or even spare parts. But they were not trying to recapture the artist's personal vision. They simply wanted to make the machines work, and their authors, with only a few reservations, were happy to comply. Comparable interference with a work of art, although it is not unheard of, is viewed as a violation of artistic integrity, and formulas for the repetition of works of art are not usually available.

Another critical difference between a work of art and an instrument of science is that the former draws attention to itself as the locus of an aesthetic experience, but the latter, even if it is beautiful, directs attention away from itself to a process or phenomenon. Thus scientists speak as if they are directly observing phenomena when they are actually observing secondary effects mediated through the apparatus. The readings on a meter or screen are identified with the process they are recording, and the apparatus, in effect, becomes invisible. The merit of an instrument lies in its capacity to perform a task, and so any modification that enhances its ability to perform that task efficiently and unobtrusively is an improvement. To modify a work of art in like manner would be a violation of it. Although a work of art may have utilitarian applications, they are irrelevant to its identity as a work of art.

The works displayed in "Cybernetic Serendipity" were treated as art by the art critics, but they fell between art and technology, and neither their subject matter nor their mode of production clearly warranted their classification as one or the other. Some of them had been produced as instruments of scientific research or for other practical ends. Some were plainly didactic and others deliberately playful. Their ambiguous status exactly fit the philosophy of the Exploratorium, which promoted that same ambiguity. Because of their intricate meshing of artistic and scientific interest, some of the works required little or no change to be displayed within either of the categories. When "Cybernetic Serendipity" closed, the Exploratorium was able to keep several works and use them as is or as models of future exhibits. Some pieces were transformed simply by removing them from the context of the "Cybernetic Serendipity" show and placing them within a series of didactic Exploratorium exhibits.

A good example of a work that underwent such contextual transfiguration is a piece originally entitled "Pendulum Harmonograph" by the industrial designer who created it. It is a machine that draws symmetrical figures. The Exploratorium called it "Drawing Board" and simplified it a little but left it essentially unchanged and included it in a sequence of exhibits on pattern formation. In "Drawing Board" two linear pendular motions combine to produce a series of curves and ellipses. The figures are called Lissajous curves after the nineteenth-century French mathematician who first devised a mechanism for recording periodic oscillations. In "Drawing Board" a stationary mechanical drawing arm fitted with exchangeable colored pens records the Lissajous figures on a sheet of paper affixed to a board that makes pendular swings beneath the drawing arm. Exploratorium visitors set the pendular platform in motion by giving it a shove, and by controlling the amplitude of its swing they determine the shape of the curves produced. Visitors can also interrupt the motion and substitute different colored pens in the drawing arm. Each resumption of motion begins a new set of patterns, and a different series of figures is imposed on the first. The same effect of coupled pendular motion can be observed in the sand pendulums that are exhibited in some museums (for example, the Boston Mu-

seum of Science). They also trace Lissajous figures in sand but, unlike the Exploratorium exhibit, produce no record that the visitor
can keep as a memento.

At the Exploratorium several other exhibits display the same
mathematical ideas as "Drawing Board." One, called "Relative Motion," was designed to demonstrate how the combined linear motions of two pendulums produce a pattern of curves. The two pendulums are suspended at right angles to each other, and the visitor
can swing them independently. The Lissajous figures produced by
their combined oscillation are not recorded as in "Drawing Board"
but are simply inscribed in space. Nevertheless, the more obvious
relation of the two pendulums makes this exhibit helpful in explaining what is going on in the other exhibit.

"Sidebands," another exhibit left over from "Cybernetic Serendipity," displays the same effect in a much more sophisticated fashion on a television screen. This exhibit, made by two British electronic engineers, invites the museumgoer to interact with the exhibit
by turning knobs that adjust the phase and frequency of the two
wave oscillations relative to one another. The screen displays are the
mathematical equivalents of the two moving pendulums manipulated in "Relative Motion" and the swinging platform of "Drawing
Board." Another knob on the "Sidebands" screen advances the
curved figures in apparent precession, each figure rotating like a
planet about its axis as it revolves in its orbit. The exhibit was bought
for the museum by the estate of a mathematics professor, Frances
R. Dewing, who clearly understood the message that the Exploratorium hoped to convey by displaying multiple variations on the same
theme. Her executor expressed her sentiments on awarding the gift
to the museum: "This exhibit brings home the relationship between
geometric truth and art, and she would have responded very warmly
to this. She felt this kinship."[17]

The ease with which the "Cybernetic Serendipity" exhibits were
integrated into the Exploratorium program underscores the opportunism of the museum's exhibit strategy. Although the exhibits were
acquired by chance and conceived independently, they were readily
associated with a network of didactic Exploratorium exhibits and,
in turn, led to others. In conjunction with the three exhibits just discussed, for example, additional exhibits were built to show how
compound linear motion and curvilinear motion are practically related. One application of that idea is the automobile differential, and
so an example of one is displayed nearby in the museum along with

an oversized model differential that can be manipulated by hand.

Exhibits rarely have one exclusive, canonic interpretation. Since the "Cybernetic Serendipity" show originally had no pedagogic purpose, the works in it were more multivalent than some of the in-house exhibits, which were designed to convey a specific notion. There was, therefore, no single correct disposition of the show's exhibits from an Exploratorium perspective, and several of them could be deployed in more than one exhibit series. Not all of the interpretations of exhibits could be foreseen by their authors, and some were certainly not intended.

One "Cybernetic Serendipity" work went through an odd sequence of interpretive shifts. The machine was originally constructed by a psychologist, Christopher Evans, as an aid in his research on how patterns (and hence significance) are judged from the fixation of an image on the retina. The operator of the machine experiences a self-administered bright flashing image followed by a disintegrating afterimage. Evans believed that the fragmentation of the afterimage reverses the hierarchical construction of the original image on the retina, and he designed the apparatus to test that hypothesis. When the piece was included in the "Cybernetic Serendipity" show, however, Evans called it "Cybernetic Introspective Pattern Classifier" because it enabled subjects to reflect on the organization and decomposition of their perceptual experience. After the show, the Exploratorium bought the machine and displayed it as a pedagogic exhibit in the vision section alongside several other exhibits on the physiology of the eye and the quasi-cognitive processes of the optic system. The exhibit, retitled "After Image," was now interpreted in a sense much closer to Evans's original purpose. Later someone also discovered that "After Image" can reveal an interesting feature of depth perception. There is no limit on the possible interpretations of an exhibit and hence on the ways it can be associated with other exhibits.

The discovery of "Cybernetic Serendipity" was itself serendipitous. It gave the museum staff a substantial body of exhibits to work with immediately and was a mine of ideas for the future. The show helped fill the museum space quickly with exhibits that coincided with ideas that Oppenheimer had put forth in the rationale, and so it laid the groundwork, both physically and intellectually, for the development of the museum.

During the negotiations to obtain "Cybernetic Serendipity" from Washington, Oppenheimer was also looking for promising exhibits from local artists. It happened that a group of artists, scientists, and technologists had recently come together to promote collaborative interests that seemed to correspond to those of the Exploratorium. The new organization, Experiments in Art and Technology (EAT), had been formed in New York in the mid-sixties by Robert Rauschenberg and others; its purpose was "to familiarize artists with the aesthetic potentialities of the new media and materials that science had made accessible, and to reintroduce scientists and technologists to the type of imagination and humanizing applications of human invention that had traditionally been the domain of artists."[18] The group was launched in New York with a successful multimedia program called "Nine Evenings, Theater and Engineering," and it was attracting new forms of industrial and corporate patronage. A West Coast branch of EAT was founded in 1969 in California, headed by John Almond, an electronic systems engineer and musician, and by Merlin Stone, a well-known feminist author and sculptor who was then teaching at the University of California and the California College of Arts and Crafts. The EAT group expressed a collective allegiance to a new experimental "systems aesthetic," which was process- rather than object-oriented. Members learned from one another about new media and materials, and they turned to academics and researchers to learn about principles of physics and structural engineering, communications technology, electronics and computers, feedback systems, and physical techniques with potential application to the arts. They had organized local seminars and lecture series by university and industrial scientists, and they responded with interest to the new museum.

The EAT organizers invited Oppenheimer to take part in their educational program, and they welcomed the Exploratorium as a resource for scientific information and technical advice. They also hoped to use it as an alternative space where artists could stage performances and display their work. Merlin Stone assembled a show of a dozen or more works by EAT members that opened together with "Cybernetic Serendipity." Like the works from "Cybernetic Serendipity," several of the EAT pieces fit so well into the Exploratorium plan that they were either purchased directly by the museum for permanent display or became models for future exhibits.

In addition to attracting the EAT artists, the Exploratorium space appealed to other experimental performing artists. The vast empty hall lent itself especially well to explorations in sound and light that would have been impossible in a smaller space. One group offered to present a series of experimental performances accompanied by verbal scientific explanations. Another group organized an antiphonal concert performed by two choirs placed at opposite ends of the building. Their aim was to capitalize on the two-second delay as sound traveled the length of the gallery between the choirs. They ran into difficulties, however, for in the dark space the distance also prevented the two choirs from seeing each other, and they could barely discern the conductor, who was trying to coordinate their singing from the center. Another sound experiment was produced on a synthesizer by the San Francisco composer Alden Jenks. He played variations on a single tone that reverberated off the hard walls surrounding the three acres of empty space. Recalling that event with some bemusement, Oppenheimer later wrote:

Alden's concert consisted of a single note that started at 8:00 p.m. and ended at 10:20 p.m. The note varied continuously as harmonics and subharmonics were added, the volume of the various component frequencies of the note changed slowly and continuously, and new components were added or subtracted to change the quality of the tone. But the note never stopped, there was no punctuation, no staccato, just one infinite legato. As the concert progressed, I began to wish, as I remembered having wished long ago on a rough trans-Atlantic voyage, that I could just "turn off the waves" for a while, even for just five minutes, and maybe then everything would be all right again.[19]

But the composer himself exulted, "I could have gone on all night."

Collaborative and multimedia productions were also performed in the museum space. A presentation involving light, space, and sound was performed by three Bay-area groups: Deus ex Machina, an electronic music ensemble; Deadly Nightshade, a light-show production group; and the Southcoast Pneumads, who produced inflatable sculptures. Their joint enterprise, "The Magic Pillow Show," had an enormous transparent, inflatable, tentlike form as its centerpiece. Lights played on its exterior surfaces and were interrupted by shadows as the public moved in and out of the interior. Air was continuously pumped into the space and made whooshing sounds as it escaped whenever the entry flap was lifted. The production alarmed the San Francisco Fire Department, which threatened to close it down, but Oppenheimer managed to allay the fears of the department's agents.

The Exploratorium had a special appeal for many of the young people who had been drawn to the unconventionalism of San Francisco. They came to the city in hopes of realizing their fantasies, and the museum seemed to them a garden of delights. But not everyone was delighted by the spectacle. Some established citizens disliked the crowds of disheveled young hippies, and others were suspicious of Oppenheimer himself. Many were simply not ready to subsidize a stranger or to try out a novel idea.

Comparatively little support was available from the new high-technology industries and electronics research companies. Although William Hewlett, president of the Hewlett-Packard Company, gave the museum his personal support and endorsement, the companies tended to be conservative in their investments; most of them ploughed their profits back into their own research and development. Oppenheimer eventually did win over the executives of some corporations, after having demonstrated the viability of his project, but his lack of enthusiasm for computers and the museum's apparent emphasis on low technology could not have escaped their notice. There was even talk of a rival high-technology museum, to be funded by the specialized electronics industries and located on the peninsula south of San Francisco in what is now known as Silicon Valley, the heart of the computer culture. But that enterprise has been long in gestation.

By the end of its first year, the Exploratorium had proven that it had potential, but continued success required a larger base of support than could be counted on from the local community. The Oppenheimers hoped that the museum would become a national resource that would bring visitors to San Francisco. Like most scientists, Oppenheimer believed in the universality of science and, therefore, that the attraction of a science museum should not be regionally restricted. Science pertains to everything, and its conclusions are true everywhere, so it seemed only reasonable that the same federal agencies and national foundations that fund scientific research and teaching in the universities should also support the museums that teach science.

Although the Exploratorium was far from achieving national, let alone universal, stature, its first year had been a productive one. The building of the physical museum was well under way. More than 130 exhibits valued at over $140,000 had been assembled, and nearly $145,000 had been raised in contributions. The two-pronged exhibit strategy had allowed the museum to flourish and develop its own style. Gradually it became less dependent on borrowed exhibits as the volume of exhibits designed and built in the museum increased. With the help of a small grant from the Alfred P. Sloan Foundation of New York, the staff launched a pilot series of exhibits on visual perception, which was expanded to become the first coherent exhibit section of the museum. As word of the museum spread, more than 150,000 people came to visit, and more than 200 schools brought scheduled tours. Visitors from abroad sought counsel on how to emulate the Exploratorium in their countries. Finally, at its June 1970 meeting, the city of San Francisco's Parks and Recreation Commission voted to extend its lease with the Palace of Arts and Science Foundation, and the city renewed its agreement to maintain the park grounds surrounding the building. The Exploratorium had earned its home.

Shops and Tools: Making Is a Way of Learning

The sounds and sights of a machine shop—the scream of cutting instruments, an occasional shower of sparks from the welding station, the pervasive smell of machine oil—are not what visitors expect to find on entering a museum. Most museums prefer to hide these noisy, dirty, and sometimes dangerous places from the public and to display only their completed and polished products. The people who work in the shops are, likewise, often treated as shadowy, faceless figures. No one knows who they are, and their names are not embossed on the museum's letterhead. But for Oppenheimer the making of things and the collaborative process of their production were important aspects of the exhibit presentation, and he made sure from the beginning that the process of constructing exhibits would be as visible and accessible to the public as the finished product. The workshops can be looked on as a microcosm of the museum as a whole, and their development encapsulates the basic themes of the Exploratorium.

The machine shop began with a few borrowed tools in a cleared space in the middle of the floor of the Palace of Fine Arts. As the museum grew, the shop expanded to include high-quality carpentry and glass-blowing apparatus, a graphic arts studio, an electronics laboratory, machines for working plastics and Plexiglas, a darkroom and enlarging equipment, and, for a while, a laser and holography laboratory. The shop staff, like the rest of the museum personnel, became increasingly specialized and professional, and some of the ossification of institutional growth was unavoidable. Yet the zest for experimentation and an atmosphere of fellowship were preserved, and the workshops remain the areas in which the original ideals and values of the Exploratorium are most conspicuously present.

Tools are indispensable to the Exploratorium's operation. Besides being necessary to construct and maintain exhibits, they are themselves a significant part of the exhibit collection. Outfitting workshop areas within the museum was, therefore, one of the first orders of business, and Oppenheimer brought as much imagination and energy to that task as to the building of museum support and structure. He and most of his coworkers loved tools and gadgets, and so some of them were displayed mainly for their historical interest and aesthetic pleasure. Most, however, were acquired to be used, and they were displayed in use as the staff performed their regular activities. The workshops were as close to the public as safety allowed, and they attracted the same folk who linger at construction sites or country blacksmith and handicraft shops. Sometimes visitors offered technical advice or asked for it, and there were frequent exchanges of machine reminiscences.

The workshops were also integrated with the museum's educational function. Training programs for the development of manual vocational skills were introduced shortly after the museum opened and had the dual merit of producing furniture and exhibits for the museum while preparing students for productive employment elsewhere. Furthermore, shop training was linked to fundamental scientific understanding, and the museum's shop apprenticeship program contributed to the upgrading of science education in the local school system.

The story of how the Exploratorium acquired its tools and staffed its workshop is another example of the museum's opportunism, showing how it drew on the resources of the community while giving something of value back to the community. The changes in human relationships and physical accommodations that took place in the shops further exemplify the museum's institutional development.

The Workshop as Exhibit

Oppenheimer's original plan called for a centrally situated and well-equipped workshop where exhibits could be fabricated within view of the public and with their active participation. He described the important place that the shop was to occupy in the museum and the educational function it could serve in a grant application to a local foundation:

One of the highest priority programs is the development of a workshop area that will be available to both the staff and to young people for the development and fabrication of projects that can be displayed in the Exploratorium. The workshop area will contain wood, plastic and metal working tools. It will also include facilities for electronics. Skilled craftsmen will supervise and instruct the young people who are working on projects in the shop area. This shop facility will be open to high school and college students throughout the area. However, in order to keep the program of manageable proportions, we will limit the use of the shop facility to those projects which are suitable for display in the Exploratorium, that is, to projects which have pedagogical or artistic merit and which are consistent with the rationale of the Exploratorium. In this way the young people working in the shop area will not only be doing things that are instructive for themselves but they will also be able to contribute to a worthwhile public educational program.[1]

Some of the tools collected for display had largely sentimental and historic value, such as the ranch tools the Oppenheimers had used during their Colorado exile and a collection of antique saws and farm implements bequeathed to the museum by a local hardware-store owner. A set of weights and measures was donated by the national Bureau of Standards, along with a quaint old shoe tester that had been found in its basement. The Exploratorium, however, was not primarily interested in collecting tools for the sake of their contemplation. It needed tools to construct exhibits. Exhibits had to be built even before there was an adequate workshop, and the earliest ones were made by Oppenheimer at the University of California's physics department and in the Lawrence Hall of Science. Immediately after opening in the Palace of Fine Arts, the Exploratorium received a small foundation grant from Ruth and Scott Newhall to erect a makeshift workspace in the museum by partitioning off a section of the floor. The grant also provided for safe though clumsy-looking overhead busbars for light and power and paid for the installation of welding and soldering equipment. Equipped with a few hand tools and electric saws and drills, and with the help of an assistant explainer and a retired machinist who volunteered to work part-time, Frank and Michael Oppenheimer set to work in that primitive Exploratorium shop.

In the meantime, Oppenheimer was borrowing and scavenging more equipment, and well-placed friends were again helpful. Edwin MacMillan, director of the Lawrence Radiation Laboratory, arranged for a loan to the Exploratorium of a large collection of materials and tools owned by the Atomic Energy Commission. The borrowed items included voltmeters and amplifiers, power supplies and oscilloscopes, lathes, lenses and mirrors, as well as chairs, table stands, cabinets, and work benches. Many of them were incorporated into exhibits, making the loan in effect permanent. Its value was estimated at $40,000.

Edward Condon came to the museum's assistance once again by initiating what turned out to be protracted negotiations to obtain some workshop machines from the Naval Radiological Defense Laboratory at Hunters Point. That San Francisco naval shipyard was closed in 1969, and technical institutions throughout the area coveted its high-powered equipment. Most of the others were after its cyclotron and Van de Graaff generator, but Oppenheimer confined his request to machine tools and apparatus, especially electronic devices and optical components that could be used in building new exhibits.[2] He obtained letters of endorsement from Senator Alan Cranston and Congressional representatives Phillip Burton and William Maillard, and even the Secretary of Defense, David Packard, intervened on behalf of the museum.[3] The naval officers at Hunters Point were sympathetic, but Oppenheimer's appeal was unsuccessful at first because there were no established legal channels for the transfer of government-owned materials to a private institution. Finally, toward the end of the year, Charles Blitzer of the Smithsonian Institution interceded with the Defense Department.[4] As an agency of the U.S. government, the Smithsonian could be the recipient of record of government materials and could technically make a loan to the Exploratorium. Blitzer took charge of the formalities for the transfer of the machine and carpentry shop equipment to the Exploratorium. With the help of all those official intercessions, the museum finally had a sizable collection of woodworking and machine tools and some components of a glass-working shop by the spring of 1970 and could begin exhibit production in earnest.

It was not until 1971, when the museum received its first National

Science Foundation (NSF) grant, that the Exploratorium itself could receive materials directly from the federal government. The federal grant made the Exploratorium eligible to apply for the various items that the General Services Administration (GSA) places on deposit in government surplus centers. That hidden subsidy was a major asset to the museum and a source of endless delight to its playful staff. The government periodically publishes lists of available surplus and excess goods, though they are often incompletely and inaccurately described. An eligible user may request objects from the lists but must first obtain clearance from the federal granting agency and must state precisely how it intends to use each item. The projected exhibit function of every requisitioned camera, hypodermic needle, screw, or oscilloscope had to be anticipated in detail. But the commodities that actually arrived from the government supply depot were sometimes quite unexpected. On one occasion, for example, an order of titanium sheets that the staff planned to use in an exhibit on oxidation turned out not to be sheets at all but ingots. They were too heavy to cut or put to any use except as pretentious counterweights to stabilize exhibits on the floor. After several such experiences, the Exploratorium sent staff members to the local surplus depots to make their selections in person, whenever they could get permission to do so.

Even after the GSA materials had been delivered, the recipient agencies were still accountable to the government for their appropriate disposition. A shift in plans meant making another petition for approval. Private dispersals or alternative arrangements for goods had to be authorized by the NSF. An elaborate bookkeeping record was devised for GSA acquisitions and their use. Despite the burden on staff time that the bureaucratic procedures entailed, the access to government surplus goods was of inestimable value to the Exploratorium. Sometimes the GSA materials inspired new exhibit ideas, and staff members generally found the foraging among gadgets productive and highly entertaining. And it assured a steady stream of technical supplies in good condition and of near state-of-the-art capability, which could be traded in and upgraded as necessary.

In addition to receiving federal assistance, the museum's workshop was funded by some local foundations committed to the vocational training of disadvantaged youths.[5] The foundations were not particularly interested in museums or in the advancement of theoretical scientific knowledge, but Oppenheimer was able to convince them that their mission coincided with that of the Exploratorium.

As a result, they helped set up the museum workshops, purchased tools and materials, and contributed for several years to the museum's student apprenticeship program. The foundations were more impressed with the Exploratorium's proposal to teach basic job skills than with its more academic objectives. But Oppenheimer made clear in his letters of appreciation that the students were learning scientific principles even as they acquired technical skills.[6]

Several local manufacturing and tool production companies, whose foremost interests were also practical, contributed goods to the workshops. Industrial corporations likewise donated raw materials for construction—aluminum, plywood, and plate glass—and others gave tools and exhibit components. Oppenheimer solicited their support at trade shows and retail conventions. Through an advertisement in the trade journal *Hardware Retailer,* he sought contributions of tools to be exhibited in the Exploratorium's first major technological exhibit program: "Tool manufacturers and distributors are asked to provide tools for the exhibit—special-purpose tools designed for special manufacturing operations as well as tools for home and commercial machine, carpentry and plastic shops."[7] The tools to be displayed ranged from simple hand tools to automated machine tools. Practical demonstrations of their use, alongside samples of the wares they produced, were planned. The exhibit was not to be commercially promotional but was to educate the public about tools and their uses.

Initially the museum's most pressing need was for drills and saws and construction materials. Not all of the exhibits were made of wood, but many were, and most did not require much precision machining. Later, the museum sought more-sophisticated exhibit components as well as computer hardware and software, video machines, and electronic devices. One of the shop employees took charge, setting aside part of his worktime to do the research and correspondence necessary to solicit in-kind support. Gifts of that nature can be advantageous to the donor as well as to the recipient. In-kind contributions are often made as tax write-offs or to clear a company's inventory, and they tend to be odd lots of obsolete design. Sometimes the items are substandard for commercial use, so the manufacturer cannot sell them, but they are entirely adequate for exhibit purposes. Commercial lasers, for example, such as those used in supermarket check-out scanners, must conform to a rigid standard. Such exactitude is not necessary for the hand-directed laser demonstrations at the Exploratorium, and so a Bay-area laser manufacturer regularly contributed its imperfect specimens to the museum. The irregularity of the in-kind donations lent a certain eccentricity that came to be associated with the Exploratorium style.

Once the workshops were equipped and functioning, their operation and staffing depended largely on the museum's educational program. Demand for good science teaching had accelerated with increased international tension and the U.S.-Soviet space race, but the schools lacked the resources to offer it. With the help of several grants, the Exploratorium workshops became extensions of school teaching programs and so filled a vital need that the schools were unable to satisfy.

In 1971 the National Science Foundation awarded $35,600 to the museum to run a high school program using its machine shop. Several high school students had already discovered the Exploratorium by themselves, and some were working there as volunteers. The NSF program helped pay for the expendable materials they used and for a staff member to give them scientific and technical instruction. The students were expected to work on their own science projects outside regular school hours, and they received no pay for their work even though it was sometimes used by the museum in exhibits. A second grant, awarded at the same time by the Junior League of San Francisco, was designed to train mechanically inclined high school students in the machine shop. The students were to be responsible for the construction and maintenance of exhibits and were also to work as explainers on the museum floor. The grant did provide for released time from school and for student pay at a rate of $2 an hour, well above the minimum wage of $1.65. The students were expected to spend about twenty hours a week in the museum, and the grant also provided for a part-time graduate student to supervise their work.

Both grants called for regular evaluation of the students' progress. The on-the-job guidance helped the students improve their manual skills and also contributed materially to the museum's exhibit development, but the programs were not entirely successful. Students tended to get stuck on practical problems and to abandon them unless they were closely supervised. They seemed to lack curiosity or ambition and depended on external motivation. The students saw the programs as job training rather than scientific education, and even the granting agencies were somewhat confused about their real intent.[8] In his renewal proposal to the NSF, Oppenheimer therefore stressed the academic component of the apprenticeship and requested that it be closely integrated with the high school science curriculum. The NSF, in turn, required that the school district assign a full-time science teacher to the apprenticeship program to teach in conjunction with the museum workshop supervisor. As a result a high school teacher regularly accompanied the students to the museum and coordinated her teaching with their projects.

The NSF program renewal provided that students be released from class to come to the museum during school hours, and they were allowed to work for school science credit as well as for pay. They could formally study an appropriate area of theoretical science while solving the practical problems associated with building a related exhibit. Some students, for example, studied plasma physics while working on an exhibit called "Glow Discharge," which shows how gas inside a tube can be forced to glow when current is applied and the air inside the tube is partially evacuated. The practical problem they faced was discoloration of the glass when excited gas atoms disintegrated the metal anode at one end of the tube. That would not have happened in a single laboratory demonstration, but with repeated use in the museum the glass tube was blackened and had to be frequently replaced. The students, together with their museum mentors, had to immerse themselves more deeply in the physics of the phenomenon than would have been necessary in a purely academic context. It was therefore easy to justify awarding high school science credit for the students' work on museum projects.

The students also worked with technologies and played with apparatus that they would not have had access to in even the most privileged school setting. Lasers were still too new and too expensive to be included in high school curricula, but the student apprentices learned their uses. They helped construct the museum's holography laboratory.

Some of the students were attracted to scientific research as a result of their apprenticeship, and a few stayed to become regular Exploratorium employees. Ron Hipschman did both. As a high school apprentice, he worked on the holography demonstration and continued to work at the Exploratorium in many other capacities while completing his formal education. He now teaches physics at San Francisco State University and is also the producer of *Laserium,* a light show that is regularly presented at the California Academy of Science. Hipschman still works at the Exploratorium and is the author of one volume of the museum's *Cookbook,* a collection of instructions for building exhibits.

Despite the improvements in the NSF High School Science Workshop program, its joint teaching arrangement was unwieldy. Although the schools had assigned a liaison teacher to coordinate their activities, most of the burden of actual teaching fell on the Exploratorium staff. The supervisor that the museum hired to oversee the students' was Richard Gagnon, an art student who had first appeared at the Exploratorium as a volunteer carpenter. His position eventually expanded to fit the more general description of shop manager, and he was responsible for developing some of the museum's most beautiful exhibits.

The NSF program ended after its second year, but it did improve the quality of science teaching in the public schools, and it set a precedent for other joint teaching programs under other grants. It also helped the Exploratorium equip the shops, purchase expendable materials, and pay for labor. It provided students with employment and vocational training, along with scientific understanding and a foundation for self-esteem. The schools gained from the availability of an external curriculum and from the substantive science education and teacher guidance that the museum offered. The shop program thus served as a vehicle to integrate the museum within the cultural and social communities of the San Francisco area and to contribute to them.

That contribution was evidently recognized by the Junior League and other private foundations, which continued to pay for the vocational training of apprentices in various departments of the Exploratorium. In less than two years, approximately a hundred students received manual training and some science education in the museum shops, and much of the staff was involved in teaching them. The high visibility of the shops at the Exploratorium reinforced the lesson that manual work is a respectable profession, an important lesson for some parents and teachers as well as for the students themselves. The apprenticeships thus represented pivotal career options for some of the students and provided a community service that schools and other social agencies are not always able to offer.

The Exploratorium took pride in the apprentice program and gave it up only with deep regret. Ironically, it was the success and growth of the museum that forced the curtailment of the program. As exhibits became more complex, their construction required more sophistication and more professional skills. New shop workers were hired for specific job qualifications rather than for general ability, and they were held to higher standards of technical achievement.

Building materials were purchased more systematically and with explicitly defined objectives. Construction materials were specified in exhibit grants, and the shop staff was accountable for the allocated goods. That left less opportunity for creative play and eliminated the luxury of waste. It left less room for amateurism and for the exploratory ventures of novices. Time had become precious. The days of scavenging for exhibit parts in junk shops and yard sales came to an end. The student apprenticeship program became a casualty of the museum's new professional efficiency. By 1974 it had become economically unfeasible. A letter from the Exploratorium's fund-raising officer expresses the reluctance with which the museum acknowledged its dilemma as it relinquished the program:

We are very much aware that these same kinds of pressures for efficient use of facilities and manpower are widespread and that relatively unproductive youth have been more and more isolated from work situations, and thought of as "in the way." The Exploratorium, by its very nature and purpose, is the last place that should succumb to these pressures. Providing an opportunity for youth to work alongside productive adults is a social necessity and not a social luxury. It should be thought of as a source of delight and not as an onerous obligation. Yet financial considerations of the past two years have led us to just such a situation.[9]

Although the high school apprenticeship program was officially discontinued, its spirit persisted. Staff members who wished to become proficient in an unfamiliar craft undertook apprenticeships in departments other than their own, for which they were paid on a reduced salary scale. A few women braved the traditionally male preserves to learn manual skills, and some explainers and other young people attached themselves to one or another skilled shop employee who was a dedicated mentor. In that manner the workshop staff made its own accommodation to performance pressure.

The success of the museum and its expanding staff and programs necessarily affected its physical appearance. In the beginning, the museum had fostered a homemade look, partly out of necessity but also deliberately, to reassure visitors that scientific understanding and technical practice are not beyond the reach of ordinary people in their day-to-day circumstances. But as the staff became more professional, the exhibits they produced looked more polished and sophisticated. As the museum acquired new equipment and a more diverse inventory of supplies, the shop that Frank and Michael Oppenheimer had hastily assembled also needed to be refurbished and enlarged. The conversion of the workshop space reached a climax in 1981, when a new mezzanine was constructed and all of the work stations in the museum were redesigned.

Electronics and New Technologies

The construction of an electronics laboratory posed special problems, the foremost being Oppenheimer's ambivalence toward the computer revolution. Because of his resistance, electronic components were used only sparingly in exhibits, and no exhibits displayed computers until 1980, when "Survival of the Fittest," an exhibit that models population growth, was built as part of a series of exhibits on exponential change. Oppenheimer had anticipated in the museum's rationale that some of the exhibits would include electronic components, but he had reservations about the computer bandwagon and mistrusted the fanaticism of its devotees. He refused to consider computers as worth displaying for their own sake and was not impressed with them aesthetically—although most tools and machines delighted him. Nevertheless, it was evident from the beginning that electronic components would be essential to the exhibits, and so Oppenheimer hired a local engineer, Bill Hearn, to set up an electronics laboratory. He too proceeded with materials bartered and scavenged through manufacturers' closeouts. But in a rapidly expanding field, parts quickly became obsolete, and exhibits composed of such nonstandardized parts were consequently idiosyncratic and difficult to repair. The exhibits appeared to be as inscrutable as the facility that housed them, and the public more dazzled than enlightened by their display.

In the whine and din of a machine shop one can discern a purpose, as workers stop and bend and carry objects from station to station. Even the most ignorant observer has a sense that things are being shaped and cut and joined, while those familiar with the machines can savor the artistry of their use. Electronics offers none of those dramatic thrills. It is based on the encoding and exchanging of information, but its manipulations are hidden from view. The uninformed observer of an electronics laboratory sees only closed boxes with gauges marked by trembling index needles and hears only unintelligible sounds. Laboratory workers sit silently, intent on oscilloscope screens. Few outsiders can identify the workers' movements or participate in their intellectual activity. It is not exciting to watch someone else think. Furthermore, electronics technicians prefer to work in an undisturbed and dust-free environment, and so there seemed little reason to put the electronics shop on display. An enclosed shop was constructed in the museum, and though the public was not forbidden entry, few visitors were likely to request it without a specific reason. The concealment of both the process of electrical engineering and its products displeased some staff members, but others were fascinated by the new technology and unperturbed by its isolation.

Oppenheimer was displeased when electronic components began to appear with greater frequency in exhibits. The new exhibits seemed to contradict the principles on which the museum had been founded. The early exhibits clearly exposed their moving parts, but electronic devices are generally hidden in sealed capsules, appearing to work as if by magic and leaving the public ignorant of how they work. Oppenheimer's opinion prevailed, and he and Hearn soon came to a parting of the ways for personal as well as ideological reasons. Hearn's successors fared little better, and the conflict caused by Oppenheimer's animosity toward electronic wizardry was not resolved within his lifetime.

However, no twentieth-century science museum could afford to disregard one of the major technological advances of our time, and as he grew older, Oppenheimer did make concessions to staff members who argued for a greater electronics presence. Computer courses were taught in summer classes, word processors and database systems began appearing in the administrative offices, and more computers were incorporated into exhibits. The public was delighted. No doubt the location of the museum, so close to the center of California's flourishing electronics industry, stimulated interest in the new technology. In 1981, when the new mezzanine was constructed, an enclosed electronics lab became a permanent part of the museum.

Workshop and display areas for other new technologies were created as necessary and feasible. An experimental laser and holography installation was set up early on by a professional holographer, Robert Sontag, under an arrangement that granted him studio space in exchange for his demonstration and teaching of holography techniques in the museum. Holography equipment is expensive and delicate, and it must be housed in an atmosphere free of disturbing vibrations and dust. Lasers, which are used in the production of holographs, have now become relatively familiar commercial items, but they were new at the time of the Exploratorium's opening, and they excited a great deal of interest, especially among young people. They were associated with fantasy and science fiction and the glamour of high technology, and they were among the most frequently stolen items in the museum collection. Because of those security problems and maintenance difficulties, the holography studio had to be abandoned as a permanent exhibit. Sontag started a commercial holography studio elsewhere in the city.

Another attempt to initiate a school of holography in the museum was made in 1971 by Lloyd Cross, a physicist who had been closely associated with the early research on lasers and masers at the University of Michigan. He had also organized the first major exhibit of holography as art at the Cranbrook Institute in Michigan in 1969. His holographic art techniques became widely known and imitated after he left the Exploratorium to found a low-cost laser resource center at Project One in San Francisco. A laser demonstration by the explainers became a regular museum feature, and a few holographic art works were permanently displayed, but the attempt to maintain a studio for their production was given up.

As the animal behavior, or biology, section of the museum grew, it too generated special technological needs. The display of marine organisms necessitated construction of saltwater tanks, and appropriate housing had to be designed for grasshoppers and other insect species. Some exhibits needed refrigeration or filtering systems or special lighting. Exhibits that displayed sophisticated neurophysiological phenomena required complex and delicate apparatus that is normally found only in research laboratories. Some of the equipment could be purchased with funds from grant awards, but most of it still had to be adapted to the rigorous conditions of the museum atmosphere, and so a biological laboratory and workshop outfitted to make and repair the necessary items became a part of the museum. Later, exhibits involving chemical processes related to the sense of smell and to sexual attraction also required specific laboratory resources. The development of the biological workshops is discussed in Chapter 4.

Words and the Museum Image

The need for exhibit labels and graphic designs became clear soon after the museum opened. Like the other shops, and the exhibits, the graphic arts workshop developed opportunistically out of crude beginnings. Staffed at first by volunteers, it soon functioned as a well-equipped, professionally staffed facility for design, printing, and reproduction. Its development too was marked by tempestuous political and ideological struggles, and it came into its own as an important department only after they were resolved.

Most people cannot take in or understand everything that they observe in a museum. They need verbal and visual aids. Furthermore, they must be attracted to the museum in the first place, by means of words and images. Oppenheimer's words projected an initial vision, but once the museum became a reality, its presentation to the public was no longer exclusively under his control. The development of the graphic arts workshop, which was largely responsible for creating the museum's image, temporarily polarized the staff but led eventually to a sharpened articulation of the museum's philosophy. Like the other workshops, the graphics workshop was a crucible in which the character of the museum was formed. But because the need for a graphics workshop was not obvious from the beginning, it struggled as much for legitimacy as for material support.

At the Exploratorium's sudden opening, there were no glossy advertisements, not even a leaflet to inform curious tourists about the Palace of Fine Arts. A few exhibits stood on the floor, and a single explainer walked among them and talked to visitors about them. There were no signs to tell people how to use the exhibits or to explain what was happening when they did. Individual staff members took it upon themselves, when they found time, to make hand-lettered signs and to modify them as needed. Whoever had the chief responsibility for building an exhibit ordinarily wrote a few words of explanation, and those statements, misspellings and all, served as exhibit graphics until something else could be contrived. The signs were crude and temporary, but it was more important to get the exhibits out on the floor, and so the makeshift labels had to do. As the number of exhibits grew, so did the confusion they caused. Visitors needed help, both to manipulate the exhibits and to understand the phenomena they demonstrated. Since the need for the production of graphic materials had not been foreseen, there was neither space nor material to do it. Nevertheless, production did get under way with the help of a few volunteers using donated supplies.

Exhibits had to be meaningfully arranged on the museum floor, as well as labeled and explained. Practical considerations such as lighting and proximity to power sources partially determined their placement, but there were also such factors as the aesthetic complementarity of exhibits and their intellectual coherence. Where possible, related exhibits were placed near one another so their relation would be apparent. However, the vast and empty space of the Palace of Fine Arts tended to overpower subtle intellectual statements. Despite the exhibits' phenomenal and conceptual links, the expanse in which they were spread out obscured their relatedness and exaggerated their differences. The museum art committee proposed a hexagonal pattern of exhibit arrangement to soften the emptiness and to integrate the exhibits visually, and a local artist erected a tubular tensegrity structure to encircle the entire exhibit space.[10] Several artists, challenged by the yawning space, volunteered to solve the museum's aesthetic dilemma, but the best solution was more exhibits.

Walter Landor, a prominent San Francisco designer and member of the Exploratorium Board of Trustees, introduced a young protégé, Cecelia Chapman, to the museum, and in 1972 she set up a rough graphics department with the help of a single high school apprentice. It was housed in a makeshift enclosure protected by a plastic roof and illuminated by a string of bare light bulbs. It contained a few drafting tables, some tools, and a multilith machine. With only those primitive facilities, the small shop began work and soon was hard put to meet the increasing demand for its services. The museum was producing new exhibits at a rate of one per week, and it needed signs to accompany them. It also needed more-elaborate exhibit explanations for distribution to the public, an exhibit catalog, and announcements to advertise the performances and other museum events that were beginning to occur with some frequency. The necessity of an in-house graphics workshop was no longer in doubt, but its status was less secure than that of the shops that produced exhibits.

The graphics department improved its physical installation during the next few years, but its staff and leadership remained unstable. Grant money was available for the purchase of suitable furniture— drafting equipment, typewriters, a typesetting device, and photo enlarger—and some items could be obtained from federal government surplus resources. No longer lettered by hand, exhibit signs were now of professional quality, laminated with a sturdy, transparent coating and photographically reproduced when necessary in the museum's darkroom. Fixtures for labels no longer looked tacked on; along with the museum as a whole, they looked polished and professional.

By 1973 the graphics staff had grown to two full-time designers and a high school apprentice. Their tasks had become well defined, and they no longer roamed the museum floor doubling as exhibit builders and maintenance workers. They rarely even wrote the descriptive material that they printed but were kept busy preparing copy and laying out pages for the continuous flow of museum publications that other people passed on to them. The pioneering days were past, and Cece Chapman took leave for new adventures.

Exhibits were beginning to crowd the floor. No longer challenged to dispel the appearance of emptiness, the museum now needed to relieve the clutter that the profusion of exhibits produced. A succession of visual designers were hired to introduce harmony into the apparent disorder. But those ventures turned out to be disastrous. The effort crystallized a fundamental incompatibility between the philosophy that the Oppenheimers adhered to and a professional aesthetic principle that visual designers characteristically seek to express.

The Oppenheimers held the conviction that the universe is complex but not unintelligible. Their pedagogic mission was to help people appreciate and enjoy that universe, and they believed that the interactive exhibits that the museum displayed were a means to that end. They were convinced that a great many exhibits were necessary to unravel the complexity but realized that the multiplicity of exhibits might add to visitors' confusion. They turned to words, pictures, and diagrams to enhance the exhibits and illuminate the connections between them. The graphics were not meant to be superficial aesthetic embellishments; they were supposed to eliminate obscurity and make the exhibits clear. By 1975 there was no mistaking that exhibits do not speak for themselves. Increasing their quantity might emphasize the world's complexity, but it did not help to make that complexity intelligible. Many visitors experienced sensory overload; some were amused by it.

Hoping that good visual design could solve the problem, Oppenheimer sought foundation support to strengthen the graphics department:

The exhibits here are not a miscellaneous collection of demonstrations, experiments and effects. They form a network . . . that can be used for learning by both the casual visitor and for teaching in a more formal way. But too many of our visitors do not perceive the threads and interconnections, even though we have had them in mind when setting up and grouping the displays. Too many of our visitors feel a sense of being lost, not merely when they first walk in the door, but when after many repeat visits, they have enjoyed and become familiar with a large fraction of our exhibits. We are concerned with perception and with science and art. If science provides a mapping of nature, and aesthetics revolves on form, then our visitors should be able to perceive these attributes through the experience of the museum as a whole. The fact that they do not reflects our lack of attention to graphic presentation and consistency. Our highest priority should be to rectify this deficiency through the development of a strong and talented graphics department.[11]

Oppenheimer hoped the graphic designers would help implement the aesthetic principle in which he believed—that there is a unity implicit in the world's diversity and that it is revealed by infinite attention to detail, thoughtfully and lovingly displayed. Science, in its devotion to accuracy and precise measurement, is committed to the belief that minute differences make a difference and that attention to the smallest detail will make manifest the unity of the whole. There is, according to that view, beauty in the plurality of the patterns of the world and order in their variety. Simplicity is not inherently more beautiful than complexity, yet an ideal of simplicity is present in the economy and order of things. The world made intelligible has an aesthetic elegance and charm that is integral to its being and irreducible to simplifying formulas. But the Exploratorium exhibits, much as they charmed the public, did not convey that ideal of simplicity. They failed to suggest connections among themselves or among the phenomena they were meant to reveal. Oppenheimer looked to good design to make those connections more obvious.

But "good design" held an altogether different meaning for the designers, and they began from an entirely different aesthetic perspective. The designers emphasized the immediate sensory impression that a perceiver associates with an experience and advocated a visual solution to what seemed to them a perceptual rather than an intellectual problem. The profusion of stimuli presented by the exhibits evidently evoked a stressful sense of noise and confusion, but skillful use of form and color could palliate that impression and impose a holistic sense of harmony. Oppenheimer regarded that as a dishonest solution to a manufactured problem. In his eyes the designers' reaction to the appearance of disorder was mindless, and their proposed correction of it was superficial. Such visual improvements would be inconsequential at best, and at worst they were distortions of the real nature of things. More tolerant than most people are of the complexities of the world, Oppenheimer was appalled at the designers' readiness to displace ingenuous confusion with soothing lies.

The Oppenheimers were acutely sensitive to the risk of visual sensationalism. They were unwilling to compromise on the issue, since the very foundation of the Exploratorium was its celebration of the authenticity of experience. They argued that although aesthetic pleasure is a genuine objective of the Exploratorium, it is trivialized when achieved by a purely ornamental formal order. They had turned to artists to provide insight into the integrity of phenomena and to express that, but they were disappointed to find that many artists are wholly preoccupied with aesthetic surface and have little interest in revealing the structure of things.

After several professional graphic artists worked out badly, the Oppenheimers gave up the idea of placing a professional at the head of the department. Frank Oppenheimer explained their decision as follows:

A head of graphics who is also a graphics person will not work in the Exploratorium. High-powered graphics people, despite their best intentions, are invariably more concerned with making a "Graphic Statement" than with solving the particular problems of graphic communication that concern us. We do not need and cannot cope with a universal graphic aesthetic that is arbitrarily imposed on this institution. Every graphics person of ambition that we have tried to work with wants to re-design the whole place, including each of the exhibits.[12]

Instead, Jackie Oppenheimer assumed control of the graphics department and ran it with the help of a longtime friend and coworker, Annabelle Fulk. Neither of them was a "graphics person" or a scientist, and the decision to put them in charge was received with consternation by some of the Exploratorium staff. Some staff members saw the appointment as a political move to consolidate Oppenheimer's power, which appeared to have eroded with the increase of museum staff and to be particularly weak in those areas in which he lacked experience. Many believed it was a mistake to place inexperienced amateurs at the head of a department that seemed to be suffering precisely from the lack of qualified leadership. The divisive ideological issues were not well understood, and many staff members failed to grasp the significance of the aesthetic controversy that had led to Jackie's appointment and to the dismissal of the professional designers. In the atmosphere of general dissatisfaction, personal and political clashes became indistinguishable, and the staff was racked with some of the bitterest disputes in the museum's history.

But Jackie Oppenheimer proved to have qualities well suited to her task. Both she and Fulk were educated laypeople who had spent their adult lives in the company of scientists and teachers. They were familiar with the language of science but could appreciate the difficulty of making it intelligible to the public. At the same time, they had a mastery of English prose style that visual artists and exhibit makers often lack. Furthermore, no one apart from Frank Oppenheimer himself had been closer to the development of the museum or understood its purposes better than Jackie. Under her command the graphics department was reorganized, and changes in the visual layout of the museum as a whole soon followed. The work of the department was once again reconciled with the construction of exhibits at an early stage. Control devices and the placement of labels could be taken into account before an exhibit was completed rather than appended as an afterthought, and signs could be affixed so as not to obstruct the use of an exhibit or its repair. By becoming involved at the production level, the graphic artists learned to understand the exhibits, their purpose, how they worked, and what phenomena they were meant to display. As a result, the artists were better prepared to describe and display the intellectual connections between them.

One step toward greater visual coherence and harmony was the introduction of color coding throughout the museum. It required a careful reappraisal of the relationships among the exhibits. In some cases the staff physically relocated exhibits, clustering those that were bound by common themes. The clusters were then identified by overhead banners, each announcing a theme—vision, color, light, sound, electricity—and each banner had a distinctively colored border. Borders of the same color identified the signs attached to the exhibits within each cluster. All descriptive and teaching materials that referred to those exhibits were also printed with the matching border. The procedure is relatively simple and uncoercive and has proved to be an effective way of giving minimal guidance to visitors who are seeking some order among the exhibits. It is not entirely satisfactory, because the sections overlap. Since phenomena such as light, sound, waves, and patterns are everywhere, they cannot be displayed in isolation. Exhibits placed under one banner could just as well be placed under another. At least it is now possible to respond to a question by sending the inquirer to a marked section of the museum. Exhibits can also be relocated or reassigned for special purposes, as, for example, when a traveling show suggests a new way of associating exhibits.

Another new unifying device was a standardized format for the text of the signs. Each exhibit was identified by a color-coded sign bearing its name in bold letters. Instructions for operating the exhibit and suggested observations to be made were printed together on a portion of the sign headed "To do and notice," and a second portion of the sign marked "What's going on" explained the phenomena that were taking place. A third portion, entitled "So what," provided historical information about the discovery of the phenomena or offered more philosophical speculation about them.[13] The signs also recommended additional exhibits where the visitor could explore the same or related phenomena. At nearby reading centers, charts and other graphic materials combined and integrated the information, and the museum produced supplementary guidesheets and pamphlets covering the same subjects.

Those and other graphic procedures went a long way toward reducing the sense of confusion and disorder that had prevailed in the museum. They brought a degree of harmony without losing the fine discrimination of detail and without imposing a misleading formal unity. Obviously such minimal organizing measures could not satisfy everyone. Some people found them unnecessary, and others thought them inadequate. Many museum visitors simply continued to enjoy themselves, examining one exhibit after another, stopping wherever something caught their fancy, without thinking or caring about possible connections between exhibits. Others wanted more structure and did not think the small formatting changes sufficient to relieve the stress of the anarchic atmosphere. It is impossible to please everyone, but that is not the museum's aim. The purpose of exhibit graphics is to help people understand why the museum constructed the exhibits and what natural phenomena they are intended to reveal. Neither the graphics nor the exhibits themselves should confine visitors to a single dictated experience.

Aesthetic and political controversies continued to erupt from time to time, but the deprofessionalization of the department's leadership did bring about closer collaboration between departments. The graphics department enlarged its museum involvement, assuming major responsibilities far beyond its earlier activities. Ironically, some of the ambitions that the professional designers had aspired to without success could now be realized, as the department took on such ventures as the construction of exhibits and the organization of programs. In particular, the graphics shop renewed its effort to produce technically excellent publications. Insofar as that entailed the marshaling of resources and qualified staff, it brought new technologies and professionally trained people into the museum. But their professionalism did not dominate the department or conflict with Exploratorium ends. In fact, when waning health forced Jackie Oppenheimer to retire, she was able to pass on the leadership of the department to a professional artist, Jad King, whose work in the Exploratorium had made him thoroughly familiar with its philosophy.

As an artist, King worked with stained glass, but he came to the Exploratorium as an illustrator, hired to draw the exhibits for a visitor survey. His line drawings revealed such careful attention to detail as well as an appreciation of the exhibits' function that the museum sometimes used them, in preference to photographs, for various other projects. He remained on the staff to work on publications. After Jackie's death, King expanded the museum's line of marketable items and increased its photographic capabilities. As more space became available to the department, thanks to the museum's capital improvement program, the size of the staff increased, and its projects grew even more ambitious. Unfortunately, King's career was suddenly and tragically cut short by death just after Frank Oppenheimer died in 1985.

Several publications were initiated by the Exploratorium and produced by the graphics department. The first catalog, written by Sheila Grinell in 1974, discussed twenty-five exhibits in detail and listed many related exhibits in the categories of light, color, eye logic, the third dimension, sound and hearing, patterns, and electricity.[14] A second catalog, devoted exclusively to sound, hearing, and resonance, was produced in 1977.[15] The principal author, Thomas Humphrey, was a physicist, recently graduated from the California Institute of Technology. His catalog was based on the weekend explainer training classes that he taught. It can be used as an introductory physics text, employing about thirty of the museum exhibits to illustrate the concepts discussed. The entire exhibit collection was finally documented in a series of catalogs by K. C. Cole, a journalist who had written an article about the Exploratorium in *The Saturday Review* in 1972.[16] Her catalogs are intended not only for casual use by museum visitors but also as a teaching aid. The first volume, on vision, appeared in 1978, and the second, on light, enhanced by color photographs, was produced in 1980. A third volume appeared in 1986, and a fourth is in progress. The catalogs are conversational in tone and rich in detail.[17]

K. C. Cole subsequently became a science writer on the staff of *Discover* magazine and published *Sympathetic Vibrations, Reflections on Physics as a Way of Life,*[18] in which she extends the style of thinking fostered at the Exploratorium to physics and to everyday life. In 1984, at its fifteenth anniversary celebration, the Exploratorium honored Cole for her popular contributions to the understanding of science.

In addition to the catalogs addressed to the general public, a more technical publication meant for builders of exhibits was also produced. The project, the *Cookbook,* is a series of recipes with annotated drawings, giving exact information on the fabrication of exhibits. Less comprehensive than the catalog, it nevertheless covers a broad range of those Exploratorium exhibits that can be reproduced. The *Cookbook* was designed as a source of exhibit ideas and to teach the techniques of interactive exhibit production by means of illustrated examples drawn from different areas of the Exploratorium collection.[19] Several volumes of the *Cookbook* were produced, the first by Ray Bruman and a second and third by Ron Hipschman. Although the authors emphasize the relatedness of the exhibits and make a strong case for redundancy in exhibit design, that message is often lost on *Cookbook* users, who can purchase individual recipes and replicate the exhibits without absorbing the philosophy that underlies them. The *Cookbook*s were nevertheless widely acclaimed, and Exploratorium exhibits constructed from the recipes are now found in science centers throughout the world.

Probably no form of publicity has spread the museum's fame more widely than the *Cookbook* or won it more friends. But people are sometimes puzzled that a museum allows its contents to be duplicated. Does that not detract from the museum's uniqueness? The question reflects a bias in favor of individuality and misconstrues the function of a science museum. Art museums tend to celebrate works that are unique and unrepeatable, but science cannot be conveyed by similarly irreproducible evidence. A good science exhibit is one that can be shared, and the Exploratorium has been enthusiastic in its efforts to propagate good exhibits.

Another publication that disseminates the museum's philosophy is the magazine *The Exploratorium,* which first appeared in 1977 as a bonus to museum members. It includes educational essays and timely discussions by staff members, as well as notices of museum activities. It began as a bimonthly, experimental, free-lance operation and subsequently became a quarterly, in-house publication, supplemented by a monthly newsletter.[20] Each issue of the magazine is devoted to a specific theme that relates to certain Exploratorium exhibits or to current programs. The topics range from baseball to bicycles to junk, weather, time, and language. Oppenheimer frequently wrote an opening essay, and guest authors are occasionally invited to contribute feature articles.

The foundation of the magazine revived on a smaller scale some of the aesthetic and political controversies that had torn the department earlier. Once again a struggle emerged between the image makers and those who favored a simple presentation that centered on content. Oppenheimer insisted that the magazine be elegant in style and format but that it avoid commercial slickness. Neither was it to appear amateurish, although it was a forum open to all staff members. After a few years of trial and experimentation, *The Exploratorium* won a reputation for excellence among science centers, and in 1982 the Mellon Foundation made a large award to the museum to promote its publication program.

It was not the usual responsibility of the graphics department to design exhibits, but that happened in the case of the Saul Steinberg exhibit. Marguerite Browne, a part-time staff artist, was asked to construct a display on the topic of balance in the visual arts. She used the drawings of Saul Steinberg to state the thesis that visual balance in a drawing is achieved by cognitive means as well as by the placement of masses and forms. The exhibit makes that point by presenting several enlarged works by Steinberg with a critical graphic element deleted. The missing feature is inscribed on a hinged Plexiglas sheet that visitors can place over or remove from the drawing so that they can view it with or without the critical element. That element—a connecting line, a question mark, the word "yes," or a rope—is the link whose presence or absence accounts for the equilibrium of the picture. Deprived of the feature, the picture loses its unity and looks lopsided because the meaning is obscured without it.

The Steinberg exhibit displays the concepts of mass and motion in terms of their cognitive significance, demonstrating that our awareness of those physical phenomena is influenced, in part, by our psychological associations with them. It reveals that a sense of movement or imbalance can be generated conceptually as a result of intellectually grasping the significance of an idea. In other words, ideas can truly "turn us around" or be "heavy" or "weighty," and are felt as such. That thesis is stated graphically by a whimsical sculpture at the top of the exhibit structure. It consists of a large and commanding figure 8 counterpoised against a smaller but more flamboyant collection of the numerals 5, 2, and 1. The two parts appear to be counterbalanced, undoubtedly because we know the equivalence of their numerical value and not simply because of the spatial arrangement of their elements. Other exhibits in different sections of the museum treat the same concepts in a purely physical fashion.

The Steinberg exhibit is linked in various ways to other Exploratorium exhibits, particularly to some in the vision section that reveal the natural inclination of the eye to seek patterns. Exhibits such as the "Random Dot Stereograms" suggest that the eye-brain system identifies patterns as a consequence of texture and form as well as significance. As some of the illusion exhibits also show, people crave meaningful order and will persistently see something they know to be physically impossible just because it makes sense of an otherwise incoherent situation. The Steinberg exhibit reasserts the complexity of visual perception and illustrates how eye and brain, nature and culture, perception and memory, operate in tandem to accomplish it.

The exhibit also has a special meaning for artists. It indicates how the often unarticulated insights of the artist express and sometimes anticipate observations made by analytic scientists. Steinberg said as much in a letter urging the National Endowment for the Arts to fund the Exploratorium's construction of the exhibit.[21] The exhibit is a particularly apt embodiment of the Exploratorium's harmonization of art and science, for through art it draws together certain themes that are repeatedly explored by didactic exhibits in other sections of the museum. Indeed, the treatment of Steinberg's drawings as patterns whose formal identity is derived from their significance foreshadowed an entire exhibit section on language that had not yet been conceived when the Steinberg exhibit was developed. The language section was later to refine the relationship between significance and perception that the Steinberg exhibit introduced. The exhibits included in the language section would emphasize the cultural determinants of significance.

In a sense the Steinberg exhibit symbolizes the reconciliation that was at last achieved between the partisans of the graphic image and those committed to letting the hardware speak for itself. The graphic arts department did become the pervasive presence that the early designers wanted it to be. Implicated in virtually all phases of exhibit conception and in all aspects of the museum's presentation of itself to the public, this small department wielded unexpected political power. It became the instrument of outreach for an expanded administrative structure with ambitious promotional objectives and public relations programs. The duties of the graphic arts department sometimes stretched beyond promotion and aesthetic presentation to the actual coordination of public events, especially those that involved collaboration with other public institutions.

Staffing the department remained a delicate issue. The controversy over image-making never wholly subsided throughout Frank Oppenheimer's lifetime. He retained a residual suspicion of those who sought to prettify the museum, but he came to value and trust those staff members who understood the Exploratorium's priorities and were willing to subordinate design principles to them.

Teachers and Learners

Each of the museum shops emerged in response to new and diverse needs, and each acquired its own hierarchically structured staff, which assumed responsibility for hiring more people and training them. As a consequence, the museum became a confederacy of independent activity centers, each pursuing its specialized tasks, with Oppenheimer as the ultimate seat of authority. Inevitably, the divisions of labor and associated adjustments in political structure led to some diffusion of the Exploratorium's original singularity of purpose. It was not possible to maintain the family atmosphere that had characterized the Exploratorium's beginnings, and struggles over power became more common. Oppenheimer withdrew somewhat from the day-to-day operation of the workshops and the construction of exhibits. As much as he loved being at the heart of the exhibit-making process, the demands of running the museum and the decline of his and Jackie's health held his attention elsewhere.

The shops thus reflect the museum's institutional growth in its positive and negative aspects. A rich assortment of activities takes place there. New exhibits are still produced, but the museum also makes copies of its exhibits on commission for other museums and produces other items for sale. Exhibits are continuously being improved, and so are the skills of the shopworkers who build them.

At the same time, class and salary distinctions between shopworkers and other museum personnel have become more pronounced, and some of the bureaucratic divisions the museum hoped to avoid have nevertheless appeared.

Two separate worlds have emerged within the museum. One is the daytime world, when the office workers are present and most interactions with the public take place. The other world comes forth at night, when the museum is closed to the public and most of the administrative staff have gone home. Then the shops, productive throughout but constantly under public scrutiny in the daytime, become friendlier centers of comradeship, fun, and teaching. Old staff members, artists, and friends renew old collaborations and begin new apprenticeships. Some of the most creative work, as well as some of the zaniest, goes on in the long hours of the night. It is undoubtedly in those nocturnal sessions that the original values that shaped the Exploratorium are transmitted and preserved most effectively. On most nights a sizable crew of staff members, former employees who never seem to go away altogether, their friends, and museum hangers-on can be found long after midnight, building exhibits, playing, and socializing. Sometimes some of them are still there when the janitors arrive to clean the museum in the morning.

The Exploratorium shops emerged out of need but have not been merely utilitarian instruments for building and maintaining exhibits. They remain expressive of the museum's central concerns and have never become isolated from each other or from other museum functions. Although the institutional growth of the museum affected the structure of the shops, the Exploratorium's fidelity to its original ideals has been insistently preserved in them. Oppenheimer refused to hide the working parts of the museum away from the public, and so the shop areas remain as visible as possible. The workshop staff still plays a major part in the conception and design of exhibits and in their evaluation. Job descriptions have become more specialized and their status more hierarchical, but the labor of the shop has not been degraded, and the shopworkers have not been reduced to instrumental status. As much as anyone in the museum, the members of the shop staff remain creative teachers and productive learners.

Chapter 4

Contents of the Museum: Creating and Experiencing Exhibits

In the course of building exhibits and observing the response of the public to them, the Exploratorium staff reached certain conclusions about what a good exhibit is and aims to be. Those principles are not dogmatic, and they do not constitute a formula for building exhibits, but their articulation helps us to understand how exhibits can be used as a pedagogic device, like a text, that enables us to interpret the world.

The Vision Section:
Model of a Thematic Exhibit Sequence

The history of the development of the vision section represents an important chapter in the Exploratorium story. Visual exhibits were among the first to be constructed in the museum, and they formed the first coherent exhibit section. They can therefore be regarded as a paradigm of the Exploratorium's exhibit philosophy. The staff learned from producing the vision section, and to a large extent it set the pattern for the production of all the other exhibit sections. As the first integrated series of exhibits devoted to a specific perceptual theme, it is instructive in two dimensions. On the one hand, it expounds a perceptual theory, essentially that explained by the psychologist Richard Gregory in his book *The*

71

Intelligent Eye.[1] On the other, it reveals an emerging exhibit strategy whose principles became more clearly defined in the process of constructing the exhibits. The aim of the strategy was pedagogic, to design exhibits that could teach the public (or rather that would induce museum visitors to discover for themselves) how visual perception takes place and how it is modified by experience.

Interaction is an important ingredient of both the visual theory and the exhibit strategy. Gregory's theory holds that visual perception is a complex integration of the perceiver's internal structures and interpretive dispositions with the stimuli that originate externally. The Exploratorium strategy is to let visitors be the laboratory subjects of their own perceptual experiments. By interacting with the museum exhibits, which provide the stimuli and the tools for observation, the subjects are able to analyze the visual process as it takes place within themselves.

No single formula or technique was sufficient to produce the range of exhibits required for a comprehensive and intelligible treatment of vision, and the issues to be explored were constantly reassessed as the exhibit collection grew. Most of the exhibits were designed and constructed in the museum by the staff. Others were based on ideas from expert consultants or from observant visitors, and quite a few were contributed, commissioned, or even accidentally discovered. All, however, had to pass the test of use on the museum floor, and many were repeatedly modified. In effect, an exhibit is never completed, for the museum constantly improves and replaces old exhibits, and new exhibits redefine the context of those already on the floor.

The story of the vision section begins early in 1970 with the receipt of a small grant from the Alfred P. Sloan Foundation,[2] permitting the museum to plan its first coherent exhibit section. There were partisans of touch, taste, and smell at the museum, who wanted to begin by exploring those more common and primitive senses, but they posed practical and cognitive problems that could be avoided by beginning with vision. Furthermore, visual perception is commonly taken as a metaphor that encompasses all intellectual apprehension. Seeing the light is a spiritual as well as perceptual activity. Vision also has been studied more and is better understood than any other mode of perception, and so the Exploratorium could draw from an ample body of research materials, not to mention a ready-made panel of medical and technical experts on visual perception among the members of the museum's board. Much of that research is comprehensible even to the inexpert. It does not require the mastery of a specialized terminology, and it can easily be validated in one's own experience. Visual phenomena are, on the whole, accessible to the discriminating, even though untrained, eye. Consequently, sophisticated experimental findings can be imparted to the public without the use of elaborate equipment.

Another reason for starting out with vision was Oppenheimer's personal experience building such exhibits and his familiarity with the field. Some of the demonstration models he had developed for his Library of Experiments and as teaching devices for the Elementary Science Study curriculum dealt with visual processes such as size-distance judgment, binocular vision, and depth perception; they could be readily adapted as Exploratorium exhibits. He had already located some inexpensive commercial products with interesting optical features that could be turned into museum exhibits without delay.

The museum's interest also coincided with a popular fascination with optical effects. They were sought in drug-induced experiences as well as in the art of the sixties, notably op-art and the psychedelic movement. Adult toys and well-made devices that produced reflections, distortions, and illusions were much in demand, and the retail market was saturated with kaleidoscopes, Fresnel lenses, rotating polarizers, and other optical gadgets. They were immediately appealing to the public and could be quickly adapted to the museum's purposes.

The staff agreed to confine the scope of the section to the study of the eye and how it registers and interprets the world of light. The next step was to consult with experts in relevant fields and, with their help, to study what was known about vision, and then to figure out how museum exhibits could impart that knowledge to the general public.

The museum followed Gregory's theory of human vision: People have two eyes, placed about two and a half inches apart and facing forward. Light reflected off external surfaces passes through the pupil and is focused by the lens onto the light-sensitive receptors on the retina at the back of the eye. When the two eyes are focused in unison, each eye registers a slightly different image. Seeing with two eyes (binocular or stereoscopic vision) is a complex activity that combines those two images. Seeing, however, is not performed by the eyes alone. The images must be transmitted to the brain, which judges and interprets them. The tiny, flat, inverted images projected on the retina are all the data provided to the brain, and from that information it judges the size, shape, distance, volume, motion, and depth of things, not to mention their reality. The visual pattern registered on the retina, besides being limited, is also ambiguous. A single, recorded, two-dimensional image might represent numerous possibilities in the external world. It is up to the brain to select the most plausible interpretation, and to do that, the brain must apply a set of rules to the data of experience. Those rules, or guiding principles, are not infallible. The brain does not apply them mechanically but relies instead on a rich contextual history, the product of its own experience. Because old rules are habitually applied to new situations, the brain's standard of correctness inclines toward conservatism, and yet it can be modified by exposure to new experience. Sometimes, however, the brain makes the wrong choice. The wrong choices are especially interesting to the student of the perceptual process because they highlight its operational design and mechanisms.

Processes at the sensory and cognitive levels of perception are so closely integrated that we cannot separate them. Gregory holds that the retina is an evolutionary outcropping of the brain and as much a part of the cognitive processing apparatus as it is a receptive medium.[3] Following Gregory's suggestion that perception is prototypic thinking, the Exploratorium adopted the expression "eye-brain" to refer to the visual system as a whole. Exhibits in the vision section also take Gregory's experimental approach to understanding the logic of perception, in particular by examining what happens when visual information is conflicting or inadequate:

We can see these signs and symptoms of error in perception—paradox, ambiguity, uncertainty and distortion—as clues to the ways the brain uses sensory information to jump from the patterns of sensory information to the so different perception of objects. When it leaps wrongly, to land in error, we can learn from the pitfalls the strategy it adopts. From our eyes' errors we can look behind the eyes and see something of the most extraordinary and the most complicated functioning system on Earth, to discover at least in outline how it solves problems far too difficult for any computer so far conceived, every time we see an object—or a picture.[4]

Many exhibits, therefore, reveal how the eye-brain handles incongruities and illusions of various sorts.

Most people are not misled by illusions. After a few investigations we are convinced that railroad tracks do not converge in the distance but remain parallel. Such anomalies suggest that despite their interdependence, perception and intellect do not follow the identical logic in their construction of reality. By examining a variety of choice situations where the eye-brain system is in conflict, we can infer the criteria by which it chooses and the order in which it ranks them.

Gregory reasons that instead of directly apprehending reality, we assemble incomplete data and construct reality according to certain internally stored and ranked interpretive dispositions. He refers to those dispositions as "object-hypotheses," some of which may be "wired in at birth" as a matter of biological economy; others are the product of experience and habit.[5] Ordinarily we pay no attention to our sorting categories, even those that are acquired. We apply them unconsciously, but we can stop and concentrate on them deliberately. Experimental research simplifies and isolates perceptual situations so that the perceiver can test the presumed hypotheses in the act of using them.

Beginning with the assumption that Gregory's account of vision is essentially correct, the Exploratorium proposed to set up a section of the museum as a public laboratory in which visitors could test the perceptual hypotheses by which distance is discriminated. In several isolated and controlled experiential situations, visitors would face a perceptual problem that required them to make a visual judgment. Some situations were so arranged that the anticipated perceptual solution would be intellectually paradoxical (as in the case of illusions). Other situations simply provided an occasion for visitors to observe and analyze their normal perceptual behavior. The exhibits were meant to show people the functional structure of their own eyes—how we use our eye-brain system to select from the rules stored in our internal repertoire and how we apply them to sensory data to arrive at probable judgments of what we call the objective world.

Oppenheimer turned for help to a member of the museum's board, Arthur Jampolsky, director of the Institute of Medical Sciences at the Smith-Kettlewell Institute of Visual Sciences. Jampolsky in turn invited Merton Flom, professor of optometry at the University of California at Berkeley, to form an advisory committee of Bay-area scientists whose research was primarily concerned with vision. The committee met with museum staff members, and together they compiled a list of visual phenomena that might be displayed. Observing that perception is, in every case, a personal event, they nevertheless maintained that it can be articulated into dozens of measurable events and subprocesses that are common and comparable because of their order and universality. Those events are the subject of experimental research, and the committee proposed to base exhibits on the laboratory apparatus used to study such phenomena. The apparatus had to be modified so that untrained museumgoers could be both researcher and object researched. Visitors would observe their own perceptual processes in action. Additional exhibits would then relate the observed events and processes to other neurological, physiological, mechanical, cognitive, and experiential events. (See Appendix 2.)

The committee initially proposed a sequence of exhibits that would plunge visitors into a disorienting environment. They were to encounter a series of illusions and odd visual effects produced by strobe lights, glasses that reverse right and left, real images and holograms, and unusual lighting effects and juxtapositions of perspective. The point of such exhibits was to suggest the interaction of expectation and judgment with immediate sensation. Intended as a prelude to the more detailed analytic exhibits to follow, they could also be appreciated simply as curiosities. Most of the exhibits that the committee suggested eventually were constructed and put out on the museum floor, but their sequencing was quickly abandoned. It was contrary to Oppenheimer's philosophy, and it would have been impossible anyhow, within the Exploratorium's wide-open spatial arrangement, to control the flow of traffic and the order in which visitors experienced exhibits. A sense of disorientation and surprise can be achieved well enough simply by providing a sufficient number of exhibits that confound expectations and demand interpretations that are possible but implausible. No artificial tricks are necessary to demonstrate that we will spontaneously interpret anomalous stimuli so as to make a plausible story, even when that leads to an unlikely conclusion, such as the appearance of a hole in someone's hand. That is exactly what we think we are seeing when we look through a tube in the exhibit "Cardboard Tube Syllabus" and try to reconcile the image received by the right eye with the conflicting evidence received by the left eye.

Another exhibit that shows how easily the eye-brain can be confused by habit is the "Ames Room." When viewed from a single critical viewpoint, the room appears to have the expected rectangular shape. In reality, one corner of the room is much farther from the viewing eye than the other corner, but that cannot be discerned from the critical viewpoint. If familiar objects of the same size—two average adults, for example—are placed in the two corners of the room, they seem weirdly distorted, since the farther one looks much smaller than the viewer expects. The eye-brain system is strongly inclined to favor the erroneous hypothesis that the room shape is normal, even though that choice entails the unlikely conclusion that the occupants of the room have changed size. The "Ames Room" is a provocative exhibit, demonstrating that there is more to seeing than the eye's mechanical response to visual stimuli.

To reinforce that lesson, the committee proposed some additional exhibits. One set of exhibits illustrated classical illusions adapted from Gregory's book and other standard research sources. A related exhibit, a set of six psychokinematic disks entitled "Circular Deformations," was independently offered to the museum by Fred Duncan, a local artist with an interest in optical phenomena. It reveals how the eye-brain system compensates when our expectations of spatial constancy are disrupted by unusual motion. Like the stationary illusions, the revolving disks let visitors choose between conflicting optical clues, showing that most people with the same perceptual background, given the same clues, will make the same erroneous judgment, even though they know that it is incorrect. Everyone employs the same internal hypotheses in the same order, and when an individual's judgment differs from the norm, it is usually possible to find contextual or circumstantial reasons that explain that person's choice. But perceptual background is important, too. Evidently perceptual judgment is culturally as well as physically controlled, since there are verifiable cultural differences in people's responses to illusions.[6] It seems to follow that our visual judgments, widespread uniformity notwithstanding, are learned rather than innate.

Other exhibit series reveal other visual dilemmas. One sequence on eye rivalry, for example, shows what happens to binocular vision when the images on the two retinas are so diverse that they cannot be fused to represent a single three-dimensional object. In the resulting confusion, the eye-brain may vacillate between alternative interpretations, and the viewer may even experience nausea. A similar effect results if the images on the two retinas are not simultaneous. An exhibit called "Professor Pulfrich's Universe" (independently contributed by artist Gerald Marks) reveals what happens when the light from an object takes longer to produce an image on one eye than on the other. The viewer looks at a complex scene through tinted spectacles that let more light through to one eye than to the other. A ball swinging like a pendulum (in two dimensions) is seen successively instead of simultaneously by the two eyes and therefore appears to be revolving in three-dimensional space. The eye-brain has adjusted to the delayed information as if the temporal difference seen by the two eyes were spatial. The unifying phenomenon of persistence of vision also helps to reconcile the confusing messages that each eye receives separately. A sequence of images on the retina is viewed as an object in motion because persistence of vision makes an enduring perceptual whole out of a succession of momentary stimuli that occur at different points on the retina. The eye-brain remembers the several images and compares them.[7] "Professor Pulfrich's Universe" includes many bizarre optical effects that capitalize on tendencies of the eye-brain system. Several simpler auxiliary exhibits were also created to isolate those perceptual processes so that visitors could study them as they experienced them.

In addition to that series of visual perplexities, the advisory committee recommended an exhibit series to explain the functional structure of the eye and also a series to analyze how the eye-brain makes its perceptual judgments. The committee advocated the use of models and photographs as well as devices for self-examination, recommending that they be displayed along with exhibits showing how a variety of light-sensitive systems operate. Human sight may be compared not only with other light-sensitive organisms but also with inanimate objects such as photoelectric cells and cameras. Exhibits can, for example, display how image formation (the process of representing an object on a surface by reflected light) is common to most optical systems. The committee members considered several devices that collect light, convey it to a sensitive surface (a film or retina) through an aperture or lens, and display it as information. They suggested exhibits to elucidate how that information is assembled and transformed into meaningful data by the eye-brain and by other optical systems.

Another type of exhibit was conceived to contemplate how the world might differ from the way we experience it. Some conditions cannot be changed, and we cannot imagine how they could be otherwise, but we can extrapolate the effect of applying certain physical laws to circumstances different from our own. In the past, such projections were confined to the realm of fantasy and science fiction. Even with the aid of computer simulation, which makes them intellectually accessible, they can remain rather thin and abstract. Museum exhibits, however, can turn them into concrete, personal experiences. How would the world look to us, for example, if our eyes were positioned differently? We cannot change the actual distance between our two eyes, but we can use optical devices to alter their angle of vision. "Wide Eyes," an exhibit commissioned from a local artist, Billy Hiebert, does exactly that. Looking through the device, we can see the world as it would appear to a creature whose eyes were six inches apart. The image on the retina remains its normal size, but the effect is disorienting. No doubt we could become habituated to that world, and the experience of it helps us to understand how different the world must appear to giants and insects with a nonhuman scale of reference.

Thanks to an obsolete surveying device donated by the U.S. Geological Survey, an even more widely separated binocular base of vision can be explored. The exhibit "Stereo Map Projector" is composed of two aerial photographs of a landscape taken from points half a mile apart and projected on a screen. The separate images are presented in rapid succession, first to one eye and then to the other, so that each eye sees a slightly different image, just as it would if the two eyes were half a mile apart. The eye-brain's persistence of vision fuses the two photographs so that the viewer sees them as a single three-dimensionally contoured surface. Such devices are in fact used in making contour maps, and they were useful during World War II for aerial detection of camouflaged Nazi factories, but today computers and other sensing devices do the job more efficiently. Although the donation of "Stereo Map Projector" was coincidental, alert staff members recognized how it might be used as part of a series on depth perception. It remains an example of the opportunistic exhibit strategy that gives the museum an air of vitality and spontaneity while demonstrating the relevance to practical life of scientific concepts.

The advisory committee could not possibly have anticipated all the sources of exhibits. Neither could it prepare a definitive list of all the exhibits to be included in the vision section. Many exhibits were tried and some were kept, and many more are still possible. The committee members tried to present a broad perspective on vision, and they were most helpful in giving the staff a sense of the state of the art. But the professional researchers were not necessarily the best qualified people to conceive exhibits, because they were in the habit of working with a more specialized audience than could be expected in the museum. Some of their proposals derived from their research and were adaptations of laboratory apparatus, which invariably had to be modified to be intelligible to the public. On the whole, the museum staff was better qualified to judge how that might be done, but a few of the advisers warmed to the creative challenge and joined in the design and construction of exhibits.

A Berkeley professor from the school of optometry put a post-doctoral research fellow to work building a giant model of the human retina that displayed the types of receptor cells and their various sensitivities. But the model was not successful as an exhibit. Even though the model retina responded to images that visitors could control by manually advancing slides on a projector screen, the exhibit was not genuinely interactive. It also left misleading impressions as to the capacities of the retina. Without a running commentary such as might be given in a classroom demonstration, the exhibit was pedagogically incomplete. Nevertheless, the staff learned a great deal about exhibit design from it. It revealed that useful lecture aids might not work in a museum where they must speak for themselves. It showed the inadequacy of two-dimensional models and the shortcomings of simulation, and it showed that the mere mechanical manipulation of a piece of equipment is neither equivalent to nor sufficient for intellectual interaction between an exhibit and its user. The exhibit did not withstand the test of performance on the museum floor and was soon withdrawn. That may well have been the most important lesson that the Exploratorium learned from its early efforts; namely, to build prototype exhibits and set them out on the museum floor for a trial period of public use. To this day, few museums revise and correct exhibits on the basis of public reaction, and few museums take seriously the effect that additions and subtractions of exhibits have on the collection as a whole.

There are many ways in which exhibits can go wrong. The Exploratorium staff learned to recognize some of them while experimenting with the vision section. To begin with, exhibits can be too complex. In the natural world, phenomena do not occur in neatly isolated packages, so research scientists must learn to segregate phenomena for selective study. An experimental exhibit illustrates that point. A diagnostic instrument was adapted for self-examination. It enabled visitors to look through a microscope at the inside of their own eyes. It was bewildering to visitors, however, because they were unable to distinguish the several parts of the eye to which their attention was directed. The museum's solution to the problem was to create separate exhibits for each of the relevant parts of the eye. In place of the single device, a group of exhibits was constructed, some derived from laboratory and medical apparatus and some from texts, to enable visitors to explore the eye's anatomy one part at a time.

It is also possible for exhibits to be so simple that they bore people. Sometimes one-dimensional exhibits are unavoidable, at least temporarily, but sometimes exhibits can be productively combined. "Professor Pulfrich's Universe" combined several visual concepts that had been presented separately in earlier exhibits. After "Pulfrich's" arrival and evident success with the public, the other exhibits could be withdrawn from display.

The staff learned that people enjoy exhibits that display phenomena but are also willing to attend to purely didactic exhibits if they are genuinely clarifying and instructive. Some of the curricular materials that Oppenheimer had developed at ESS to analyze stereoscopic vision were explicitly pedagogic but turned out to be easily adaptable to museum use. One such exhibit was designed to teach the so-called stereo rule, the standard by which the eye-brain decides which of two objects is closest to the viewer. According to the rule, if two objects look closer to one another in the viewer's left eye than in the right eye, the left object is closer to the viewer. If they look closer to each other to the right eye, then the right object is closer to the viewer. The two objects will appear equally far apart to both eyes if they are the same distance from the viewer.

That principle is conveyed by a simple exhibit, "Stereo Rule," which eliminates all other extraneous depth clues so that viewers must judge distances solely on the basis of the rule. A related exhibit called "Reverse Distance" shows that people are biased in favor of the evidence of binocular vision and will rely on the stereo rule even when other depth clues conflict with it. The exhibit reverses the right-left images to each eye so that following the rule leads to the wrong conclusion. Nevertheless, operators of the exhibit regularly ignore the contradictory evidence. Looking through a construction of prisms, they try to join two rods that seem to elude them. Only when they close their eyes or avert their gaze do their hands lead them to success, guided by kinaesthetic instinct. Other exhibits in the museum reinforce the same conclusion: that visual, and especially binocular, clues tend to be favored over others, even when more accurate spatial indicators are available. The series of exhibits makes a cumulative statement that might be taught didactically in a science lecture. Museum visitors can learn, through a personal, physical experience, what the stored visual hypotheses are and the order of their application in making visual judgments.

The public reception of such exhibits, however, made it clear that didactic exhibits require a great deal of reinforcement. A single exhibit or exhibit series that analyzes visual experience is insufficient and must be supplemented with exhibits that offer a synthetic review of the entire visual process. Many exhibits were designed to make one or more specific points, but then it would become apparent that an interesting phenomenon had been overlooked or that an important connective principle was not well explained. Staff members began designing exhibits to fill those gaps and to summarize complex processes that had been explored piecemeal.

"Eye Balls" is one of those summarizing exhibits. A simplified model of the eye-brain system, it reviews the complex process of binocular depth perception. To use the exhibit, a visitor stands at the point that the brain would occupy in the system and faces two objects from behind a pair of model retinas. The observer sees what the brain would "see" there, a pair of inverted images on each retina. But in addition to the retinal images, the observer also sees the right-side-up world that only an omniscient outsider could see and recognize as the source of the images. By moving the outside-world objects along a track that brings them closer to or farther from the model retinas, the visitor can observe how the images on the retinas change in size. Those changes are the clues from which the brain ordinarily judges the comparative distances of the objects. But the visitor is more privileged than the brain and can also see that the objects themselves have not changed size but have only changed their position relative to the retinas. The model thus displays the conditions under which size discrepancy and binocular application of the stereo rule are used in making distance judgments.

"Eye Balls" is a good teaching exhibit. It provides a visual summary of the principles that can be inferred experientially from other exhibits. It does not offer new information, but it helps visitors synthesize what they already know or could have learned from the other exhibits. Gap-filling exhibits such as "Eye Balls" are educationally valuable, for they recapitulate and place in coherent order ideas that may have been haphazardly assimilated. Exhibits that evoke new experiences and express novel ideas may be more exciting than the pedagogic reviews, but the gap-fillers are no less necessary. The Exploratorium staff learned that a balance of exhibit types was most effective pedagogically. Some exhibits, like the classroom demonstrations, are meant to convey received knowledge; others, like the instruments for self-testing and self-examination, are designed to help the visitor analyze experience; and the gap-fillers collect and synthesize what is known. Still other exhibits allow visitors to participate at the forefront of research and introduce them to the process of experimentation, which is at the heart of scientific inquiry.

In seeking exhibit ideas Oppenheimer spoke to leading scientists at some of the foremost research centers on vision. Several of them were intrigued by his project and helped the museum in various ways. Richard Gregory, whose theory underlies the entire vision section, was a frequent and useful consultant. Edwin Land, founder of the Polaroid Corporation and inventor of the Land camera, was another. Land is well known for his relativistic color theory and for his experiments on the eye's reaction to light intensity. He and some of his associates gave advice and materials to the museum for the construction of several exhibits that embody his theories. "Green Tomatoes" (the exhibit on Land's contextual color theory) and the "Grey Step" series (derived from his experiments on the effect of boundaries, or their absence, on our awareness of brightness) are among the more elegant and successful of the museum's exhibits and have helped propagate public understanding of Land's vision theory.

Another prominent scientist who contributed original research material to the museum was Bela Julesz, an experimental psychologist at the Bell Telephone Laboratories. Julesz had done some important experiments demonstrating the brain's ability to synthesize significant stereoscopic patterns from apparently random arrays of dots separately presented to each eye. Although no familiar shape or contour is presented to either eye, the different displays are fused so as to produce a three-dimensional perceptual experience. He concluded that textural clues and brightness coherency are sufficient to suggest depth and volume to the brain so that it sees spatial form even when there is no image of a figure on the retina. Julesz arranged for Bell Laboratories to give the Exploratorium a set of his computer-generated random dot stereograms so that visitors could repeat the experiments. A visitor who looks at the stereogram with only one eye, or even with both eyes under normal circumstances, sees a meaningless mosaic of dots, but if a visitor looks at the dot array through cross-polarized glasses, each eye discerns a different pattern, which binocular fusion merges into a three-dimensional whole. Most people see a single, three-dimensional figure that appears to emerge slowly into view. The exhibit does not prove anything. It is an experimental tool, like a piece of laboratory equipment, that allows people to make perceptual observations that have yet to be interpreted. Such research indicates that the perception of depth is time dependent and that people vary in their ability and in the time they need to recognize a figure.[8] "Random Dot Stereograms," unlike "Eye Balls," is a conceptual instrument for making new discoveries. As such, it is also illustrative of some of the less well understood techniques used in the practice of science.

We do not ordinarily think of museums as centers of experimental research, although many museums are repositories of collections used for scholarly inquiry. As traditional preservers of culture, museums are expected to present only the conclusions and results of completed research. The Exploratorium, however, invites its staff to pursue original and pedagogic research and to share that process with the public. As a result, new exhibits may be generated. The museum provides the apparatus and creates an atmosphere in which experimentation is possible, and staff members are encouraged to advance their understanding of phenomena and to develop exhibits that will, in turn, help the public to understand those phenomena.

One exhibit that grew out of staff research some years after most of the vision section was in place began with some puzzling questions about binocular fusion. The project was initiated by Sally Duensing, one of the Exploratorium schoolteachers, and Bob Miller, whose museum career began as an artist. They set out to explore how our two eyes blend their separate and sometimes markedly different images to produce a single fused perception. How, especially when the images are incompatible, does the brain select only certain elements from each image? Are the two images wholly superimposed and somehow averaged, or do some features command more attention than others?

Duensing and Miller studied the literature on the subject and then began experimenting with a simple stereoscopic device that they designed to present a different image simultaneously to each of a viewer's eyes. Their subjects reported visual experiences that combined portions of each image, apparently selecting and eliminating features on the basis of their relative interest. Duensing and Miller found that faces tend to take priority over crossed lines, and familiar figures dominate meaningless shapes. They also found that parts of a fused image can be erased. A movement of the subject's hand, for example, can wipe the image away, but some parts of it are harder to eliminate than others. When a face image is wiped away, the eyes tend to remain eerily present. Duensing and Miller were fascinated by the phenomenon of partial erasure, and it, rather then the original concern with fusion, became the focus of their investigation. They published their conjectures in the psychology journal *Perception,*[9] and the article elicited several scholarly responses. The apparatus that they used in their experiments became an Exploratorium exhibit called "Cheshire Cat," so named in honor of the Lewis Carroll creation who appears and disappears, leaving behind only a toothy smile. The phenomenon that they identified also became known in the professional literature as the Cheshire Cat effect.

The "Cheshire Cat" exhibit was definitely not among those that the original planners of the vision section had contemplated, but its topical interest and the manner of its construction were in keeping with the strategy and ideals that Oppenheimer had set forth in the rationale. As a research project, "Cheshire Cat" extends the study of binocular vision beyond optical geometry and physiology to more-speculative psychological realms. It poses questions regarding the extent to which affective and cognitive factors influence our perceptual attention even at the most primitive level. It suggests that a proper understanding of perception must include cultural and historical information that is often excluded by the mechanistic reductions of experimental science. But those issues are hard to discuss and even harder to submit to laboratory tests. Museum exhibits cannot resolve the problems or give conclusive answers, but they can bring perceptual inquiry into the public domain, broaden the base of exploration, and help enlarge its scope to include matters of a philosophical and humanistic cast. Duensing and Miller did not begin with that intention, but the exhibit they produced invites the curiosity of others about the cultural context of vision.

This chapter has focused on exhibits that have to do with depth perception or the experience of three-dimensionality. But exhibits were also created to show the eye's responsiveness to edges and contrasts, the effects of fatigue and inhibition, color vision, light polarization, and a great deal more. Generally, exhibits were built in series that guided visitors from experiences to theoretical explanations of them. The procedure recalls the design of an experimental program in a research laboratory. Given Oppenheimer's academic background, it is not surprising that such a model should underlie the Exploratorium's philosophy of exhibit construction, but that is not the model ordinarily adopted by museums. Exploratorium visitors are not told how the world is. They are invited to find out for themselves. They are shown experimental procedures and conducted through the reasoning by which evidence is gathered and assessed.

They are urged to be skeptical and critical and to demand clarity where observations are obscure or connections are poorly made. Above all, they are not expected to accept a statement on someone else's authority. It is assumed that they will want to discover the truth for themselves and, having done so, will wish to share it. In 1971, when the first-year pilot grant to develop the vision section expired, the Sloan Foundation was convinced of the merit of exhibit-based teaching. (See Appendix 3.) The foundation renewed and increased its commitment to the Exploratorium exhibit program, and the museum continued to produce chains of coordinated exhibits on vision and other themes. The staff had learned a great deal in the process of creating the vision section and was able to apply those lessons to its later development. Certain broad principles of exhibit design and construction had emerged, as well as ideas on how to make them pedagogically effective.

One principle that was affirmed clearly and early was that exhibit-making is a single, integrated process and should not be subdivided into distinct operations of conceptualization, design, fabrication, and assessment. Many museums have separate departments for each activity, and some hire outside contractors to handle various phases of the process. The necessarily sequential procedure is costly and inefficient and allows little opportunity for correction or improvement after a phase is completed. The Exploratorium experience showed that an in-house, integrated exhibit-making program was more cost-effective and expeditious. It produced exhibits of better quality that were easier to maintain and repair. They were also more fully understood by the museum's staff members and therefore had intellectual as well as practical advantages.

Another rule was that the process is open-ended. Exhibits are always subject to revision or replacement, and the presence of new exhibits can modify and redefine the significance of old ones, as in the case of "Professor Pulfrich's Universe" and its satellite exhibits. In the early days of the Exploratorium, when the staff was small and everyone shared responsibility for everything, the process of exhibit-making was under constant review by the entire staff, and that proved to be an important advantage. Exhibit-making was never hidden away in the bowels of the museum but was itself an exhibit on display.

The Exploratorium's experience with expert consultants was also illuminating. During the initial contemplation of an exhibit series, the museum benefits from the research and specialized knowledge of its academic advisers. But their expertise often cuts them off from popularly held opinion about the subject. Those at the forefront of research and even the theoreticians with the best overview of a field are not necessarily in the best position to conceive exhibits that make sense to a lay audience. Since scholars do not habitually rely on exhibits alone but use their models and demonstrations to supplement written or spoken words, they are not accustomed to designing an apparatus that will speak for itself. In the museum, unaided exhibits must attract an audience and stimulate visitors to ask and answer questions they would not have thought of before. Experts can formulate ideas and criticize their implementation, but a competent museum staff is best qualified to translate those ideas into comprehensible and concrete embodiment.

A related museum principle is that the judgment of the public as well as that of the creators must be taken into account in the evaluation of exhibits. No matter how ingenious the conception or design, if an exhibit fails to interest the public or if people cannot understand or manipulate it, it is an unsuccesful exhibit. The Exploratorium found it useful to build prototype exhibits and try them out on the museum floor for three months or longer while closely observing people's reaction to them. Since the same staff members who design and build exhibits are also on the floor maintaining and repairing them, they are in a good position to judge which features of an exhibit are not understood and which frustrations are common among visitors. The staff members who work closely with the public, especially the teachers and explainers, are also well placed to propose modifications that respond directly to public need. To make sure that everyone is familiar with the exhibits, the museum encourages all staff members—including administrators, janitors, and office personnel—to attend exhibit meetings, where new exhibits are discussed and tested. Everyone is also urged to take a turn in the regular "floorwalk," a tour of the museum, laid out in sections, in which any dysfunctional exhibit is noted, minor repairs are made on the spot, and suggestions for maintenance or improvement are recorded. As the quantity of exhibits and the size of the staff increased, such generalized participation in the workings of the museum became less feasible but also more essential to maintaining the organic character of the museum.

The commitment to general comprehensibility requires that the museum be responsive to suggestions from external as well as internal sources. Unsolicited proposals and contributions from outsiders (such as the devices spontaneously contributed by artists) must always be welcomed, though not uncritically accepted. Successful exhibits are sometimes inspired by other museums or may be suggested by books and reference works. Regardless of their origin, they must withstand the test of use.

Ideally, exhibits should maintain a delicate balance between provocation and satisfaction. The viewer should feel aroused to probe and ask questions without being made to feel foolish, ignorant, or managed and should experience personal gratification from the process of inquiry without becoming complacent. To accomplish those aims in a practical way, exhibits must be free of misleading gimmicks and distortions. They must not give false information, and they must avoid overloading the visitor, even with true information. They should be neither excessively complex nor oversimplified. They must make their point with clarity, and yet not make it so didactically that the visitor is prohibited from contemplating alternatives. An exhibit must demonstrate the desired phenomenon, without obscuring the ambiguities inherent in the natural world. Visitors who are led to expect something that does not materialize are likely to become irritated. Poorly designed exhibits can also make visitors feel managed and resentful, a reaction sometimes expressed in the form of inadvertent or malicious damage to the exhibits. Visitors tend to push exhibits to their physical limits, turning knobs as far as they will go—and maybe a little beyond—just to test what the machine can do. Such behavior is part of the learning process and should not invariably be viewed as malevolent.

Since the museum's invitation to explore and manipulate exhibits is meant to be taken seriously, the exhibits must be constructed to withstand aggressive treatment. They must be sturdy and safe enough to endure ingenious abuse and yet sensitive enough to respond to fine adjustments. Exhibits must be flexible. Ease and economy of repair are often more important than indestructibility. It is essential that a maintenance staff be on hand at all times to keep exhibits in repair, because breakdowns, which are necessarily frequent, demoralize visitors and leave them in doubt as to whether the fault is with themselves or with the exhibit. Overzealous experimentation is sure to cause some damage, and pilfering of removable parts of exhibits must also be expected. Exhibits must be physically accessible to people of all ages and sizes without being hazardous. Their working parts should be as unobstructed and as visible as possible, even at the sacrifice of exhibit cosmetics.

At the Exploratorium there was a struggle over exhibit aesthetics, almost from the beginning, between those who favored an elegant appearance and those who preferred a homemade, funkier look. The former argued for homogeneity, while the latter maintained that the self-evident functionality of things is beautiful and has pedagogic impact as well. They made a strong case for unpretentious simplicity—not to be confused with ineptitude. Their point was that scientific apparatus is distinguished by the sophistication of what it does and not by its formal appearance. In the early years, when the museum was struggling to survive, that aesthetic of simplicity was expressed in the use of clumsy wooden two-by-fours, plastic tubing, yard-sale furniture, makeshift hardware, and other scavenged exhibit components. Later, when there was more money for materials, the exhibit style did shift toward greater external elegance, and the humble look remained more as a matter of nostalgia or of principle than of need.

The staff also discovered some pedagogic principles while developing the vision section. Learning from exhibits is different from learning from books or lectures, and it requires certain circumstances. First of all, there must be an abundance of exhibits that deal with the same phenomenon, or what Oppenheimer called "redundancy." The term is often employed pejoratively, but here it is meant in a positive sense. Repetition, especially under varying conditions, helps secure understanding. Furthermore, since museum visitors come and go as they please and wander among exhibits without direction, there is no assurance that everyone will look at all the exhibits in a section or see them in any particular order. Phenomena as complex as depth perception must be shown in a variety of contexts if both their unity and diversity are to be understood. The eye-brain has so many different ways of discerning depth and chooses among them in so subtle a fashion that the process cannot be adequately explained by only one or two exhibits. Several exhibits are required even to make the point that the eye-brain chooses from many interpretations and that its choices commonly, though not invariably, are good ones.

In addition to their redundancy, exhibits can also have a plurality of uses. Although an exhibit must make its intended point simply and unambiguously, one exhibit can, nevertheless, present several ideas. A single exhibit can be a part of several separate learning chains, and indeed, it is difficult to prevent people from making whatever connections they like between exhibits. Many of the exhibits in the vision section illustrate several different phenomena and can be used in conjunction with various groups of exhibits to teach altogether different concepts. The clustering of exhibit groups on the museum floor reinforces particular relationships just because people are likely to move from one exhibit to the next, but there is no coercion to follow a prescribed route. Alternative ways of connecting exhibits are often included in written materials about the museum. Often the most illuminating discoveries are made when an exhibit is taken out of one context and placed in another.

By the same token, it is important that exhibits allow visitors to explore their limits as well as their potential. If they cannot observe the disappearance as well as the presence of an effect, then they cannot truly grasp its significance. The exhibit "Critical Angle" illustrates the point. Many museums display the bending of light as it passes through a medium and show how, at a critical angle, it is reabsorbed into the medium, but they do not show what happens to the light beyond that point. In the Exploratorium exhibit visitors are given greater latitude to play with broad and narrow light beams, to break them down into their spectral components, to divert them, and to watch the colors of the spectrum disappear as each reaches the critical angle and is internally reflected. The exhibit states that at a certain point the behavior of the light changes, but it also allows visitors to fiddle with the light beam so that they can see how it bends before and after it hits the critical angle. That flexibility lets visitors experiment with the bending of light as a general phenomenon and so appreciate the drama of its behavior at the specific critical angle where refraction becomes reflection. Incidentally, such flexibility in exhibits tends to reduce the injury done to them by visitors who try to force exhibits beyond a narrow range. If they are free to satisfy their curiosity, most visitors will reach a natural and personal conclusion without passing from inquisitiveness to violence. Perhaps there is a broader lesson to be drawn from the observation that the imposition of excessive constraints inspires reactive violence.

No doubt the most obvious educational principle learned from the vision section is that exhibits must be stimulating and interesting, but it does not follow that every exhibit will appeal to everyone or that all visitors should be excited by the same things. It is natural for patrons of art museums to linger over some works and pass lightly over others. Science museums are no different, and it cannot be expected that exhibits will be universally attractive. The Exploratorium's aim is to appeal to the broadest possible audience in a multiplicity of ways. If exhibits are sufficiently numerous and flexible, just about everyone can find something engaging in the museum.

A final pedagogic principle is that exhibits must reward repeated attention. Just as the experience of a good work of art can change with each viewing, an exhibit should reveal different aspects of reality when it is approached differently. Exploratorium exhibits are designed for return visits, and the museum's practice of selling admission tickets that are good for six months is intended to encourage repeat visits.

The vision section is one of the most important in the Exploratorium. It was the first to be developed and so laid the foundation of the museum's exhibit philosophy and defined its educational goals. From it the staff learned how to articulate a theory and how to communicate it materially, and they picked up some practical and pedagogic lessons along the way. Its exhibits were made to let people see how they see and discover how they judge the world through their visual experience, illuminating the perceptual theme set forth in the museum rationale. As the exhibit collection grew, a strategy for the rationale's realization emerged as well.

The Biology Section: Perceptual Patterns Extended

People tend to think of perception as a capacity peculiar to living organisms, especially to animals. Perception, however, can be broadly defined as the ability to discriminate and react to patterns, and that ability is found throughout the inanimate world as well as in living creatures. Reminding ourselves of that continuity may deepen our understanding of perception, but most people find the study of perception most fascinating among creatures with whom they can identify and feel a community of experience.

When the Oppenheimers founded the Exploratorium, they wanted to call attention to common features in the variety of perceptual adaptations of animal and plant species, including human beings. But the Exploratorium would not become a zoological or botanical garden, nor would it house collections of specimens. It was to be a museum of science with a specific concentration on perception. Nevertheless, insofar as the Exploratorium does include plants and animals, it resembles those other types of institutions in certain respects, and it shares some of their problems.

The decision to restrict the range of biological exhibits was partially dictated by the theme—perception—that was to be the museum's centerpiece, but it was also a matter of prudence, since the Oppenheimers did not wish to come into conflict with those biological institutions that were well established and already providing scholarly resources to the Bay area. And there were practical constraints. All biological collections require curatorial staffs with practical biological knowledge and appropriate research skills that are different in kind from the abilities required to construct and maintain exhibits that are entirely inanimate. Biological exhibits require special care and maintenance and raise distinctive pedagogic and psychological concerns. People react with special intensity toward creatures that are or might be alive. They are as likely to be cruel as compassionate and may inadvertently or malevolently injure captive organisms. The Oppenheimers soon found that even their limited biological collection faced the problems common to displays of living organisms. They had to raise funds to support such difficult collections and to hire staff with the skills required for their maintenance.[10]

The biology section that gradually developed has a distinct character that expresses the Exploratorium philosophy and also reflects the stylistic preferences of the two people who successively headed the department. Of the various subjects that the museum encompasses, biology was least within Oppenheimer's area of competence, and therefore he was forced to delegate authority over it. He nonetheless had firm convictions regarding what should be exhibited, and the biology section exemplifies better than any other section his notion of the extended walk in the woods. Its exhibits enable people to experience biological phenomena that are too small, too obscure, or too rapidly changing to be apprehended by the unaided human apparatus. The biology section, like the vision section, has also featured exhibits that allow visitors to make introspective comparisons. Viewers can observe a process as it occurs in another organism and then attend to the same or a similar process taking place in themselves. Although the biology section remains far from complete, it continues to stretch visitors' experiences beyond their everyday limits, and it persists in drawing attention to the unity of perceptual experience not only between organisms but also inside them.

In the first phase of exhibit construction, individual organisms were displayed in conditions that approximated their natural habitat, where visitors could observe their behavioral adaptation to their environmental circumstances. In the second stage, a new department head introduced a neurobiological focus. Exhibits were built to repli-

cate laboratory conditions and, by showing minute sections of organisms, to demonstrate how communication takes place within the
organism and between its parts. That phase received steady and significant support from a foundation whose income was derived from
the manufacture and sale of microbiological and medical instruments. The foundation's assistance may have influenced the number
and sequence of exhibits with a neurobiological theme, but the
choice of subject matter was clearly congruent with the interests of
the staff and the educational objectives of the museum.

In recent years, new and experimental exhibits have been designed
on audition, olfaction, reproduction, and embryology. Not all experiments have led to successful exhibits, but even the failures are
often educational and represent ways of overcoming some of the
particular problems of biological exhibition. Those exhibits that survive the rigorous museum test often offer answers to practical dilemmas. The problem of how to store the living animals needed for exhibits, for example, was solved by displaying them in a seminatural
habitat. That way the public can observe the natural life cycle of the
organisms in one exhibit and in another exhibit examine certain characteristics of the organisms' perceptual behavior. A few permanent
natural history displays are therefore present as adjuncts to the more
analytic perceptual exhibits.

Some exhibits compare human perceptual experience with that of
other organisms and highlight the continuity between them and such
nonbiological forms of sensitivity as the photoreactivity of pigments, the permeability of membranes, and the ability of various
substances to polarize light. Graphic references to those exhibits connect the biology section with the other parts of the museum and direct visitors' attention to them.

The first step toward founding the department was taken in 1972,
when the NSF awarded a grant to the Exploratorium that included
salaries for staff with biological expertise, as well as funds for exhibit
construction. Oppenheimer hired Dr. Evelyn Shaw, a curator and
researcher on leave from the American Museum of Natural History,
in New York. Her primary research had been in the field of marine
biology, and she was particularly interested in how animals change
their behavior in response to modifications of their environment or
as a result of conditioning or learning. She gave the name "Animal
Behavior" to the new section, and a banner bearing that title continues to hang over what is now generally identified as the biology department. Shaw hired an assistant, Charles Carlson, a recent gradu-

ate from the University of California biology department, and together they researched the first animal exhibits and accumulated materials for their construction.

Shaw set out with the guiding principle that good scientific experiments can be transformed into exhibits that the public can manipulate in an authentic laboratory atmosphere. Her experience suggested that marine organisms would be appropriate research material. Their variety and manageable size, their economy and aesthetic appeal, and the comparative ease of access to them and ease of maintenance made them suitable as museum exhibit prospects, provided that an appropriate habitat could be constructed for them. If sufficient precautions were taken, the public could observe and even handle the organisms with little hazard to either the animals or the people. By studying the creatures, museumgoers could gain a firsthand impression of scientific research and also learn something about animal behavior.

Constructing a habitat turned out to be a major hurdle. The help of expert consultants and funding from an external source had to be solicited to enable the staff to build a large tank in which synthetic seawater could be circulated, filtered, and maintained at appropriate temperatures. But once the seawater storage system was completed, the collection of specimens and experimentation with marine exhibits could begin. Shaw designed the first three exhibits to display marine organisms in an environment as close as possible to their natural habitat and to show how the animals adapt to what they perceive as changes in their environment.[11]

The first exhibit, called "Brine Shrimp Ballet," displays the light-sensitive behavior of the tiny brine shrimp *Artemia*. Visitors can watch through a magnifying glass, or with the unaided eye, as the animals swim about in a glass tube and can observe how they shift their bodies toward or away from light sources at the top and bottom of the tube.

At first Shaw and Carlson believed that brine shrimp react to the wavelength of light, and so the exhibit was designed to alternate the wavelengths of the light. Red and blue lights were flashed to provoke behavioral reactions of attraction and aversion in the brine shrimp. But further observation suggested that the animals respond to light intensity rather than to wavelength, and so the exhibit was redesigned. The tank was illuminated with white light that could be turned on at the top or the bottom. By switching between the light sources, visitors could observe that the majority of the brine shrimp adjusted to the light shift by reversing the direction of their movement, always presenting their ventral side to the more intense illumination.

Adult brine shrimp are photonegative in their natural environment, but their young are photopositive. The stage of their life cycle and seasonal changes affect their phototropic patterns. It would be confusing to try to reveal all the complexities of their light sensitivity in a museum exhibit, and so the Exploratorium exhibit included only adult brine shrimp with as homogeneous a life history as possible. The sophisticated experimental controls used in a research laboratory cannot be duplicated under exhibit conditions, but Exploratorium visitors are still able to manipulate one variable of the exhibit sufficiently to see the basic phototropism of the brine shrimp. "Brine Shrimp Ballet" has remained essentially unchanged as an exhibit and has continued to please and instruct museumgoers.

Shaw's second exhibit, "Featherworm," displayed an organism with both light and tactile sensitivity. The featherworm shrinks and retracts into a protective tube when a shadow is cast over it or when the side of the tank is tapped. The tapping produces vibrations that are conducted through the water and irritate the organism, warning it of danger. The animal's reaction is easy to observe, but unfortunately, featherworms rapidly learn to ignore false alarms. Having survived a few trials and discovered that the shadows and vibrations in the museum environment do not signify menacing predators, the featherworms become complacent and unresponsive. Although that is an interesting discovery from the point of view of research on animal learning, it spoils the effectiveness of the museum exhibit. In addition, the featherworms did not transplant well, and duplicating the conditions of their natural habitat was beyond the resources of the Exploratorium. The exhibit was discontinued.

"Featherworm" did illustrate some of the special difficulties that attend biological exhibits. Although all exhibits require a certain amount of trial and error, designers can count on inanimate objects to remain more or less constant in their behavior regardless of changes in their external circumstances. Unlike living organisms, they do not learn or adapt. But living organisms can change their character rather dramatically in a new environment, so preliminary trials are an unreliable index of their future behavior. The adaptability of animate behavior may distort the very thing that the exhibit was meant to display. The featherworm, having adjusted to museum conditions, ceased to manifest its usual adaptive responses, and so it was not a good exhibit of perceptual behavior. Shaw and Carlson were forced to reject several other exhibit ideas for similar reasons.[12]

Their third exhibit, "Flatfish," was also ill-fated. It was meant to demonstrate the ability of some organisms to camouflage themselves to escape detection by predators. Flatfish swim along the bottom of the ocean, changing their body coloration to match that of the sand beneath them. They can also bury themselves in the sand, leaving only their protruding eye stems visible. Even the eyes serve as a form of camouflage, for they resemble the spots on the tail of the sand shrimp, the predator that feeds on the flatfish.

To show the flatfish's ability to change its color, the exhibit displayed the fish in a series of adjoining tanks, each of which had sand of a different color on the bottom. In the confined space, the fish were obliged to change color rapidly and were invariably caught with their coloration in transit, so that it never conformed exactly to that of the sand over which they were swimming. Since the fish were therefore not effectively camouflaged, the point of the exhibit was lost. Shaw and Carlson then tried placing several flatfish in separate tanks, each with a different color of sand. The fish did assume the same color as their habitat, but now the exhibit was static, revealing three distinctly colored fish populations in three different environments. It was not possible to observe the fish in the act of assuming their protective camouflage, and so again the point of the exhibit was lost. That exhibit was also withdrawn, and the biologists continued to search for more effective ways to display animals that use camouflage and adaptive coloration. The entire museum staff was invited to take various animals home and to observe their behavior under different conditions. For a while everyone was keeping pet chameleons and other exotic creatures that could survive captivity without becoming neurotic or being drastically altered by it. The museum had become an animal behavior laboratory in which everyone was collaborating to create feasible display procedures.

Meanwhile, the marine organisms were displayed in a connected series of tanks. A large central tank housed a seasonally shifting population of animals in a relatively naturalistic habitat. At carefully supervised satellite tanks, visitors could touch and handle some of the animals. A team of apprentices and high school explainers helped Carlson construct and maintain that exhibit. They replenished the supply of organisms on regular diving expeditions, sometimes in collaboration with teams from nearby biological institutions. They collected the animals and then reconstituted as familiar an environment as possible for them within the museum. The apprentices were getting valuable practical experience as well as learning about marine ecology, and some of them later pursued biological studies in college and graduate school. Others remained as employees of the Exploratorium and became a part of its department of biology.[13]

Shaw began developing some exhibits that would allow visitors to compare their own perceptual behavior with that of the marine exhibits. A pair of exhibits, "Moving Stripes I and II," illustrates how fish and human beings adjust to an environment of alternating light intensity. A group of striped fish of the species blue acara is placed in a circular tank with a striped background of stylized waving reeds painted on the walls. The tank revolves, and the rate of its rotation can be controlled by the visitor. The fish swim faster or slower, conforming to the speed of the moving stripes. Since the fish themselves are striped, their adjustment of velocity probably is a product of evolutionary adaptation with a camouflaging function. At any rate, it diminishes the visibility of the fish, whose stripes appear to merge with the background.

The second "Moving Stripes" exhibit shows the human adjustment to the same situation. It is less dramatic, since people respond only with their eyes rather than the entire body. The observer can follow that response by closing one eye and placing a finger gently over the eyelid. Since the motion of both eyes is coordinated, the observer can feel the eye as it follows the moving stripe for some distance and then jumps quickly, shifting its focus back to its starting position. Visitors can also see the same scanning shift in the eyes of other people who are watching the rotating tank. Unlike the fish, which move their bodies in rhythm with the environmental motion, humans achieve a compensatory illusion of stability by panning along the retinal image. The same mechanism enables dancers performing pirouettes to avoid vertigo by focusing their eyes on a fixed point. Several exhibits in the vision section elucidate related visual phenomena. There are also examples in op-art, which capitalize on the same tendency of our eyes to move from edge to edge, creating an experience of stability by regularizing motion.

The "Moving Stripes" exhibits have proven successful, but like Shaw's previous exhibit projects, they posed more animal behavior problems to be solved by the museum staff. The constant rotation of the tank and its accelerations and decelerations were fatiguing to the fish. To relieve them, a second, identical tank was constructed, and the two tanks were coupled by a timing mechanism. The paired tanks were set to revolve alternately so that the fish inside would have intervals of rest. An additional stationary storage tank was used for relief and also displayed the acara under more natural circumstances.

It was evident from "Moving Stripes" that animals need rest and that animal behavior cannot be continuously observed. Some behavior must be evoked by relatively stressful interventions, but the museum obviously cannot permit painful or injurious stimulation of the organisms by the public, nor can it allow people to provoke dangerous behavior on the part of the animals. Even if some mildly aggressive or defensive reactions by an animal can be tolerated, additional measures are still necessary, as in the case of the flatfish, to keep the creature from becoming habituated to or fatigued by the stimulation. Any interference with an animal's natural response might jeopardize its survival, and it certainly debases the cognitive integrity of the exhibit and raises doubts about its pedagogic merit.

Public reaction to animal exhibits is capricious. People enjoy seeing creatures behave in an animated fashion, but the same people are repelled if they believe the animal is being treated cruelly. They like to think they are observing animals in a state of nature, but they become bored and impatient if the animals are sleeping or inactive.

Translating laboratory experiments into exhibits the public could manipulate turned out to be a challenging task. Interactive biological exhibits cannot be left unsupervised, as most other Exploratorium exhibits are, and living organisms cannot be uninterruptedly available to visitors; the animals need rest and sometimes have to be replaced entirely. Unlike the physics exhibits, which require only basic maintenance, biology exhibits demand constant care and protection. They present security problems akin to those of art museums. A partial solution has been to offer periodic demonstrations of the organisms, during which explainers remove some of the animals from their tanks and show them off to the public. Visitors are allowed to handle the animals only on those occasions. The practice, which is followed by many zoos, obviously diminishes the spontaneous access of visitors to the exhibits, but it also spares the animals a good deal of abuse.

The replacement of exhibits by demonstrations is not confined to the biology section. It is done wherever hazards or security problems exist. Lasers, for example, cannot be handled by the public without risk of loss and injury, and so they are demonstrated by explainers at hourly intervals. Demonstrations are particularly successful in the biology section for a variety of reasons. Despite the public's fascination with animals, people often feel squeamish and uncomfortable with them, and the self-possession of the adolescent handlers seems to put visitors at ease. Watching a teenaged explainer reach into the tank and pick up a sea slug can reassure the visitor that perhaps the creatures are not so slimy and repulsive after all. Visitors are emboldened by the confidence of the young people, but the explainers also teach them to exercise caution and kindness in their treatment of the animals. Demonstrations have been employed wherever they seem the safest and most effective form of pedagogy, but in general, the museum's policy has been to let the public interact as freely as possible with the exhibits. Some of the exhibits require no handling by the visitor at all; interaction is sometimes a grasping by the intellect rather than a physical manipulation.

One hourly demonstration that always draws crowds is the dissection of a cow's eye. Visitors stand by, at first repelled by the operation, as the explainers themselves were before they learned how to perform it. But they soon forget their distaste and succumb to wonder. Invariably, when the demonstrator isolates and extracts the clear, round, transparent lens from a mass of blood and tissue, a ripple of excitement passes through the audience. At that moment the more theatrical explainers hold up the lens for the audience to look through at a tiny inverted image of the scene around them. Everyone can then appreciate how the world is represented on our own retinas—in upside-down miniature. Exhibits in the vision section and in the displays of optical instruments help clarify that optical phenomenon, but nowhere is it more dramatically revealed than in this biology demonstration.

Children often request the lens or other parts of the eye to take home with them, but the museum does not encourage that practice, since it is likely to lead to an unappetizing litter of forgotten souvenirs. Instead, the Exploratorium includes the cow's eye dissection in most of its school demonstrations and teacher training workshops so that children can perform the procedure in their own classrooms. One reason for the success of the Exploratorium's demonstration is the freshness of the cows' eyes. Many adults associate laboratory dissections with the pickled odor and cloudy appearance of the specimens used in school labs. An Exploratorium staff member picks up a fresh selection of cow eyes every day from a local slaughterhouse, and so the specimens in the demonstrations are firm and clear, and the image they capture is bright and wondrous.

Shaw wanted to show how some animal perceptual behavior transcends the human capacity, although it does not exceed what we can know or infer indirectly with the help of instruments. Bats, for example, find their way in the dark with a type of sonar that we can reproduce only artificially. An even stranger creature is the elephant fish, displayed in the exhibit "Electric Fish," which generates an electric field from its tail and emits signals that it uses to probe deep water, much as we might use an artificial sounding apparatus. The elephant fish normally lives in deep water, where there is not much light to see by, and so its electrical probe is useful to it. In the museum the fish is displayed in partial light, and so the utility of its sensing apparatus is not always clear to visitors. The signals that the fish emits are discernible to humans only through a detection instrument—the signals produce a clicking sound over a loudspeaker and visible pulses on an oscilloscope. The fish, presumably, has direct control over the signals and intuitively responds to the information that it receives back from them. (Human beings transmit electrical impulses within our bodies, but we do not normally control them, and we have little consciousness of them.) Observers can only conjecture what the fish is "thinking." As an exhibit, the display leaves too much to the observer's imagination. It does, however, suggest that there are perceptual pathways and ways of knowing that we do not possess and may never understand.

When Shaw left the Exploratorium to teach at Stanford University, Charles Carlson succeeded her as head of the biology department. It was his ambition to make some of the latest experimental work of the neurobiological laboratories accessible to the museum public, extending the museum's perceptual theme to the communicative interactions inside an animal's nervous system and between its parts.

Once again it was difficult to obtain and care for the necessary specimens under museum conditions. Carlson consulted with researchers at the University of California, and some of their graduate and postgraduate fellows worked with the Exploratorium staff to set up neurobiological exhibits drawn from their experiments.[14] Richard Greene, a young neurophysiology student from MIT who had just learned how to implant electrodes into brain cells, joined the Exploratorium staff and taught his new colleagues the technique. Exchanging information and learning procedures from one another, the young professionals were quickly caught up in the excitement of helping the museum staff expand the biology section. They were hampered by the lack of adequate laboratories and sophisticated apparatus and by the museum's noise and dust (which specialized laboratories are generally protected from). They also had to tailor the neurobiological exhibits to be used by the inexperienced public, a bold undertaking given the cost and delicacy of neurobiological techniques and equipment.

Carlson and his associates were advised to appeal to the Grass Foundation, the highly reputed family foundation of a Massachusetts corporation that had built a small fortune from the production of medical instruments. After receiving Carlson's letter of inquiry, several members of the family paid a visit to the Exploratorium and took an instant liking to the biology project. They made an initial contribution of laboratory equipment and subsequently entered a long and close association with Carlson and the biology department. Eventually the foundation funded a coherent exhibit program. Although the Grasses controlled the purse strings, they had a truly enlightened policy that encouraged genuine experimentation and self-criticism.

By its own account, the Grass Foundation was interested in science education but had little experience with its public dissemination.[15] Mary and Ellen Grass were particularly impressed by the museum's use of actual neurophysiological experimental procedures instead of simulations. They made substantial grants of funds and materials to support the laboratory-learning environment and provided for the documentation of the exhibits and their evaluation as teaching tools. The Grass family expected that the Exploratorium exhibits would serve as models for other teaching institutions, and the foundation repeatedly invited Carlson and his staff to neurophysiological meetings, where they were asked to demonstrate the exhibits they had constructed. The advice the Exploratorium had solicited from experts paid off in the form of exhibits that transformed the neurophysiological laboratory procedures and made them accessible to the public. For the biology staff, the exposure and professional credibility that followed from attending the meetings enhanced their ability to keep up with current research and to improve the exhibit collection.

The first neurobiological exhibit that Carlson and his staff built with the help of Grass Foundation equipment was "Crayfish Stretch Receptor." It shows how the brain of an organism monitors the activity of another part of its body. The interactive exhibit allows visitors to push a prod that bends a tail removed from a living crayfish.

The movement of the tail normally transmits an encoded electrical impulse that nerve fibers carry to the brain. The brain receives a multitude of such messages from every part of the tail and integrates them to determine where every one of its tail segments is and how fast they are moving. In the Exploratorium exhibit, an electrode attached to one nerve fiber of the crayfish intercepts the message as it travels from the tail to the brain and displays the electric signal visibly on an oscilloscope and audibly as a clicking sound heard through a loudspeaker. The intervention procedure is a standard laboratory technique, familiar to neurobiologists and here slightly modified for ease of manipulation. The visitor who initiates the tail movement observes the effects of that movement from the point of view of the crayfish's brain. The brain, however, is not present in this exhibit, for only the tail is displayed. The severed tail section is refrigerated in an artificial bloodlike solution. It remains responsive for a day or two, and the biology staff has learned to replace it well before it ceases reacting.

"Crayfish Stretch Receptor" was hailed by professionals as a tour de force of exhibit construction, for it involved difficult laboratory techniques and delicate procedures. However, it also disturbed people in a variety of ways. Many people were confused by the apparatus, believing that the implanted electrodes were used to administer a shock rather than simply to monitor an electrical impulse that takes place normally in the organism. The Exploratorium staff decided that more exhibits that clarify the microelectrode technique would help resolve such confusion. Some visitors were also disturbed by the presentation of a severed part of an organism, and people occasionally objected to that and to other exhibits on humanitarian grounds. The staff learned to prepare the specimens with particular care, avoiding the display of dead or expiring organisms, which can evoke near pathological audience behavior.

Public reaction can be unpredictable and sometimes irrational. One incident sounded a sobering, if ridiculous, note that changed the way the staff assessed exhibit proposals. The event in question concerned a predecessor of "Crayfish Stretch Receptor." The "Buzzing Fly" exhibit showed how a nerve impulse, initiated in the brain, is translated into muscular activity. (The crayfish exhibit shows the reverse procedure, beginning with a muscular manipulation that is then transmitted as an electrical impulse to the brain.) The ordinary housefly produces its familiar buzzing sound by beating its wings in flight. The wings are moved by the thoracic muscles, which in turn are activated by nerve impulses. In the exhibit, visitors used a tiny motor-driven brush to gently stimulate the nerve endings on the abdominal hairs of the fly, initiating the neural message that signals the muscles to commence the flight motion. To increase the dramatic effect of the beating wings, the sound was amplified, but some visitors thought the loud buzzing was the fly's screams of pain. In fact, no harm was done to the fly except that it was briefly being tickled and was unproductively exercising its wings. The resulting torrent of letters and protests included one from a Los Angeles psychiatrist who charged not only that the exhibit was unethical in its mistreatment of animals but that it also threatened to traumatize children by exposing them to such inhuman cruelty. Local radio and television stations took up the cause, and Oppenheimer and Carlson were summoned to interviews and debates with antivivisectionists, where they had to defend the probity and the humanitarian commitment of the Exploratorium.

It was not easy to apply the lesson of the "Buzzing Fly," since the public sympathy had been so misdirected. Stroking the fly's abdominal hairs did not injure it in the slightest. On the other hand, some other exhibits must cause at least minimal pain to organisms, and yet they do not evoke any outcry whatsoever. Nonetheless, the public outcry was sufficient to persuade the museum to discontinue the "Buzzing Fly."

One exhibit, called "Watchful Grasshopper," has caused no alarm and even pleases the public, even though it entails the presumably painful implantation of electrodes into the animal's stomach. The procedure is performed as humanely as possible in the laboratory, out of the sight of the public, and the animal does not scream in pain when the electrodes are inserted, but it does flail its legs about and clearly does not relish the operation. Afterward, however, it is able to hop about freely even with the implanted electrodes, and once they have been removed, the grasshopper can live out its natural life, unimpaired, in a storage cage in full view of the public. The purpose of the exhibit is to display the animal's visual reaction to motion. The electrode, implanted near the grasshopper's ventral nerve cord, intercepts the message that passes through its nervous system when a moving object enters the animal's visual field. If a visitor waves a hand across the grasshopper's line of vision, the animal's neural response is traced as a series of pulses on an oscilloscope or heard as an amplified crackling. However, like the featherworms in the earlier exhibit, the creatures soon adapt to or become fatigued by the museum crowds and stop responding. The grasshoppers must be frequently replaced with fresh, unhabituated ones.

"Watchful Grasshopper," like some of the earlier animal behavior exhibits, also has its human counterpart that allows visitors to compare their motion-detection capacity and peripheral vision with the grasshopper's. No electrodes are implanted in the visitors' nervous systems, however. The "Peripheral Vision" exhibit simply shows behaviorally that humans respond in much the same way as grasshoppers to intrusions at the limits of their field of vision. It reveals that humans, like other organisms, may be oblivious to a stationary object that is barely within visual range, but if the object begins moving, it stimulates more rods (a type of receptor cell on the surface of the retina) and is then perceived. The person may be unable to discern what the moving object is; the brain merely concludes that something is moving. That capacity clearly has adaptive value, helping creatures to capture prey and to avoid predators, but like the grasshoppers, humans are subject to fatigue and will cease responding if they are excessively stimulated.

In addition to teaching people about their perceptual behavior and that of other organisms, Exploratorium exhibits were also designed to help people understand laboratory procedures and the instruments used for research. Neurobiological apparatus is especially mystifying because of its delicacy and because of its indirectness. The observations made by means of implanted electrodes are actually readings from oscilloscopes or needles on gauges. Researchers do not directly see an electrical impulse or the contraction of an individual muscle fiber; they only infer its occurrence from indications on calibrated devices, and so they must know how to interpret the signals that are seen or heard. But the uninformed public has no way of knowing whether the blips and wiggly lines across a screen represent a signal that is being introduced into a system or one that is emitted by it. Without additional information, people cannot discern what is being recorded or measured. Thus the exhibits that employ those devices are inherently less accessible than some of the animal exhibits that display large-scale responsive behavior.

Inscrutable exhibits are not confined to the biology section, but people seem to tolerate such exhibits when they relate to the infinitely small or the infinitely large or to vastly distant events. Visitors expect biology to be more human-scale and accessible, and they tend to resent or ignore biology exhibits that leave them confused. Their disenchantment sometimes translates into a generalized hostility toward science.

The staff decided that some didactic exhibits were needed to help people overcome their misgivings about the procedures and gadgetry of neurobiology. Staff members had observed that visitors sometimes believe they are measuring their own activity when they press the button that bends the crayfish tail or when they pass a hand through the visual field of the watchful grasshopper. Some people wonder if pressing a button sends an electric shock into an exhibit preparation. They cannot tell what produces the blips on the oscilloscope. Some people are afraid to touch the exhibits at all, fearing they might get a shock from them, although the museum makes every effort to eliminate that possibility. The staff designed a series of exhibits to do two things: differentiate the electrical transmissions that take place within an organism (between its nervous and muscular systems), and distinguish between electrical impulses introduced from outside a system and those emitted by it.

Everyone is acquainted with the small shocks a person can receive from a doorknob on a crisp, wintry day. The muscles contract involuntarily and withdraw from the unpleasant stimulus. The "Grasshopper Leg Twitch" exhibit demonstrates the same process in another creature. The visitor administers an electric shock to a muscle in the severed leg of a grasshopper, which reacts with an involuntary movement. The leg kicks or contracts, depending on which muscle is stimulated. Incidentally, although a shock is applied in this exhibit, there has been no protest against it to compare with the furor over the "Buzzing Fly." Nor has there been an outcry over the obvious mutilation caused by severing a leg. The detached leg retains its capacity to react for eight to twenty-four hours after removal from the grasshopper's body, and the grasshoppers appear to continue to function normally, even minus a leg.

Complementing "Grasshopper Leg Twitch" is a set of exhibits that demonstrate the converse effect, the production of electrical impulses as a result of muscular activity. "Crayfish Stretch Receptor," discussed above, exemplifies the process in a nonhuman organism. It is harder to illustrate in humans, because most people resist being attached to electrodes, which is necessary to demonstrate the effect. The staff, however, invented an exhibit with a system of electrodes that visitors can apply easily and painlessly to their own forearms. The "Electromyogram" exhibit measures the electrical impulses that a person produces by making simple hand movements, such as opening and closing a fist. It is an adaptation of a harmless medical procedure that all hospitals use to measure muscular activity. A closely related exhibit, "Heartbeat," is also derived from medical procedure. Here again, the exhibit measures the effect of muscular exertion. The visitor pedals a bicycle, which accelerates the person's heartbeat, generating an electrical signal that is transmitted by means of electrodes in the handlebars of the bicycle to an oscilloscope and an audiomonitor. As the visitor's exertion changes, the frequency of the electrical pulses varies visibly and audibly with the changing rate of the person's heartbeat.

The exhibits demonstrate, in crayfish or in humans, how bodily movements, whether voluntary or not, are expressed as electrical impulses that can be observed and measured. They have the secondary purpose of displaying machines that visitors are likely to find relatively familiar and unmenacing, even though the manner of their operation might not be understood. The machines are commonly used in medical diagnostic procedures, and the exhibits may help to answer technical questions that people are sometimes reluctant to ask their physicians. Another by-product of the exhibits is their lesson of unity. Throughout nature organisms communicate among themselves and within themselves by recognizing, preserving, translating, and transmitting patterns. In organisms with a nervous system, electrical signals deliver patterned messages by way of nerve fibers to and from the motor apparatus. Other organisms have different ways of moving information from one part of the body to another.

With the encouragement of the Grass Foundation,[16] Carlson and his staff continued to explore the subtleties of neurobiological research, and particularly its communicative aspect. Indeed, they were determined to construct an entire miniature neurophysiology laboratory in the museum. The staff would be able to implant electrodes into a single nerve cell of an organism in the laboratory before the museum's public hours. They could then set the preparation up on a microscope slide in a glass case, with the eyepiece placed outside the case so that the public could focus on the slide through the microscope and see exactly what the neurobiologist sees. The exhibit shows how the internal electrical activity of the nerve cell is generated when a stimulus above a minimum threshold is applied, and how the cell's firing transmits electrical impulses at varying frequencies to neighboring cells. Visitors are able to adjust the stimulus from outside the apparatus and observe the resulting wave image on an oscilloscope. The exhibit design was ambitious, requiring the same attention given to the design of a research laboratory. In addition, it had to be fortified to withstand the Exploratorium conditions—to protect the apparatus from vibration, dust, humidity, fluctuations in voltage, and even the extraneous radio waves that come from other exhibits in the museum. It also took time to investigate which organisms were comparatively simple in structure, sturdy enough, and most accessible to experimentation. Again, consultation with academic researchers proved indispensable.[17]

The exhibit went through several prototypes and redesigns. When it was finally completed, it was called the "Language of Nerve Cells," and it does display the fundamental communicative interaction that underlies all animal perception. It is an effective pedagogic introduction to neurobiological research, and Carlson was invited to demonstrate the exhibit at the 1977 meeting of the American Neurobiological Association. Educators there were amazed that such fragile and sophisticated apparatus could be encapsulated for museum and classroom use, and afterward Carlson received many requests to build replicas of the exhibit for schools and teaching laboratories. He and his associates later developed an accompanying exhibit, "Nerve Impulse," to display the compound path of numerous electrical impulses along the length of an entire nerve cord, rather than within a single nerve cell. Users can vary the voltage that stimulates the nerve cord at one end and can observe the changing frequency of firings recorded at the other end.

The educational effectiveness of the exhibits is hard to assess. The "Language of Nerve Cells" never attracted large crowds. In an account submitted to the Grass Foundation, Carlson noted that approximately 5 percent of the museum's 560,000 annual visitors interacted with it.[18] The exhibits certainly do not evoke the kinship that visitors tend to feel toward some of the whole-animal displays. Some people are drawn to the neurobiological exhibits for irrelevant reasons—they enjoy the flickering lights on the oscilloscope, for example. On the other hand, some local neurophysiology professors regularly bring their classes to use the exhibits as adjuncts to their laboratories. The Grass Foundation commissioned follow-up and audience-evaluation studies, and so a questionnaire was distributed inviting visitors to express their reactions to the exhibits and make suggestions for their improvement.[19] Their responses revealed that people had difficulty understanding the exhibits, and so more graphic explanatory aids were provided, complete with photographs and diagrams that related the exhibits to other exhibits in the museum. Those materials are helpful to people who use them, but most visitors come to play with exhibits and not to read about them. For some visitors, the museum's ambient noise and confusion prohibit careful study, but the possibility is there for those who wish to apply themselves.

There is a great deal left to be done in the biology section. The neurobiological series is concerned with the fundamentals of animal perception. A few exhibits also display plant tropisms and plant sensitivity to heat and touch. Botanical exhibits on germination and on the medicinal applications of plants were planned from the beginning, but those topics still await imaginative development. Some exhibits were produced on the topics of cell differentiation and reproduction, processes that involve a precognitive ability to recognize and select. An early exhibit using sea urchin eggs did not survive the museum test, but a more recent one that displays the development of a chick embryo has been highly successful. Sexual attraction is another perceptual experience, and an exhibit on insect pheromones shows how a chemical produced by the female moth is detected, even in minute quantities, by the male moth, who will struggle against strong winds to pursue it. That exhibit is one of the few that the museum has been able to create on the sense of smell, an area that poses special problems.

Microscopic organisms present another area for exhibit exploration. One exhibit, "Giant Microscope," allows visitors to peer through a microscope at a set of rotating slides containing microorganisms that have been collected from the lagoon outside the Exploratorium. Like the marine animal displays, this exhibit changes seasonally and gives visitors a glimpse of the local ecology. There is also an exhibit of phosphorescent bacteria, visible to the unaided eye only by their shimmer. Although there is a natural connection between their light-productive capacity and some of the other exhibits on light absorption and emission, the phosphorescent bacteria are somewhat isolated, and the educational linkages that might be made have not yet been fully explored. Exhibits showing bacterial multiplication, for example, would be useful in the teaching of basic genetic and microbiological concepts and would also relate to the museum's mathematical section on the concept of exponential growth.

Animal social behavior, one of Evelyn Shaw's original interests, is another promising area of exhibit development. There have, from time to time, been proposals to display ant colonies, bee hives, and other creatures that collect in organized groups. Such suggestions are as likely to come from artists and community activists as from scientists. Some staff members have urged the Exploratorium to develop exhibits that promote an environmentalist position or seek to raise ecological consciousness. Because of its style and the spirit that pervades it, the Exploratorium has always been subject to pressure to espouse moral and political causes, and some people believe that the museum has an obligation to educate the public in practical matters of science and social policy. But Oppenheimer believed that the educational mission of the Exploratorium did not lie in advancing specific political causes. Its aim was not to give people the right answers—even when he believed he knew them—but to help them gain the confidence to make discoveries for themselves. The Exploratorium, he insisted, was committed to the free play of the imagination and not to the business of getting things done.

Politics was not the only impediment to ecological exhibits. They require space and pose maintenance problems, and a few people were concerned about health risks and the possible annoyance of buzzing insects. Visitors are directed to explore the grounds and the lagoon outside the museum, and many do stop there to picnic or feed the ducks and pigeons. One artist-in-residence made a project of identifying and labeling the more interesting plants and animals in the area surrounding the Exploratorium. In recent years various artists, including the Exploratorium's own Peter Richards, have used the fog, the weather, the ocean tidepools, and the waves of the sea as components of art works. In characteristic Exploratorium fashion, they have blurred the distinctions between art and nature, artist and scientist, inside and outside the museum, to stretch our consciousness of the relationships among all those concepts.

The biology section has continued to amplify the theme of human perception. Evelyn Shaw was the first to fix a focus, on the adaptive behavior of marine animals in their environment. Charles Carlson turned a spotlight on the environment within the organism and the communication that takes place between its parts. Both types of exhibit brought a new order of complexity to the museum that continues to challenge the intellect and skill of the museum staff. With the help of interested supporters and the advice of the academic and professional community, the biology department is developing a genuinely innovative and educational exhibit program.

Teaching Physics Through Phenomena: Electricity

There is no such thing as a standard museum experience, nor is there a single prescribed pathway for gaining the most benefit from one. People come to museums to be amused and entertained and to spend agreeable time with family and friends. They also come to learn, and even though museums can serve a variety of other functions, they are, above all, educational resources.[20] Museum exhibits are designed with the expectation that someone is going to learn from them, and so a hypothetical observer is clearly anticipated in their fabrication. The Exploratorium's ideal museum learner is one who interacts with exhibits serially, using them in combination to test out and amplify ideas that are picked up from one exhibit and modified by another. In this section I will discuss how several exhibits related to physics are used to elicit that learning experience.

The central theme of the Exploratorium is perceptual phenomena, but the exhibits that feature those phenomena are not necessarily what casual visitors first notice on entering the museum. Many visitors see the museum as a vast three-dimensional textbook illustrating classical physics. Actually, there is no single exhibit section devoted to physics, but most of the phenomena that elementary physics texts cover—motion, heat and temperature, sound, light and color, electricity and magnetism—are what we perceive in the world and what science teaches us to perceive in accordance with its rules and conventions.

Frank Oppenheimer came from the physics classroom and had worked on the reform of science curricula. He saw the Exploratorium as a way to complement the formalism of science teaching in the schools by bringing physics back into the realm of everyday objects and experience. The exhibits in the Exploratorium display natural phenomena partially isolated from the complexity of the natural world but not abstracted to the extent characteristic of academic physics laboratories. The exhibits are supposed to bridge the gap between our intuitive but imprecise acquaintance with the world of phenomena and the exact, though indirect, measurements and abstract generalizations that are identified with science.

Science students perform experiments in class, but they are rarely taught to explore the world, and fewer and fewer of them come from environments where observation of nature can be taken for granted as a normal part of human experience. In a way science has led to a decrease in curiosity among ordinary people. We have become so accustomed to living in ignorance of much that is complex that the "simple questions" that can revolutionize science no longer intrigue us—"The genius of men like Newton and Einstein lies in that: they ask transparent, innocent questions which turn out to have catastrophic answers. Einstein was a man who could ask immensely simple questions."[21] Students are told what questions to ask and in what order to ask them. They learn science as a disciplined mastery of concepts that have little to do with the world in which they live. Many terminate their education with the conviction that science is an arcane skill with useful applications but little further value. Their textbook knowledge includes the standard illustrations—the 1940 collapse of the Tacoma Narrows Bridge as an example of resonance, the stability of the Leaning Tower of Pisa as an illustration of center of gravity—but they do not learn to relate the classic formulas to such prosaic observations as the violent bouncing of the teakettle on the stove or the automatic lunges one makes to retrieve one's balance on a moving bus. Exploratorium exhibits are meant to lead the museumgoer's attention back to the phenomena.

Sometimes all it takes is a simple instruction, without any apparatus. One exhibit on sound, for example, consists only of a sign that invites visitors to stand in the center of the domed rotunda outside the museum and clap their hands or shout, while listening to the sound reverberate from the curved surfaces. Everyone recalls similar experiences of reflected sound. We have all been intrigued by the sound of our own voices coming back to us in a cave or from across a mountain valley. The Exploratorium sound exhibit reminds us of those familiar experiences and links them to other exhibits that analyze and explain them.

From the rotunda one is directed inside the museum to other exhibits that explore the sound of one's reverberating voice. "Focused Sound" is an exhibit that shows how two large parabolic mirrors reflect sound waves to a particular point where the visitor can hear the sound more clearly than at any other point. A listener close to one of the mirrors will not hear a word whispered nearby, but the same whisper is clearly audible at the distant reflective point, just as a visual image is reflected clearly only at a specific optical point and not throughout the pathway to it.

Another exhibit, "Echo Tube," further analyzes the same experience of sound. The apparatus is simply a long, hollow cylinder. A noise projected into the narrow tube bounces back with its component wave frequencies broken down sequentially. Normally, complex echoes moving through relatively unconfined spaces return intact, because all the sound waves travel at the same speed. Inside the narrow, 200-foot-long echo tube, however, the sound waves move along different pathways. The larger low-frequency waves ricochet off the walls of the tube and are delayed and distorted, while the small high-frequency waves travel straight up and down the tube and return without delay. The listener hears separate echoes, one after another, as a series of distinct and strange sounds. The exhibit is also likely to evoke childhood memories of shouting into culverts and hollow places and listening to the odd sounds that came back. We all noticed those things as children, but many people no longer even think of them with wonder, and few reflect on them as matters of scientific interest.

Obviously not all of the concepts of physics can be expressed in terms of exhibits that refer to child's play or everyday experience. Contemporary physics investigates phenomena that are far too big or small or remote or temporary to be directly experienced—elementary particles, for example—and to apprehend those phenomena, physicists employ research tools, both physical and conceptual, that are not related to ordinary experience. Some of the objects that physicists study are artifacts brought into being by the detection process itself. The objects are nevertheless real in the context of the conventions of physics, and their investigation arises out of historical questions that are rooted in direct observation.

The laboratory equipment used in such inquiries is likewise an outgrowth of simpler tools whose experiential functions can be traced. Physicists accustomed to certain instruments may regard them much as a naturalist treats a hand-held magnifying lens or a calligrapher a brush. The device becomes an almost invisible extension of the user's sensory capacity, so that the observer knows the world through the device without knowing the device and without recalling that the conclusions are inferred from secondary information. Since the physicist's apparatus, however, has little if any application outside the laboratory, it is unfamiliar to most nonscientists. They do not see "through" it; for them it is as opaque as the reality it is supposed to illuminate. A science museum can help demystify that equipment by displaying it in the context of its origin and its current use and operation, at the same time reconciling science with ordinary experience and guiding visitors to an appreciation, if not an understanding, of the concerns of modern science. One way of doing that is to expose the devices that scientists use, to name them, and to show how they work. It is helpful simply to see what kind of contraption a bubble chamber is and to observe what happens when a particle is tracked by it. The Exploratorium's first display of the Stanford accelerator initiated an expository tradition that the museum has maintained ever since.

More important than demonstrating the operation of physical equipment, however, is encouraging people to think about and feel comfortable with the concepts of physics that are pervasive in everyone's experience, even though they may seem painfully abstract. We all know what it feels like to move, but we become alienated from motion when we study it as something that happens to objects. From the stance of science it makes no difference whether a moving object is a ball or a baby; the depiction of it is abstracted from the experience of it. Waterfalls, falling babies, and fallen arches are all subject to the laws of gravitation. Newton's laws apply to colliding billiard balls and to projectiles in space. They apply to ourselves as well, but we tend to abstract them and to forget that we too are moving objects.

The Exploratorium exhibit section on motion approaches the subject experientially. Visitors learn about rotational motion, for example, by setting themselves spinning. Riding on one of the museum's gyro exhibits, visitors can feel rotational inertia acting on their bodies; they cannot help but notice the effort it takes to stop spinning or to turn around in the midst of a spin. No one suggests that having such an experience is a lesson in physics or is equivalent to understanding Newton's laws, but it might stimulate visitors to learn about Newton's laws, especially if the museum invites them to reflect on additional exhibits integrated into the section. The Exploratorium "Momentum Machine," for example, gives riders a thrill while it helps make sense of the strange sensation one has if one extends an arm while spinning—and slows down—and then draws the arm in close—and speeds up. Those exhibits present experiences we might have in a playground or amusement park, but the museum supplements them with didactic exhibits and written or verbal explanations. Obviously one can ignore the explanations and just enjoy the exhibits. That is also a successful use of the museum.

The concreteness of museum exhibits makes them more interesting than textbook illustrations and more versatile than classroom demonstrations. They can be mixed and matched and presented in various orders, depending on the needs of the audience. The museum staff can also vary the manner of the exhibits' use to conform to special projects. The Exploratorium has, for example, assembled a sizable body of exhibits that can be combined in several ways to explain the complex subject of electricity.

Electricity is a particularly challenging topic. It is phenomenologically inaccessible, although electromagnetic forces are pervasive and play an even larger part in the physical universe than gravitational force. Electrical forces hold all matter together and account for its physical and chemical properties. Furthermore, the transmission of information between the nerves and muscles in living organisms is an electrical event, and thus all of the automatic and deliberate activities of plants and animals are electrically controlled. There is little in the universe that cannot be considered an electrical phenomenon, and yet we have almost no intuitive sense of what to make of it. Apart from the unpleasant sensation of being shocked, we do not know what it means to *feel* electricity.

The applications of electricity are so pervasive in modern industrial and domestic life that we have almost ceased to be aware of them. Nevertheless, most people do not understand electricity well. Many are frightened by electrical phenomena, and although we constantly use and repair and discuss our electrical appliances, they seem beyond ordinary comprehension. Of the various ways in which electricity is formally taught, none seems to cover the matter completely and most are quite unsatisfactory. Science museums have tried to tackle the problem, and many, like the Exploratorium, have developed exhibits on electricity. Most are borrowed from physics texts and tend to be one-dimensional.

The language of electricity has become a part of the modern vocabulary: volts, ohms, and amperes are as familiar as inches and pounds, and our emotional expression abounds with "shocks," "charges," and "turn-ons." But the concepts behind the words are notoriously difficult for people to grasp. Students and practicing electricians tend to learn by heart the formulas that relate electrical units to one another, and few people know what the names of those units signify. Even fewer can connect the profusion of electrical instruments that fill our homes and workplaces with the brilliant nineteenth-century conceptual synthesis that united all matter and energy under the descriptive heading of an electromagnetic field. How might that sprawling subject be rendered comprehensible?[22]

Like the proverbial fish in water, we are surrounded by forces whose universality disguises their reality. Since the negative and positive electrical forces in the universe are almost perfectly balanced, most objects are neutral in charge, and people are not aware that electrical forces play any part in their behavior at all. It is much easier to think of ourselves as living in a sea of air than as surrounded by charged particles. We are more aware of gravitational force acting on us than of electrical attractions and repulsions, although at the atomic level they are more significant.

Electrical force is known to be polar, but charge (positive and negative) is not directly discriminated. It is known by its effects. The force between like charges is repulsive, and that between unlike charges is attractive. When charge is transferred to or from a neutral body, that body becomes charged. When charge flows through a conductor between bodies of different electric potential the imbalance of electric charge creates a current, whose presence is inferred from its effects. Most people are so accustomed to using these effects—the movement of an indicator, a glowing light, a spark—as evidence of the presence of charge or current that they ignore the mediation and confuse the evidence with its cause. Colloquial discourse adds to the confusion, suggesting that there is some mysterious electrical substance that behaves like an ordinary fluid.

The Exploratorium staff was intrigued by the challenge of teaching the public about this elusive phenomenon, but the first exhibits, based on standard textbook models, were not successful. Museum visitors ignored them. As before, the staff turned to specialists for help. In 1981 the NSF sponsored a conference at the museum, bringing together scientists, educators, historians, exhibit designers, and others to brainstorm on the topic of how to make electricity clear and accessible to the general public.

The conference participants began by reminiscing about their own childhood discovery of electricity. A few fondly recalled electric trains and household appliances they had eviscerated and dissected. Some of the women remembered anxiety and frustration, their fear of objects that were fragile and dangerous, and how they had been put off from becoming better acquainted with them. Everyone agreed that unless people are made to feel at ease with electrical phenomena rather than frightened by them, they will not discover the astonishing unity of nature that the study of electricity can reveal. One of the first objectives of the museum therefore was to overcome the fear and discomfort that the phenomenon evokes.

The panel fantasized and played with exhibit ideas. One imaginative proposal culminated in an actual exhibit called "Pacific Gas and

Leather." A simple leather belt on a pulley system represented what customers pay for when they buy electricity from a utility company. Objects that do work could be attached to the belt and made to function, demonstrating that utility customers are not really purchasing a commodity with their monthly payments.[23] We do not buy a quantity of electrons the way we fill a gas tank with fuel. Consumers pay for the privilege of attaching their devices to the system that keeps electrons moving. Nothing is consumed, however, for the electrons pass right on and are reutilized.

But beyond that one concept, how could a series of museum exhibits capture the strange and elusive nature of electricity? In the end, the panel was unable to come up with a coherent exhibit program. Leaving the task of synthesis to the visitor, they suggested several exhibit sequences that they hoped would capitalize on whatever existing associations visitors might bring with them and whatever guidance the museum staff could provide to link the exhibits to those associations.

Individual staff members often follow a preferred approach to electrical phenomena, reflecting the guide's educational history and current interests. Robert Semper, a physicist and deputy director of the museum, begins his tours of the electricity section with an academic explanation of electromagnetism. At "Pluses and Minuses," an exhibit on static charge, he rubs an ordinary Ping-Pong paddle on a cloth surface and then moves it among some apparently inert polystyrene chips, galvanizing them into frenetic movement. Some of the chips cling to the paddle, while others are repelled, depending on whether their charge is the opposite of or the same as the paddle's. Semper explains that the apparent stability of nature is largely due to the unseen equilibrium of opposite charges, and its instability is due to their imbalance. In the exhibit Semper creates an imbalance of charge simply by rubbing the paddle on his clothes or hair. The homey exhibit duplicates the effects of everyday experiences—the crackling of hair when you run a comb through it, the spark produced when you reach for a doorknob after scuffing your shoes across a rug, the obstinate clinging of a silk dress as you try to pull it on or off. Those are all situations where an object has either more or fewer electrons than protons and is accordingly negatively or positively charged.

Moving to another exhibit, called "Giant Electroscope," Semper invites the visitor to create an imbalance of charge by applying a current to a pair of loosely hanging wire threads. The current adds electrons, negatively charging both wires so they swing apart. If the visitor then intervenes to create a conductive pathway, the excess electrons escape from the wires. The extra electrons redistribute themselves, and a balance of protons and electrons is restored. The wire threads drift back to their neutral, loosely hanging state.

Semper points to a number of related exhibits that show how friction charges various substances by rubbing off electrons, causing objects to repel one another if their charge is the same and attract each other if they are oppositely charged. He explains how humans put electricity to use by deliberately upsetting the balance of charge within a system, thereby inducing it to work to reneutralize itself. Similar destabilizations occur without human assistance in the natural world, sometimes producing dramatic electrical effects such as lightning storms.

Some exhibits display how we use different forms of energy—water, wind, solar, or nuclear power—to separate positive and negative electric charges and hold them apart. The separated charges, as they return to neutral balance, constitute a carrier of stored, or potential, energy that may be put to practical use. The visitor is thus led to reflect on the nature of electricity—what it is—as well as how electrical forces account for the chemical and physical properties of matter. Many exhibits show the variety of ways that people have devised to collect energy by separating charges in neutral materials, and how that energy can be stored indefinitely and discharged at will when the separated charges are allowed to reunite. The Exploratorium plans to add exhibits to remind the visitor of the variety of techniques for creating and controlling imbalance of electric charge and for storing and transporting the energy that results. Such techniques have important industrial applications. Semper's tour guides the visitor from an understanding of the nature and universality of electricity to an appreciation of the ways in which people use it as a carrier of energy to perform productive tasks.

Tom Tompkins, another staff member, begins his tour with a user's approach to electricity. Tompkins is an exhibit builder and manager of the Exploratorium machine shop. He confronts electricity as an engineer who seeks to regulate the flow of electric charge for practical ends, and so he talks about it in terms of power and its distribution. He explains how an electromotive force drives a flow of charge through a circuit and how its passage is sustained, diverted, or hampered by different contrivances, and he points out exhibits that illustrate what the contrivances are and how they operate.

We tend to think of electricity as a fluid that can be stored and moved about; the word "current" reflects the historic roots of that idea. The analogy between an electric current passing through a wire and a stream of water in a riverbed is not perfect, but it is adequate for most purposes. The streams are alike in their inclination to follow the path of least resistance, but they are unlike in that the wire is not a hollow vessel. The current does not pass through or fill empty space. A wire is a solid substance, composed of randomly distributed protons and electrons. Their composite charge is neutral, but if parts of the wire differ in potential, charge is conducted along the wire, causing a current as long as the difference in potential is maintained. An electric current resembles a fluid in moving from a higher potential energy state to a lower one and in needing a form of pressure to keep the end states different. In a water system, a pump keeps the fluid circulating through a system of reservoirs by maintaining a difference in water levels. An electromotive force is the equivalent of a pump that separates positively and negatively charged particles at opposite terminals in a system, creating a difference in potential and so moving the current between the terminals.

Tompkins draws the analogy between the fluid system and the electrical circuit and illustrates his explanation with a working model. The exhibit "Electrical Analogy" displays a fluid reservoir system next to an electrical circuit.[24] Visitors are able to control the flow in each system by changing the motive pressures at critical points. They can watch the levels change in the reservoir system, and they can see a corresponding change of current flow, as measured by an amp meter, in the electrical system. The model is a helpful starting point for explaining the relationships among the current that passes through a circuit (measured in amperes); the electromotive force, or pressure, that causes it to move (measured in volts); and the resistance offered by the medium that the current passes through (expressed in ohms). All electrical appliances operate by means of circuit elements that control the amount of current transmitted along wires by increasing or decreasing resistance. Some Exploratorium exhibits make plain what happens to those elements when any part of the system—the pressure (voltage), the amount of current, or the resistance—is varied. Visitors can alter one or two of those variables and relate the effect to the movement of needles on a gauge or the intensity of a glowing light, just as they would recognize signals of changing ratios in their electrical systems at home—the lights flicker when someone turns on an appliance, or a fuse blows out if too much current is drawn.

The Exploratorium displays schematic models that show how appliances work in a generalized fashion; other exhibits show how particular appliances are devised to do certain things. Some exhibits are also meant to reveal the organization and distribution of electrical energy as it is transmitted and transformed from large-scale to small-scale operations and from public resources to private installations. Tompkins's explanation of electric power includes an account of the use of transformers to change the ratio of voltage to current so that electricity at dangerously high voltage levels and low current can be transported safely and cheaply from remote power plants over great distances to cities. Transformers at substations outside the cities then reverse the ratio again so that machines and appliances in factories and homes can be safely plugged into the system and operated at high current and low voltage.

The Exploratorium staff is still trying to invent ways to make the energy distribution system more evident. Unlike a stream of water, however, a stream of electrons is not easily displayed apart from the wire that encloses it, and its behavior as a current can be seen only in its consequences. Although ingenious exhibits already illustrate much that electricity can do, none yet reveals exactly what electricity is.[25] The electricity section still lacks the immediacy of some of the other exhibit sections and is far from complete, but Tom Tompkins's approach to the subject through variously engineered electrical devices does help people gain some understanding of an enormously useful resource.

Darlene Librero, coordinator of the explainer program and the staff member who probably has more direct contact with the general public than anyone else, likes to explain electricity through familiar working appliances. She takes people to such recognizable objects as light switches, doorbells, heating elements, and small motors. Everyone knows what they are, but most people never really think about how they work. The Exploratorium exhibits analyze the operation of the appliances and let observers watch what happens while a current is run through them. Then people can follow the process, ask why certain steps occur, and even fiddle with alternative possibilities. With some exhibits the visitor can alter one feature at a time and so explore the practical effects of increasing or decreasing current flow or changing its direction. Not everyone takes the time to play with the exhibits, but anyone can gain a feeling for the give and take of electrical phenomena and relate them to their own experiences. Frank Oppenheimer enjoyed telling about a woman who went home from a museum visit and rewired a broken lamp. There is no exhibit at the Exploratorium that would have taught her exactly how to do that, but many exhibits might have conveyed the principles involved and also given her the confidence to undertake the task. Oppenheimer liked the anecdote because it illustrated the museum's ability to empower people; it also suggests that the exhibits help people understand how things work.

Visitors can learn from "Motor Effect" and "Generator Effect" that motors and generators are the converse of one another. An electric motor uses current to produce motion; a generator uses mechanical motion to produce an electrical current. In one exhibit, visitors make a motor work by passing current through a wire in a magnetic field; in the other, they make a generator work by moving a wire through a magnetic field to induce a current. Generated current provides electrical power, and motors maintain and redirect the power by the interaction of a magnetic force and a charged wire rotating within it. Other exhibits display common ways that electric motors perform work and how a motor's revolution can make things move or change.

Librero finds that visitors respond well to the practical examples and are able to proceed to more abstract concepts. Having observed the connection between electric charge and magnetic field, and having used that interaction to make doorbells ring and motors spin, people can begin to think about more sophisticated electromagnetic phenomena. They can even begin to imagine electronic events that do not rely on current passing through conducting wires.

Librero invites visitors in the electricity section to take the next step by crossing the museum floor to the Einstein section. There she, like the other guides, draws attention to the universal and fundamental nature of electrical charge and its separation. The electrical activity of atoms is called excitation and de-excitation, and it occurs when an electron is raised to a higher energy level or dropped to a lower one in relation to the atom's nucleus. When excited, atoms emit energy in the form of photons, and each chemical element has a characteristic pattern of emission, a color fingerprint, that can be recognized with the aid of a spectroscope. We employ that phenomenon in neon signs and fluorescent lights. Gases confined in sealed glass tubes are excited by electrons discharged from electrodes. Since different types of gas atoms emit light at different wavelengths, each tube glows with its gas's distinct color. The process of excitation and de-excitation can be explained only by quantum mechanics, but it is illustrated by the exhibits.

Librero guides visitors to an exhibit called "Photoelectric Effect." The name refers to a phenomenon that was described but not understood in the nineteenth century, namely, the capability of light to eject electrons from metal surfaces. In 1921 Einstein won a Nobel prize for his work explaining the effect, and his explanation established the particle theory of light. The theory maintains that light, like electric charge and like the mass of pure substances, consists of discrete quanta. The exhibit appears to be similar to the "Giant Electroscope" in the electricity section. To operate either exhibit, the observer first applies a current, to create an imbalance of charge, and then discharges the stored charge. In "Photoelectric Effect" a pair of gold-foil leaves corresponds to the two suspended wires in "Giant Electroscope." The imbalance of charge causes the two parts to swing apart, and in both cases they collapse together again when equilibrium is restored. The gold-foil leaves, like the wires, hang loosely. The difference between the two exhibits is in the manner in which the balance of charge is restored. In "Giant Electroscope" a physical contact, or grounding, is required. The visitor's hand or a conducting instrument draws away the extra electrons. In "Photoelectric Effect," the excess charge is removed by shining ultraviolet light onto the surface of the plate on which the invisible electrons are stored. The light, in the form of photons or quanta of energy, knocks the electrons off the plate. Librero's purpose in drawing the visitor's attention to "Photoelectric Effect" is to indicate that electromagnetic forces are transmitted even without conducting materials. No wires are necessary. That phenomenon too must be explained by quantum mechanics, but like other exhibits in the Einstein section, "Photoelectric Effect" reveals unexpected forces throughout the universe.

Librero's electrical tour ends where Semper's begins, with the universality of electrical forces, within and outside the atom. Visitors can proceed from here to exhibits on atomic spectra that give further clues to understanding the structure of the atom and the electrical interactions that take place within it.

It does not really matter how a tour begins: in the manner of Semper with the fundamental nature of electricity and the forces that hold atoms together, or following Tompkins, with the distribution of electrical power, or with Librero, examining familiar appliances. Each starting point might eventually lead museumgoers along the same route and to the same exhibits.[26] Alternative pathways, some of which have undoubtedly not been thought of, are also possible. The Exploratorium encourages the development of as many alternative approaches as possible to the subject of electricity, as to all other areas of science. To keep opening new pathways, the Exploratorium must produce many new exhibits and improved teaching materials.

Having built up an exhibit repertoire that includes many of the classic topics of the standard physics curriculum, and having achieved a reputation for the quality of its educational resources, the museum began to fulfill Oppenheimer's hope that it would become an adjunct to the schools. The elementary schools were the first to use the exhibits in conjunction with classroom teaching, but as the number and sophistication of exhibits increased, individual high school and college teachers also began to bring their physics classes to the Exploratorium and to use the exhibits for more advanced courses. Some teachers devised syllabi that regularly referred to exhibits in place of laboratory demonstrations. A few teachers taught entire courses in the museum, using the exhibits to study the phenomena and the classroom space to conduct lectures. Several Exploratorium staff members were invited to teach physics courses in regional schools and colleges, and teacher-training workshops were organized to help teachers plan science curricula that used the Exploratorium exhibits.

In 1983 the Exploratorium developed a middle school teacher-training workshop program designed to teach such basic physics concepts as physical optics, the wave and particle characteristics of light, the quantized nature of the atom, separation of charge, electricity, magnetism, vibrations, and sound. The program was intended to facilitate firsthand science experimentation among the teachers and to help them develop intuitive models that would suggest new experiments to be conducted in the classroom. Two physicists with university teaching experience were hired to run the workshops, and the training program was expanded in the following year to include high school as well as middle school teachers. The course soon qualified for accreditation as a physics course within the state university system. The Exploratorium became officially affiliated not only with the state teacher-training establishment but also with its formal science-teaching program.

As the Exploratorium began to supplement the public educational establishment, it developed exhibits to conform to the school curricula. Still, experience remains the essence of the museum pedagogy, and the new exhibits continue to complement our experience of the natural world. The staff has found that even abstract concepts of physics can be introduced at an experiential level, although the experience is often that of a laboratory rather than of the directly observable world outside. The museum experience is, of course, brief and unpredictable, and it is not always possible to know what, if anything, the visitors are learning. But staff members are confident that museum exhibits can stimulate people to appreciate the doing of science as well as its reported conclusions.

The Exploratorium is committed to the demystification of today's world and today's science. It has stressed that the discoveries of the laboratory are no more and no less genuine than those of the open fields. The behavior of subatomic particles is as natural as the fall of apples, though less readily perceived. That is why it has seemed important to display the special devices used in the study of science, although that aim has been limited by the huge size and cost of contemporary experimental procedures. The Exploratorium has sought to maintain state-of-the-art quality in its exhibits, but above all, it has aimed to design exhibits that mediate between the physical phenomena of the world and the experience of those who wish to understand them.

Teaching Without Schooling, Learning Without Experts

Since no single part of the museum is more committed to education than any other, the Exploratorium has never had a separate department of education. The museum as a whole is dedicated to teaching and learning, and that is what everyone at the museum does. The old teach the young and the young teach the old, and professionals and amateurs teach each other. Visitors who are perfect strangers join in discussing exhibits with staff and end by teaching one another. People usually come in groups—children bring their parents after a school field trip, teachers bring classes, local residents bring their out-of-town friends, tourists bring their in-town hosts, families and friends come together—and they all show each other things and explain them to each other. Staff members too are constantly learning from each other and from the public.

Although Oppenheimer's unconventional educational philosophy precluded expert educators, Oppenheimer was eager for the museum to collaborate with other educational institutions. He cherished a vision of shared cultural stewardship, in which all the cultural agencies of the region—libraries, parks, radio and television stations, museums, and art centers—would assume joint responsibility for educating the general public. The founding of the Exploratorium was a step in that direction, and education has remained the museum's primary mission.

In contrast to classroom routines or film and television programs, museums offer the learner the opportunity to stop at will, to loiter and repeat, to ignore what does not stimulate, and to share what seems interesting. Oppenheimer put part of the blame on museums. Despite their potential, many have not taken themselves seriously as teaching institutions and many are more interested in things than in people. But the public, he believed, must share the blame, because so many of us do not think anything we do on our time off can be useful. How can we evaluate the educational outcome of play? he asked. How can we determine the social benefits of sightseeing? Even without adequate measures, there are some things we know— "People built fires to keep warm long before Galileo invented the thermometer." Oppenheimer argued that we must have faith in the educational effectiveness of museums; they are important if only to relieve some of the immense burden that our schools cannot possibly bear alone.[1]

Some of the Exploratorium activities were to be carried out in conjunction with schools and formal teaching institutions, but Oppenheimer refused to identify any part of the museum's activities as more educational than any other. In his eyes every exhibit and every conversation was educationally important, and no one program was preeminent. Nevertheless, among the programs that were instituted, some were explicitly addressed to schools, offering science courses at elementary, middle, and high school levels, as well as to teachers. Some teaching programs were also designed for the museum's staff and for various special groups of visitors. Workshops and training sessions were tailored to specialists and nonprofessionals with particular interests, including parents and museum interns. In fact, the Exploratorium has striven to dispel the assumption that education is exclusively for children and that playful hands-on activities like those at the Exploratorium are only for the young and uninhibited. It has focused as much on adult as on juvenile education. Finally, an educational enterprise that assumed increasing importance as the Exploratorium's reputation grew was the dissemination of the museum's philosophy.

Spreading the philosophy to other museums, to teachers and administrators, and to state funding agencies was a major effort. Oppenheimer waged a battle for recognition that changed the nature of science education and benefited students and museums. The proess also left its mark on the Exploratorium, for there were compromises on all sides. The several teaching programs instituted by the museum changed considerably in response to economic and political, as well as pedagogic, pressures, some of which were beneficial. At any rate, it is clear that the Exploratorium's educational philosophy, like its exhibit philosophy, was imaginatively opportunistic. In no way did it fulfill a predetermined course.

When the Oppenheimers opened the museum, they hoped for cooperation with the San Francisco Unified School District, and circumstances were on their side. A sudden, politically influenced surge of interest in science education had put considerable public pressure on the schools to upgrade the quality of science teaching. Their resources for such improvement were limited, and so the school administrators and science supervisors welcomed the opening of a new science museum in the community. Teachers too were enthusiastic, because many of them had been conscripted into science teaching even though they were ill prepared. They lacked confidence as well as material resources, and they hoped the museum could help them instill in their students an interest in science that they were not able to generate in themselves.[2]

Oppenheimer's original plan was to build classroom space inside the museum and to bring classes of children and their teachers there for intensive science training using the exhibits. But there were no funds for the project, despite the endorsement of the local teaching establishment, and so the museum settled for less ambitious pedagogic practices, including apprenticeship programs that brought in a few students at a time to work under the supervision of shop staff.[3] Those programs enabled the schools to expand their science resources and helped students learn basic scientific concepts as they acquired vocational skills. Field trips were also introduced almost as soon as there was anything to explore in the museum, and they too were popular with school systems. Oppenheimer came to an early agreement with the San Francisco Unified School District to set aside special hours for school trips so that the children could have the run of the building without inconveniencing other museumgoers. As a consequence, the museum served as a school adjunct, open exclusively for school trips on several weekday mornings.[4]

Educators disagree about the value of field trips. Teachers often regard them as a cathartic release and schedule them at the end of the semester, when their own and their students' enthusiasm for classroom learning has all but dried up. They pack the children into a bus and carry them off on an excursion, memorable more often for the bus ride than for the cultural content of the place they are visiting. The children tend to behave like uncaged captives, liberated from the classroom, and they overwhelm the staff with their noisy energy. Each class comes only once, but the museum staff endure hundreds of such invasions. No wonder they sometimes question whether the ordeal is worth the trouble. Museum professionals have also expressed reservations and have proposed tests, questionnaires, and interviews with students and teachers, as well as material checks on the use of exhibits, as means of evaluating field trips. But since no one is sure what the field trips are supposed to accomplish, attempts to measure their effectiveness are problematic.[5]

Still, the Exploratorium staff believed something could be salvaged from the chaotic field trips. As the children flitted from exhibit to exhibit, they did get an overview and a sense of the museum, sometimes spotting one or two exhibits that intrigued them, and some of the children came back after the trip with parents or friends to give the exhibits more attention. Mindful of that behavior and hopeful that an initial visit would whet students' appetite for systematic study, the Exploratorium staff decided to begin all of its intensive teaching workshops with a preliminary, supervised field trip. Since field trips can account for as much as 30 percent of a museum's attendance, it is important that they be handled with courtesy and well-informed guidance. At first the regular staff and volunteers were able to handle the school groups, but as their volume grew, the Exploratorium had to hire and train additional staff specifically to lead field trips.

The museum needed a sustained and intimate connection with the schools if it was to provide more than occasional recreation for students. The first real breakthrough into the schools came about by chance in 1971. Leni Isaacs, an Antioch College intern who worked as a part-time guide in the museum, was also teaching music in a nearby Mill Valley school. Having learned of that school's enrichment program, in which parents and other members of the community taught the children their special skills, she arranged for the Exploratorium to take charge of an enrichment course in science. The voluntary course quickly became popular not only with the students but also with their parents and school staff. It was taught by two volunteers supervised by Sheila Grinell, who had originally been hired to teach the museum's staff of explainers.[6]

The course ran for ten weeks, meeting in alternating sessions at the school and at the museum. Every time the class met at the school, the Exploratorium teachers came laden with Grinell's bag of tricks—two large suitcases full of lenses, mirrors, prisms, magnifiers, filters, tuning forks, pipes, and noise makers, and a variety of household objects that reflected and resounded. But the children much preferred going to the museum and playing with exhibits there. The class concentrated on the senses, and the museum exhibits and classroom demonstration materials were its text. The children also brought materials from home. The collection of props evolved and expanded as the teachers carried it back and forth from museum to classroom. Gradually a kit of materials was developed that could be loaned to schoolteachers for prolonged classroom use. Grinell worked with the teachers and parents, involving them in the children's exploration. Everyone was so delighted with the program that in the following year the school allocated funds for its repetition and to pay for a bus to take the children to the museum.

Soon neighboring schools were requesting similar programs, and it became necessary to hire someone for the sole purpose of overseeing the museum's teaching activities. The School in the Exploratorium (SITE) thus began with the appointment of a professional math and science teacher whose first assignment was to coordinate the students' museum experience with their regular classroom activities.[7] SITE was to be a program for the direct teaching of children. It was originally subsidized out of the museum's operating budget, with some contributions by parent groups and the individual schools, but Oppenheimer hoped that local or regional school systems would eventually take it over and incorporate it into their regular science program. That never happened, but SITE continued and survived in a somewhat different form. It ultimately concentrated less on the direct teaching of children and more on the training of teachers and the development of curricula. The shift reflected the educational priorities of some of the agencies that finally funded the program, as well as the general economic perception that more students could be reached by educating their teachers than by working with the limited numbers of students that could be brought to the museum.[8]

In the early stage of the SITE program, the Exploratorium teachers volunteered their time and had no educational resources to work with other than the museum exhibits. The children sat on an old red carpet or on wooden park benches in the middle of the busy museum floor, while the maintenance staff worked and repaired exhibits around them. Despite those primitive physical conditions, the teachers were able to design elegantly flexible curricula that used the exhibits to teach optics, light, visual perception, color, waves, and sound.

The workshop series usually began with a visit by one of the SITE teachers to the children's classroom. The teacher described the museum to them, and then the children visited it on a field trip. A series of return visits followed, each with a special focus. The children's work was supervised by Exploratorium teachers, as well as by their regular classroom teachers. A typical fifth-grade session might concentrate on the bending of light, presenting the students with a variety of transparent and perforated materials, a laser and white light source, mirrors, and concave and convex lenses. There would be some discussion of the physiology of the eye, including the cow's eye dissection and examination of its lens. Sometimes the children were sent on a scavenger hunt among the exhibits or outside to find examples of the phenomena they had discussed, and sometimes they sat in a group and made up stories about them. Other group projects might include the construction of simple things—a pinhole viewer made out of a paper cup, or a kaleidoscope model using a pair of pocket mirrors—that could easily be reproduced by the children at home or in their regular classroom.[9]

The chief objective was to show children and teachers how to carry the ideas they learned in the museum outside onto the streets and into their homes and schools. Classroom teachers were expected to review the principles communicated by the exhibits and to discuss the experience of the workshops with the children after they returned to their schools. Having seen their own images magnified on concave surfaces and miniaturized on convex ones, students were more prepared to grasp optical principles than if they had only seen diagrams in a textbook. In the same way, dealing with hearing and the other senses, the children were encouraged to notice the vibration of ordinary things, to listen to the sounds they make, to touch and feel them, and to note the differences between them and their effects. Simple experiments could be done at home or in school, using ordinary materials such as rubber bands, paper clips, and soda bottles. Children experimented together, and with the help of their teachers, they kept track of their observations and those of others, especially where they disagreed. Classroom teachers who needed help could also turn to the SITE staff for advice between visits.

The SITE teachers began experimenting with supplementary projects for the children to take to their homes and classrooms. They helped the children make simplified copies of the exhibits and designed additional classroom exercises and worksheets that classroom teachers could use with the children. They also mailed idea sheets to teachers before the first class field trip, suggesting follow-up activities the class could do between visits. One project on shadows, for example, suggests: "Pick a spot on the school yard for each child. Stand on the spot at the beginning of school, recess, lunch, before going home, etc. Have another child draw the shadow and mark the time. Have them talk about the position of the sun and varying shadows. Make shadow drawings and see if someone looking at them can tell what time of day it is."[10] Another project, on sound, gives a simple recipe for making ear chimes, out of a wire coat hanger and two pieces of string, and suggests how to change the sound by varying the shape of the hanger. The regular classroom teachers were particularly pleased with those simple curricular aids because their versatility allows slow learners to progress at their own speed, while more advanced students can also find challenges at their level.[11] The challenge to the Exploratorium was to create aids for the teachers that would be genuinely liberating, instead of replacing one set of prescriptive principles with another.

Word of the SITE program spread through Marin County and San Francisco, and soon more schools from greater distances were asking for workshops for their students. Some of the schools also wanted the Exploratorium teachers to organize follow-up activities and to train regular teachers to implement them in the classrooms. The SITE teachers instituted monthly teacher nights, free to participating schools, so classroom teachers could preview exhibits and prepare themselves for field trips or classroom activities following a workshop. The informal sessions obviously filled a need, for they quickly expanded to become regularly scheduled teacher-training courses. Their reputation spread to some of the local colleges and universities, which invited the museum to offer credit-bearing courses to their students in science education.[12]

Clearly, teachers in the school systems lacked knowledge of science, but more important, they did not believe that they, personally, could learn from phenomena or from exhibits. They could not hope to instill that confidence in their students since they did not have it themselves, but that was exactly what was expected of them. Their almost desperate search for a formula and for skills that they could immediately pass on to their classes was at odds with the Exploratorium philosophy and with the museum's rejection of the role of experts. The cult of expertise was a powerful obstacle to the museum's campaign to empower the learners.[13] The schoolteachers preferred to regard the Exploratorium as an authoritative resource, and they expected to receive the same respect from their young students. If the museum was to have a liberating effect on the teaching of science to children, it first had to change the attitudes of their teachers.

Another major difficulty was funding. Until 1973 the museum teachers were either unpaid or underpaid, and the expenses of the SITE program were taken out of the museum's operating costs. The museum attempted to obtain public funding or to use city sabbatical or master-teacher credit programs that would pay teachers to work with the museum, but local resources were already strained. Although the schools were happy to accept the museum's enrichment program, they could offer no remuneration or support to the museum in return. Finally, in 1973 the Rockefeller Brothers Fund awarded the Exploratorium $35,000, which paid the salaries of the teachers and funded the production of a lending library of exhibit replicas and teaching materials.[14] A year later a large, three-year grant from the Ford Foundation gave SITE permanent status as a museum program.

Although those national foundations supported the Exploratorium, they did so at first with reservations, for they were not yet convinced that museums were properly qualified educational institutions. Their explicit aim was to upgrade the quality of American education overall and of science training in particular. They were wary of the Exploratorium proposal because, like the state and federal agencies, they were skeptical that education could take place anywhere except in schools. However, the situation was desperate enough to warrant some outrageous solutions, and the foundations hoped the museum might be a catalyst that would stimulate educational recovery in the schools. The foundation support was therefore contingent on the museum's sustained interaction with local school systems.

The Ford Foundation insisted that its contribution be matched by a local contribution. Unfortunately, times were hard. School enrollments had declined, and citizens were rebelling against the rising costs of education. In the courts and at the polls, citizens were challenging the use of property taxes to support the schools. The concept of publicly funded schools was in jeopardy as affluent white parents fled the ethnically mixed cities and enrolled their children in private suburban schools. The state's educational bureaucracy was shaken by political struggles and a rapid turnover of personnel. Assurances of support for the Exploratorium program from one office would be countermanded by another.[15] Correspondence was delayed, commitments denied or forgotten, and even promises of classroom furniture, equipment, and paraprofessional staff assistance had to be repeatedly renegotiated. At last the San Francisco Unified School District arranged to transfer some of the workers assigned to the city under the federal Comprehensive Employment Training Act (CETA), but the sum the school district had pledged to pay for school field trips was never appropriated. Although no one disputed the excellence of the Exploratorium's teaching program or the need for improved science teaching in the schools, the state was unable to meet the Ford Foundation's challenge.[16] A letter from the 1977 Speaker of the California State Assembly to the state superintendent of schools describes the dilemma:

School districts are supportive of the program—S.F.U.S.D. is even committed financially, but because the Exploratorium is a regional resource, no one school district or school districts in combination have been able to agree on a support formula. There are not only inner-district and inter-district policy questions involved, but even more basic questions regarding the statutory requirements which might allow or preclude school districts from financial obligations to an institution without official educational status.[17]

The museum's independence of the official school system made it ineligible for support by it.

Although the state later contributed to the Exploratorium as a regional science resource center serving the public schools,[18] SITE never did become an adjunct to any state or district educational agency. It did become central to the museum's teaching commitment, and it continued to receive irregular support from various state, local, and federal agencies as well as from some private foundations, even after the crucial Rockefeller Brothers and Ford Foundation grants expired.

The granting agencies insisted on a program of teacher training, as distinct from the direct education of pupils. Their reasoning was that the improvement of a single teacher's capacity is eventually passed on to thousands of students. By contrast, the benefit to even a few hundred children who pass through the SITE program must be viewed as a wasteful indulgence. Though reluctant to accept that apparent regression to authoritarianism, Oppenheimer was forced to see the merit of its logic by the foundation officers and by members of the Exploratorium staff who appreciated its implications for classroom teachers.

The SITE staff included some former schoolteachers whose pedagogic priorities agreed with those of the foundations. They understood the torment of undereducated teachers who cannot teach what they do not understand and who are often overburdened by school authorities on the one hand and at the mercy of students on the other. Those experienced teachers also understood the psychological and political jeopardy in which classroom teachers were placed by the Exploratorium's original SITE workshop. Since conventional education depends so much on power and the maintenance of control, the playful experiential atmosphere that the Exploratorium promoted was threatening to teachers. Many remained deferential toward the museum "experts" and could not tolerate the prospect of diminished authority over their students, and they were unable to take advantage of the liberating environment that the museum offered. Moreover, many of the teachers had been taught to think of science as a body of facts to be dogmatically imparted. Their aim was to absorb as much as they could as quickly as possible and to pass it on intact to their students. They were not eager to question authority. School administrators, too, were not invariably pleased with the seemingly anarchic atmosphere that the Exploratorium style fostered. It seemed, therefore, that the museum's work with teachers must take precedence over its direct teaching of children, and that the Exploratorium would have to reshape its pedagogic expectations in light of the realities of the school world. Perhaps the greatest impact of the Exploratorium's educational philosophy was on the dozen or more SITE teachers themselves, and through them it ultimately did affect the teaching establishment.

The SITE staff became preeminently curriculum consultants. In workshops they helped schoolteachers construct their own science curricula using the museum exhibits, and then they helped the teachers implement the curricula in their classrooms. The Exploratorium still holds classes for children, especially in the summers and for specially funded projects. But for the most part, school-related programs are conducted at the schools and through the classroom teachers, with the SITE staff serving an advisory role. SITE also extended its service to include middle and high school science courses as well as elementary general science. The SITE teachers had to develop greater scientific sophistication and scope, and the museum needed a wider range of exhibits in mathematics, biology, and chemistry to accommodate the middle and high school curriculum. As the staff became more experienced, other educators and institutions frequently consulted with them on the preparation of educational proposals.[19] The staff members became itinerant consultants, invited by state agencies to evaluate proposals or to testify at hearings on educational matters. By 1984, the SITE teacher-training and other educational services had become so indispensable to the schools that the state legislature passed a bill requiring the superintendent of public instruction to designate eligible nonprofit agencies such as the Exploratorium to serve as regional science resource centers and to allocate funds for their educational services.[20] In that and other ways, the Exploratorium's educational philosophy was gradually propagated far beyond the walls of the museum.

Within the museum, the SITE teachers have continued to play a critical communicative role. Because of their interaction with the educational sector and a considerable portion of the public, they are especially well placed to evaluate exhibits and to judge which scientific concepts are unclearly or inadequately represented. Sometimes they recommend improvements in exhibits, and occasionally they design and construct exhibits of their own. The SITE staff works closely with exhibit designers and maintenance staff, as well as with all other departments in the museum. In the process, they have acquired an impressive array of skills, useful in a variety of professional capacities. Some former SITE teachers have moved on to administrative positions within the museum, and others have left the museum to take up new careers. None has returned to conventional classroom teaching.

The Exploratorium is as committed to the education of its staff as it is to that of the public. One of its most innovative and educational projects is the explainer program, which trains high school students to become museum floor staff and exhibit guides. At the Palais de la Découverte, the Oppenheimers had been impressed by the college students who demonstrated exhibits, and they made up their minds that young people should play a similarly prominent role in the Exploratorium. One aim of the program was to benefit the students, for they would learn by helping to construct and maintain the exhibits and especially by teaching the public how to use them. Another aim was to provide an additional connection with the schools, since the students were recommended to the program by high school counselors. It was also hoped that the museum's visitors would see the confidence of their young guides as proof that science is not altogether inaccessible to ordinary human beings.

The explainer program swelled the museum's attendance by young people. San Francisco's school population was a mix of ethnic origins. If the museum could draw its explainers from that population, and they, in turn, introduced their friends and relations to the Exploratorium, it could reach segments of the community that museums often ignore.[21] School counselors sometimes had to be persuaded to set aside their inclination to recommend white, middle-class students for the museum positions, but the Exploratorium staff regarded the explainers as a vital link between the museum and the world outside.[22] Concurring with that judgment, the National Endowment for the Arts in 1973 awarded the Exploratorium explainer program a grant under the Wider Availability of Museums program.

When the museum was opened, one young woman was hired at once as an explainer, and others came soon afterward, some as volunteers. The explainer program began formally in the fall of 1969, with the help of a small grant from a local family foundation. The superintendent of the school district endorsed the program enthusiastically, and the counseling departments of the city's high schools agreed to refer explainer candidates to the museum each semester. The initial grant of $15,000 was sufficient to pay the minimum hourly wage to thirty students and to pay a supervisor, Sheila Grinell, to coordinate their work. The job required Grinell to be a camp counselor and surrogate mother as much as a manager and teacher. She had to maintain order and sometimes arbitrate complex personal problems, but she found the students responsive and eager to assume the responsibilities of learning and teaching. They were not hired on the basis of their knowledge of science but rather on their ability to interact with the public. They had to be talkers, because the most important part of their job was to approach people and engage them in conversation about the exhibits. Being able to converse in languages other than English was an asset, too. Reflecting the mix of the San Francisco population, explainers have been chosen for their fluency in Spanish, French, Chinese, German, Italian, Filipino, Japanese, and several other languages, and they continue to be selected in part for their ethnic variety.

The explainers are the sole museum floor staff, responsible not only for welcoming visitors and collecting donations but also for opening and closing the museum, turning the power on and off throughout the building, expelling stragglers, reporting seriously dysfunctional exhibits to the technical staff, and taking care of minor repairs by themselves. They perform demonstrations, such as the cow's eye dissection and the laser show, and attend to exhibits such as "Drawing Board" that require special supervision. They must know the museum well, and they are trained intensively on two consecutive weekends before beginning their job and then each weekend for an hour before the museum opens. They read whatever written material is available on the exhibits and are encouraged to play with the exhibits on the job and to learn from the questions asked by the public. They learn from each other too, as well as from the entire museum staff. Incidentally, the explainers are often good evaluators of prospective exhibits. Naive users themselves, their job also gives them the opportunity to observe the public interacting with exhibits, and so, like the SITE teachers, they are in a position to recognize the weaknesses of exhibits and to suggest improvements.

Most explainers work at the museum for only one semester, although a few have stayed on for a second term or have returned later to work in another capacity. A few explainers have grown up in the museum, learning skills and advancing from job to job as the museum grew and its staff expanded.[23]

The explainer program was an immediate success. More than forty students worked as explainers during the first year, and by all standards it was a most economical undertaking for the museum, since no other guides or security staff were necessary. The expenses of the program remained well within the initial grant, even with a raise above the minimum wage and including the cost of the red jackets worn as uniforms. The Rosenberg Foundation, which made the grant, renewed its support, and an array of other benefactors has funded the program since then. Among the supporters are the Sloan Foundation, the Junior League of San Francisco, the Rockefeller Brothers Fund, the National Endowment for the Arts, and the City of San Francisco through the Mayor's Youth Fund. All have been impressed by the explainer program for different reasons and have found something worthy in it that corresponds to their own funding interests.

The high school students have profited from the program in several ways. Quite a few have improved in their school work, not only because of the scientific material that they must learn but also because their interest is aroused. They acquire a new sense of the relevance of their learning and become motivated as never before. Some have been inspired to pursue new fields of study, and some who had no college plans have decided on careers in the arts or technical fields as a direct result of their experience at the Exploratorium. Their work at the Exploratorium is a first job for many of the explainers and the first time they have been taken seriously and treated with respect in the adult world. They learn about human interactions as well as about science. As Darlene Librero, the present explainer supervisor and herself a former explainer, puts it, "They have to become observers before they can become teachers." Many explainers find friendship and sometimes romance among their fellows, although occasional ones have been socially maladapted and unsuccessful. Their most typical complaints concern the difficulty of drawing people into conversation about the exhibits. Supervisors have usually been former explainers and so have been sensitive to the embarrassment of going up to strangers, as well as to other problems that the explainers face.

The public, on the whole, has responded well to the explainers. People who might have been intimidated or put off by exhibits are set at ease by the explainers' facility with them. The students' youth and enthusiasm seem to make science more accessible and human, and it emboldens audiences to ask questions they would not have dared put to more formidable mentors. A few visitors will bait and test the explainers, and some prefer to be alone with the exhibits. Most visitors, however, appear to appreciate the explainers' lack of pretension and the relaxed tone that they give to the museum.

The explainer program has played a less tangible part in negotiating urban social relations. By hiring a large proportion of women and minority students, the museum encourages their pursuit of science and sends a message to the public that no one is to be excluded for reasons of race or gender. Furthermore, in giving visible and responsible employment to young people, the museum conveys its confidence in them. An apparent consequence is the museum's relatively low incidence of vandalism and property damage, which is commonly found around schools and public institutions and is typically associated with alienated youth.

By 1972 the high school explainer program had become a permanent fixture, funded as a regular component of the museum's operation. It was also beginning to attract nationwide attention. A description of the explainer and SITE programs was included in a study by the Council on Museums and Education in the Visual Arts, later published as *The Art Museum as Educator*.[24] Other museums began to emulate the explainer program. Some wrote to the Exploratorium to ask how to recruit students and how to instruct them. Many simply copied what they saw. Few, however, have granted their explainers as much autonomy as the Exploratorium has or given them the exclusive responsibility for introducing the public to the resources of the museum.

Because they are students themselves, the high school explainers are able to work at the Exploratorium only after school and on weekends. On the weekday mornings when the museum is open to school groups and field trips, a second group of young people, called morning explainers, is employed to welcome the busloads of visitors and escort them about the museum. The morning explainers are beyond high school age, but most of them have no scientific training or professional museum skills. Some of them are college work-study students or interns, and some are young mothers or graduate students or artists. Like the high school explainers, they attend a series of intensive training sessions and learn how to operate the exhibits, and they too are urged to become familiar with all parts of the museum. Some of them gravitate into full-time museum jobs, and many find that the job, however poorly paid, has given them a new perspective on their capabilities.[25] Their work is, in some respects, more difficult than that of the afternoon explainers, because they must deal with large groups rather than with individuals, and classroom teachers often abandon their unruly charges to the care of museum guides. Morning explainers are occasionally inspired teachers, but their duties are often custodial.

It has been more difficult to obtain funding for the morning explainer program than for the more innovative high school program. The chief source of support has been the minimal per-student payment that the schools make for the field trip service, which hardly covers the cost of keeping the museum open in the mornings, much less the salaries of morning explainers. Pressed by economic hardship, schools have been unable to pay for bus transportation and other support services, and field trips have declined.[26]

But a variety of other groups are taking their place. Morning explainers escort college and professional students—optometrists, architects, physicists, theologians, and artists—and less conventional learning groups—the elderly, the handicapped, neighborhood and special-interest societies, and new immigrant groups that sometimes lack a common language. The versatility of the exhibits and their interactivity make communication possible even when verbal exchange is at a minimum. Such groups find ways to use the exhibits that conform to their own ideas and that the Exploratorium staff sometimes is unlikely to have thought of. Staff members often see groups of people moving purposefully from one exhibit to another, clearly following a pattern known only to themselves.

An exemplary use of the exhibits for a special-interest group was a workshop on sensory impairment. It was organized in response to a mother's disappointment that the Exploratorium did not offer summer courses for children with learning disabilities. In 1979 museum staff members, working in conjunction with the Garden Sullivan Motor-Sensory Rehabilitation Center, organized a series of workshops to address the problems of children with learning disabilities. The workshops were set up not for the children but for parents, teachers, and the helpers who work with children suffering from minimal brain dysfunction or neurodevelopmental problems.[27] One of the difficulties those children face is the invisibility of their impairment, which prevents other people from appreciating or responding appropriately to what may seem to them to be a mental defect. The workshop allowed the adults who work with the children to experience the motor-sensory distortions that are normal for the children. A separate workshop session was devoted to vision, hearing, touch, and the vestibular system, which relates to bodily awareness and balance. At each session participants were first given a preliminary explanation of the relevant sensory area, its function, and its environmental integration and then taken in small groups to exhibits where they could experience the frustration and confusion of those senses. They had to confront such questions as: What happens when the cadence of heard speech is slowed down, or run together, or so distorted that words lose their normal phrasing? What does it feel like to be unable to select meaningful sound patterns from a background of noise? What if you are unable to recall a short-term sequence of events, such as the words of a single sentence? Most of the participants had never before come so close to sharing the experience of the children they cared for. They had known it only as an abstract condition, but now they began to understand the isolation of their children and to empathize with them as no intellectualization of the problem had enabled them to do. The workshop reached only a restricted group of people with a special interest, but it made a profound impression on their lives and the lives of others close to them. Being able to serve such a need was gratifying to the staff, and the incident illustrates how the rich exhibit resources of the Exploratorium can be custom-designed to suit unusual pedagogic ends.

The Exploratorium's unconventional techniques began almost at once to attract attention throughout the world. Governments and individuals were interested in starting similar museums in India, Spain, Japan, Israel, Venezuela, Australia, the People's Republic of China, and many cities in the United States, and they sent representatives to the Exploratorium to find out how to do it. Everyone who came wanted to learn how to build and use interactive exhibits. They had many questions, and they tried to find answers by following Oppenheimer and the staff around the museum asking for explanations. The planners of new museums and science centers asked for a great deal more practical advice and information than could be included in the *Cookbook,* and sometimes they sent technicians and curators to San Francisco to learn exhibit techniques by direct observation in the Exploratorium shop. The demands on staff time became overwhelming, and it was apparent that some kind of formal training program was necessary. Beginning in 1977, the Exploratorium received two overlapping grants to introduce internship programs at the museum.[28] Both came from agencies that were interested in furthering education but had previously supported only certified, degree-granting institutions. One was for faculty who wanted to design experiential techniques for the improvement of teaching, and the second grant was to train museum personnel to use hands-on techniques that foster learner involvement. The agencies were concerned with the state of adult education and were particularly impressed by the creativity and practicality of the Exploratorium's experiential teaching. The internship programs were to demonstrate how unconventional teaching approaches can be incorporated into academic and museum settings, and the Exploratorium was to assist other institutions by training their staffs in the use of its methods.

Interns were to come in pairs and with a commitment of support from the institutions they represented. They were to spend a residency at the Exploratorium, observing its practices and also realizing a project of their own design. A series of follow-up visits by Exploratorium staff to the interns' home institutions was included in the plan. Hundreds of people arrived during the first year, some with independent financial backing. They came for varying periods and at irregular intervals. There were academic physicists, biologists, psychologists, college and museum administrators, science technicians, exhibit designers, and builders. Some of them came back several times. Many expressed dissatisfaction with the authoritarianism of conventional educational systems and wanted to learn how to create and use interactive exhibits to achieve a more liberating education. But many were unable to assimilate the freewheeling atmosphere of the Exploratorium. They wanted an orderly package of training skills and were put off by the museum's apparent carelessness.

During the first year of the internship grants, the Exploratorium's training strategy was simply to give the interns the run of the museum. Quite a few interns found that bewildering and were paralyzed by the lack of a structured program. The museum staff also began to find the constant interruption of their work by interns' inquiries intolerable. The following year the program was reorganized to run only during the summer months, and the interns were invited to come in groups rather than individually. They were housed collectively and taken as a group to meet with key members of the museum staff, who briefed them on various aspects of the museum's operation. Afterward they were again left free to observe and interact with museum activities as they chose and to undertake projects of their own. In the training groups the interns developed a temporary cohort spirit, and their group identity helped them to learn from one another and, as a body, to confront the Exploratorium staff, whose sense of mission could sometimes be overwhelming. As a working unit the interns could speak to the staff more as colleagues than as disciples, and everyone profited from that shift in perspective.[29]

The necessity of explaining their work to the training groups obliged the staff members to become much more self-conscious and articulate than they had been before about their manner of operation. They had to answer questions about what they did and how they were doing it, and also why they were doing it. As a result, many staff members became sensitized to alternative ways of functioning and were drawn into dialogue with the interns. Since the staff members were, on the whole, young and had little experience with any museums other than the Exploratorium, their conversations with the interns stimulated their thinking. It led some of them, for the first time, to appreciate how innovative the Exploratorium's exhibit philosophy actually is. It also caused some to become more acutely critical of it and to take a more active part in shaping museum policy. Indirectly, the program had the effect of diffusing authority in the museum. Because everyone had a part in articulating the museum's policy and programs, Oppenheimer ceased to be its sole spokesman. As a result, staff members were able to advance professionally, and several could move beyond the Exploratorium into the larger museum community. The connections forged through the internship program helped individual staff members to make career changes and paved the way to greater interaction between museums.

The dialogue between staff and interns continued at a weekly lunch seminar, open to the entire museum staff. In the early sessions, the interns reported on their museums or their research or related work experience. Then staff members responded by talking about projects of their own, sometimes unrelated to the museum. The sessions were collegial and informative. They became so popular that even after the interns left, they continued as a forum on a less regular basis, and occasionally the speakers were museum guests or eminent friends who happened to be visiting the Bay area. Exhibit meetings were also voluntary and open to any staff members or interns. At these meetings, projected exhibits and those in process were discussed at length and in concrete terms. Anyone could express questions, doubts, suggestions for improvement, analogies, observations, and proposed explanations. Sometimes the sessions were harshly critical of exhibits and sometimes wildly playful. Often they led to exhibit improvements or to altogether new exhibits. The meetings gave the interns an excellent opportunity to observe and take part in the Exploratorium's exhibit strategy.

At the core of that strategy is the belief that exhibits do not function apart from a context. There may be no single correct interpretation of an exhibit, but the museum must have a reason for displaying the exhibit, and that reason must be discernible by the public, even if the visitor chooses to disregard it. A museum establishes its character through the exhibit decisions that it makes, and they are made relative to its purposes and limitations.

In using the Exploratorium *Cookbook* and imitating its exhibits, museums do not necessarily adhere to its philosophy. Some museums pick and choose from the exhibit repertoire, sometimes making fundamental changes for reasons of space or economy. Attributing the success of the Exploratorium to the cleverness of its exhibits, they copy the most entertaining ones without preserving the integration with other exhibits that makes them effective in the Exploratorium, and they ignore the principles of redundancy and repetition that are at the heart of the Exploratorium's educational philosophy. In some museums the selection of exhibits is governed as much by principles of interior design or efficiency as by pedagogic needs. Museums that rely on outside agencies to construct exhibits are often stuck with a display that is made according to a predetermined and irremediable concept. Such exhibits are often the product of insufficient resources combined with the lack of a clear sense of purpose.

Without a well-equipped shop and a vigilant staff it is almost impossible to keep up the continuous fine tuning that makes interactive exhibits truly responsive. Since interactive exhibits are subject to hard use, museums without the means for their adaptation and repair tend to resort to defensive measures that make the exhibits less manipulable. Reliable simulations that remain fixed may be substituted for the real phenomena, and graphic explanations may displace less predictable experiments. Faced with the challenge of efficiency and economy, museum administrators sometimes fail to see the pedagogic compromise implicit in the choices they are forced to make.

Would-be innovators in academic centers may meet with similar difficulties, as some of the interns discovered when they returned to their colleges and requested funds to construct exhibits for teaching. They found that research funds are easier to obtain than support for educational experiments, which are not perceived as a form of research. They also discovered that imaginative teaching using exhibit material is not the high road to tenure. Academic administrators, like their museum counterparts, tend to prefer the sleek and polished look of untouchable exhibits to the unfinished appearance of exhibits whose exposed parts are an invitation to probing fingers. Safety- and cost-conscious administrators worry about lawsuits and insurance premiums and are leery of allowing hordes of unskilled users close to delicate apparatus.

Thus, although the internship program has introduced many people to the Exploratorium's exhibit philosophy and helped other institutions to embark on innovative programs, not everyone who is exposed to it is convinced of the value of that philosophy or chooses to adopt it. There can be no doubt, however, that in a relatively short period the Exploratorium style set a pattern for science museums all over the world, and indeed for museums in general. Most science museums have now set aside a "discovery space," frequently for children, where visitors can manipulate instruments, look at microscope slides, or touch animals. Many museums exhibit artisans at work or invite artists to demonstrate their technique. Often they give lectures about their work and help visitors try their hand at it. As far away as the Questacon in Canberra, Australia, or the Singapore Science Center, the idea has taken root that young and old alike can learn science by experimental play, that learning is best accomplished by doing, and that the process is enjoyable.

Helping teachers to teach and learners to learn remains at the top of the Exploratorium's priorities, and all its programs and exhibits are designed to that end. Museums and science centers are but a few of the many educational opportunities that are now available to the out-of-school adult population. Self-help books and magazines, workshops, and a proliferation of television series are beginning to rival the schools in educational impact, but they all confront the same handicap, fostered by the science establishment, that any type of informal science study is taken to be mere entertainment and not quite serious. Although the nonschool teaching agencies have not yet won the status of the conventional teaching centers, they have won the hearts of the populace, which uses them to satisfy a multitude of educational needs. They have all benefited from Oppenheimer's long struggle to free museums from the red tape that prevented them from being recognized and remunerated as the cultural enrichers that they are.

To help create a sense of community among the alternative agencies that have assumed responsibility for informal public science education, the Exploratorium organized a conference of media-based science educators in 1981. Journalists, popular authors, and science writers and producers for radio, television, and film came together to discuss their common concerns and to help one another teach science to the public.[30] The conference led to some stimulating collaborations, including a television program on the Exploratorium. The *Nova* film, "Palace of Delights," was produced for the national Public Broadcasting System and has been viewed by many people throughout the country who have no other experience of the Exploratorium.[31] The conference was one of several events that the Exploratorium initiated for the advancement of science education.

Oppenheimer never succeeded in persuading the state to include the museum as an official part of its educational system, but he did make some progress in gaining official recognition of the informal cultural dissemination system he had advocated in his earliest museum proposals. He argued persistently that state funds should be made available "to finance the adjunctive educational systems, the museums, the libraries, the media and parks." He believed that "teachers and students alike could orchestrate the use of these adjunctive educational opportunities to provide a quality and richness of education at all levels that would be far superior to anything now in existence. The frustrations of the classroom would diminish and the finest talent in the land would participate in one phase or another of this expanded conception of public education."[32] The extent to which museums now have become extensions of classrooms is some measure of the success of Oppenheimer's effort to integrate all aspects of science education.

The Exploratorium has served as a model for museums throughout the world, and Oppenheimer has emerged as a museum hero. In June 1982 he won the American Association of Museums' Award for Distinguished Service to Museums. The award was particularly gratifying since at the time of its founding in 1969 the Exploratorium was not even eligible for membership in the American Association of Museums. Oppenheimer was specifically honored for "the impact of [his] ideas and methods on museums and museum education." The Exploratorium was hailed as "a mecca for all those who, regardless of discipline, have an interest in learning."[33] Oppenheimer, in his acceptance speech, reiterated his belief that museums are educational institutions and commented that there is no essential difference between the preservation of culture by museums and its transmission by education. Both schools and museums, he said, must strive to find ways to help people discover and absorb the world for themselves.

Frank Oppenheimer, 1912-1985, the founder and director of the Exploratorium, San Francisco Palace of Arts and Science. Photograph by Lisa Law, 1984.

Picturesquely located at the foot of the Golden Gate Bridge, facing the Marin County hillside, the Exploratorium is housed in the Palace of Fine Arts, designed in 1915 by Bernard Maybeck. Photograph from the Exploratorium files.

Frank Oppenheimer at approximately age three with his brother Robert, age eleven. Photograph courtesy of Judith Oppenheimer.

Jacquenette Quann Oppenheimer (Jackie) at Perro Caliente, the Oppenheimer's New Mexico ranch, around the time of Frank and Jackie's marriage in 1934. Photograph courtesy of Judith Oppenheimer.

Frank and Jackie, working their cattle ranch in Pagosa Springs, Colorado, where they were banished from 1949 to 1959, during the height of the McCarthy period of political hysteria. Photograph courtesy of Judith Oppenheimer.

When the science teacher of the Pagosa Springs High School resigned, Oppenheimer agreed to teach general science to its 300 students. His hands-on teaching curriculum led to a lifelong interest in teacher education. Photograph from the Exploratorium files.

Constructed to celebrate the opening of the Panama Canal in 1915, the Palace of Fine Arts was a part of San Francisco's Panama-Pacific International Exposition, and devoted citizens have repeatedly saved it from demolition. Photograph from the Worden Collection, Wells Fargo History Room.

The Exploratorium interior in 1969 was a vast, empty space, ideal for unusual acoustical effects. Uncluttered by exhibits, it was a site for performance pieces and concerts, as well as borrowed materials from NASA and the Stanford Linear Accelerator Center. Photograph from NASA.

The Astronaut, a holdover from the exhibit of technology used in the 1969 *Apollo 11* lunar landing, remained at the Exploratorium long after that borrowed exhibit was returned to NASA. Drawing by Jad King.

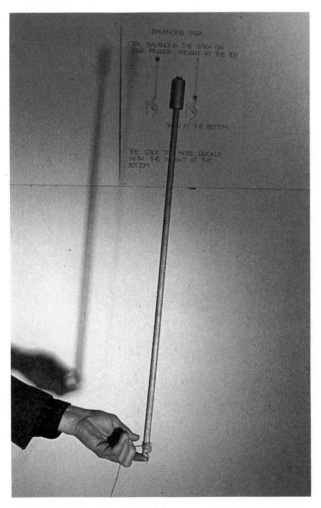

One of the earliest exhibits, "Balancing Stick" relates to momentum and the perceiver's reaction time. Oppenheimer made the exhibit at the Lawrence Hall of Science and demonstrated it at the luncheon held for prospective supporters of the museum in 1968. Photograph by Jon Wilson.

The Exploratorium model of
the Montgomery glider was
flown in 1911. It was loaned
to the museum by the University of Santa Clara, where
Montgomery taught physics
and studied flight. Drawing
from a brochure celebrating
John J. Montgomery Day,
October 31, 1963; courtesy
Arthur Dunning Spearman,
S.J.

"Drawing Board" was originally a part of "Cybernetic
Serendipity," entitled "Pendulum Harmonograph" by its
inventor, John Ravillous.
Slightly modified, it is used
by the Exploratorium as a
visitor-activated drawing
machine that inscribes Lissajous curves. Photograph by
Jon Wilson.

"Relative Motion" shows how
two pendulums swinging in
perpendicular opposition produce a curved effect. It is a
useful didactic exhibit. Photograph from the Exploratorium
files.

"Sidebands" was created by two electrical engineers for "Cybernetic Serendipity." Visitors manipulate wave frequencies on a CRT screen to produce slowly varying, rotating patterns. The exhibit was purchased for the museum by a donor. Photograph from the Exploratorium files.

The oversized "Differential" displays the interaction of types of motion and shows how such principles are practically applied. Photograph by Susan Schwartzenberg. Inset shows gear mechanism that transforms motion of differential. Photograph from the Exploratorium files.

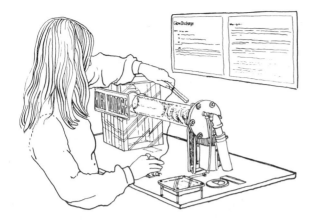

"Glow Discharge" started as a high school student project. Built by apprentices under supervision, it required that they learn carpentry and electrical wiring as well as some plasma physics. Drawing by Jad King.

"Survival of the Fittest" illustrates population growth and reveals the large difference that a small advantage makes. It was conceived as a part of a series of mathematical exhibits on exponential change and was the first museum exhibit to use a computer display. Photograph from the files of the Exploratorium.

To the uninitiated the view of an electronics shop is unenlightening. There is minimal movement or disturbance and only the sound of clicks and beeps. Photograph from the files of the Exploratorium.

Jackie Oppenheimer with Annabelle Fulk in 1977, editing the museum catalog, viewed through the window of the graphics workshop. Photograph by Marvin Glaser.

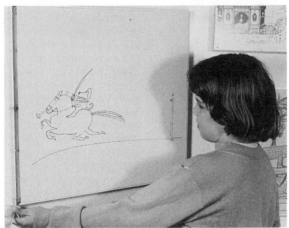

Steinberg's horse and rider set off in great haste, but with the addition of the leash shown on the Plexiglas overlay, they are visually constrained. The exhibit, conceived and built by the graphics department, shows how meaning is conveyed by images. Photographs from the files of the Exploratorium.

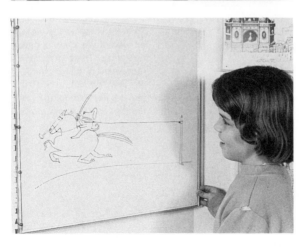

Visual balance is achieved in the conceptual sculpture above the Steinberg exhibit because the visitor intuitively does the summation and sees the small 8 as equivalent to its large counterpart. Photograph from the files of the Exploratorium.

"Cardboard Tube Syllabus" is a simply constructed exhibit, made originally out of paper towel tubes, that shows how the eye-brain system uses various strategies to judge the world from too little, too much, or contradictory information. Photograph by Esther Kutnick.

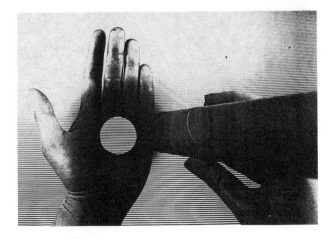

The "Ames Room," originally designed by Adelbert Ames, Jr., is deceptively shaped to capitalize on the essential ambiguity of objects. The room looks normal until objects are seen within it. Their size seems strangely distorted, a consequence of the perceiver's misplaced reliance on habit. Note the apparent change in the baby's size depending on its location. Photograph from the Exploratorium files.

Artist Gerald Marks produced the complex "Professor Pulfrich's Universe," revealing the subjective distortions that occur when a perceiver with binocular vision gets nonsimultaneous messages from the same object. Photograph from the Exploratorium files.

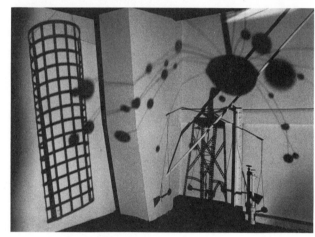

In "Reverse Distance Perception," the images presented to the left and right eye are exchanged, leading the viewer to misjudge their comparative distance. The exhibit reveals the hierarchical order of cues followed in making stereoscopic judgments. Drawing by Jad King.

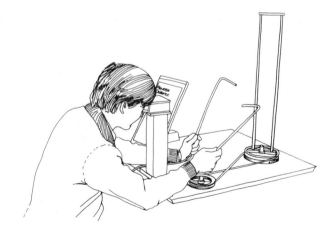

A typical gap-filling exhibit, "Eyeballs" makes the world visible from the point of view of the brain comparing the size of images on the retina to infer the relative distance of objects.

According to research by Edwin Land, the eye's judgment of black and white is independent of the absolute amount of light that reaches it and is less influenced by gradual changes of intensity than by abrupt light changes. Sharp edges make the difference, as is shown by the exhibit "Gray Step I," when the juncture between gray and white areas is obscured. Photograph from the files of the Exploratorium.

The "Cheshire Cat" exhibit, designed for the Exploratorium by two staff members, was developed out of their research on binocular fusion and the eye-brain's ability to exclude and erase conflicting information. Photograph from the files of the Exploratorium. Inset diagram from "The Cheshire Cat Effect," S. Duensing and R. Miller, *Perception* 8 (Spring 1979).

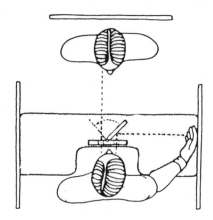

"Brine Shrimp Ballet" was
the first successful exhibit of
the animal behavior section.
The inset shows the organism's photosensitive
response. Photographs by
Susan Schwartzenberg.

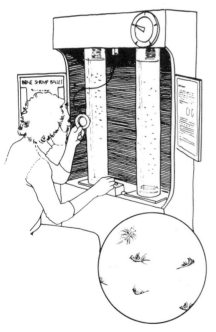

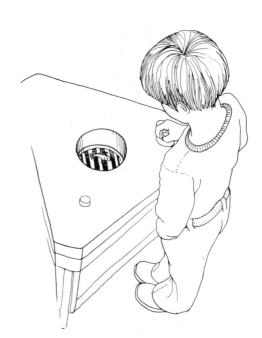

Blue acara swim around a
cylindrical tank, keeping time
with the moving stripes on
the tank walls. Moving
Stripes I and II show the
optical-kinetic reaction of
humans and fish to a moving
environment. Drawings by
Jad King.

The fish tanks store marine organisms in a natural habitat and are a seasonally changing exhibit. Explainer demonstrators supervise public interaction with the animals. Photograph from the files of the Exploratorium.

The "Cow's Eye Dissection," one of the museum's most popular demonstrations, changes squeamishness to fascination when the clear lens is exposed. Photograph from the files of the Exploratorium.

A prod to the tail of "Crayfish Stretch Receptor" sends a message from its muscle to its brain, which is intercepted by an electrode and displayed. Drawing by Jad King.

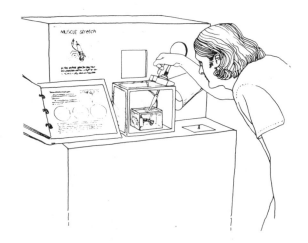

Implanting an electrode in the animal's belly for the "Watchful Grasshopper" exhibit is a delicate task, performed apart from public observation. But the creature hops about freely afterward, keeping an eye on its audience. Photograph from the files of the Exploratorium.

In "Grasshopper Leg Twitch" the detached leg kicks when an electric stimulus is applied to it. The leg remains responsive for as long as twenty-four hours. Photograph by Susan Schwartzenberg.

Electromyogram (EMG) shows that human muscular activity, such as bending one's hand, produces electrical impulses that, like the crayfish message, are audible and visually recorded on the oscilloscope. Drawing by Jad King.

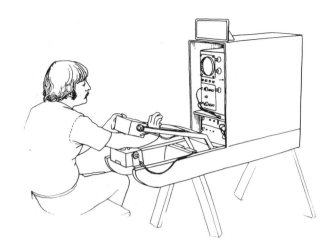

The "Language of Nerve Cells" is a miniature laboratory that allows visitors to observe the transmission of electrical impulses between nerve cells. Photograph from the files of the Exploratorium.

A simple exhibit, "Clap Your Hands," sends visitors outside the museum to listen to sound reverberate off the dome of the rotunda. Photograph from the files of the Exploratorium.

The whimsical "Pacific Gas and Leather" exhibit lets customers know that all they are purchasing when they pay for electricity is some temporary redistribution of electrons. Photograph from *Cookbook III.*

The familiar phenomenon of static electricity is recalled by clinging polystyrene chips in "Pluses and Minuses." Photograph by K. C. Cole.

Teachers and students in a workshop learn about optics and color by examining the paths of light beams and the effect of varying and obstructing light sources.

"Motor Effect" puts a current through a wire to produce mechanical movement, and "Generator Effect" uses a physical effort to create an electric current. Drawings by Jad King.

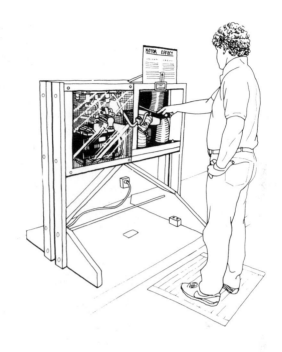

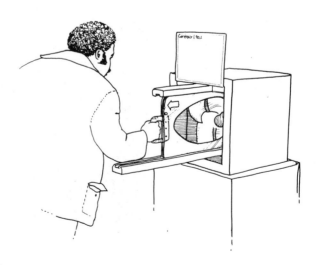

In "Shadow Box," visitors' gestures are briefly frozen in a phosphorescent afterglow. Photograph from the files of the Exploratorium.

An early project of the artist-in-residence program, Richard Register's "Tactile Tree" is an unforbidden tree of life, often aswarm with exploring children. Photograph from the files of the Exploratorium

Visitors interact with Parker's sculpture, "A.M. Lightning," by directing the stream of excited gas molecules with their hands. Photograph from the files of the Exploratorium.

To many people the "Sun
Painting" best expresses the
character and style of the
Exploratorium, and the interactions of science and art
and of people with exhibits.
Photograph by Nancy Rodger.

"Water Vortex" funnels from its clear surface to its base, dwarfing and distorting the appearance of the observers surrounding it. Photograph from the files of the Exploratorium.

"Wave Organ," an environmental work of art by Peter Richards and collaborators, is a serene spot on the San Francisco marina where the sounds and sights of the bay can be absorbed.

Chapter 6

The
Mutual
Enrichment
of Art
and Science

Speaking to a group of physics teachers at a meeting in San Francisco in 1972, Frank Oppenheimer pointed out that artists and scientists, in different but equally fundamental ways, seek out patterns in the natural world and sensitize others to them. Scientists, like artists, validate their work aesthetically, and both make intellectual choices that are "governed by a sense of concordance with nature."[1] Science and art together are needed for a full description of the world. The prevailing belief that they are dissonant and incompatible distorts and misrepresents them both.

The works that artists produce shape our apprehension of the world just as the discoveries of science do. Art helps us to see and hear and feel the world, and sometimes to conceptualize it. Artists are expert perceivers. They often show us phenomena that we have failed to note before, and reveal them with such indisputable definition that science is thereafter compelled to explore and understand them.[2] Artists give us the world with an immediacy unobtainable by science, but no less than scientists, artists are bound by canons of testing and experimentation. They render a representation of experience whose vindication lies in its resonance with the experience of others. The Exploratorium deliberately intermingles the perceptions of artists with those of scientists and resolutely denies the preeminence of one over the other or even a sharp distinction between them. Though known in the museum community as a science center and classified as a museum of science by the public, the Exploratorium calls itself a museum of science, art, and human perception, and its board retained the formal title "Board of Directors of the Palace of Arts and Science Foundation" well into the seventies.

From the beginning, the Oppenheimers sought contributions to the museum from artists as eagerly as from scientists. Exhibits were selected for their aesthetic interest and also for their compatibility with the themes of the Exploratorium. Some artworks served as seeds to bring forth a series of didactic exhibits that analyzed a phenomenon. Artworks in every medium have been exhibited at the Exploratorium. Some were single performances, and others remained on long-term display. Some were commissioned, and many were donated. Many were produced through the artist-in-residence program. The artists benefited from the technical resources of the museum and, in exchange, created works that are now permanently in the museum collection. Quite a few of the artists who got their start in the Exploratorium went on to achieve fame in the art world.[3] The exhibits that artists made often complemented didactic exhibits that explained and analyzed natural phenomena, but sometimes the work of an artist preceded analysis and generated a new line of inquiry.

Although artists usually sign their works or are otherwise credited with authorship, the practice has been a matter of dispute at the Exploratorium. Since the works are placed among the other museum displays, some people feel that they should not be singled out for special attention as art. Others believe their identification is a matter of courtesy to the artists, whose livelihood depends on just such notice. Some staff members believe that it highlights those works as productions of "professional" artists and so trivializes the aesthetic merit of the exhibits that are not so labeled. The existence of such a controversy underscores the extent to which art and the aesthetic dimension of science are, like education, everybody's business; the Exploratorium could not contain them under the purview of a special art department. The graphics department does employ visual artists with specific productive skills, but other artists work throughout the museum in many capacities, and the graphics department does not have authority over the aesthetic expression of the museum as a whole. Aesthetic quality is an ever-present and often hotly disputed concern in all the museum's enterprises, for simplicity and intellectual elegance are at the heart of intelligibility.[4]

The Exploratorium chose to celebrate its official opening with the arrival of the British art exhibit "Cybernetic Serendipity" in October 1969. Frank Oppenheimer pointed out then that artists have traditionally made people more keenly aware of nature and have sometimes provided a more meaningful introduction to complex natural phenomena than scientists are able to offer. That show seemed to bear out his observation. "Cybernetic Serendipity" emphasized aspects of nature that have traditionally been the stronghold of scientists and engineers and have until recently been ignored by artists. In fact, several of the works were produced by people who were also scientists and engineers and who were enjoying a double identity. "Cybernetic Serendipity" and the accompanying show, "Experiments in Art and Technology" ("EAT"), reflected new ways in which artists and scientists were being inspired by structures and correspondences that lie beyond commonsense experience. In the past only scientists had contemplated the little-known aspects of matter; now they were drawn into the lexicon of art. Oppenheimer welcomed the show to the museum as expressive of a new aesthetic intention:

Today's artists depict the polarization of light or the interference of waves in the same spirit that Corot painted trees or Rembrandt painted faces. Because of this pattern in art, one's appreciation of science and technology is changing. The bright streaks of cosmic rays in the neon spark chamber of the Stanford Linear Accelerator exhibit suggest kinetic art and optical sculpture. Hopefully the Exploratorium can capitalize on the trend, in order to make the discoveries of 20th century scientists more accessible to the general public.[5]

The show conveyed wonder and enthusiasm and considerable amusement at the things that can happen in the contemporary world. It was meant to arouse people's curiosity about new materials and their capacities, and it did not matter whether the objects that accomplished that end were the products of artistic insight or of scientific experimentation.

Even before the opening, the Exploratorium had acquired a reputation as an alternative exhibit space and performance center, and a series of unconventional art events took place there during the first few months of the museum's existence. Artists were drawn to the experimentalism of the Exploratorium and to Oppenheimer's energy and inquisitive intelligence. Many artists were eager to collaborate with scientists and technicians and to learn from them, and a rapport between the museum and the San Francisco arts community developed rapidly.

Some of the early artworks are still in the museum. They are scattered throughout the exhibit sections on light, color, sound, and vision. They illustrate phenomena such as light polarization and refraction, the formation of images, and how television works. They include laser exhibits and holograms, which were still a novelty when the museum was founded. The works of art help visitors who may be confused and put off by new technologies to experience them playfully and in a familiar context. The artists' exploration of new concepts and unfamiliar facets of nature entwined with old ideas and familiar emotional expression help set visitors at ease and invite them to share in the fascination with phenomena that scientists have long enjoyed.

The museum was also able to link present knowledge to the dreams and projects that scientists and artists have shared in the past. It happened that IBM had made, as a commercial promotional show, a collection of models of machines and devices built according to Leonardo da Vinci's technical and scientific sketches. It was exquisitely suited to the Exploratorium's synthesis of art and science, and the museum mounted the display enthusiastically.[6] The exhibit included some devices that were realized only centuries later. There was a paddle-wheel ship (that came into being only when steam power was developed in the nineteenth century), a three-rotation-speed gear system (foreshadowing the modern automobile transmission), a variety of measuring instruments—one for the tensile strength of wire, another for wind velocity, one for humidity—and a surveying device to calculate the angle of slope. There was also a prophetic ornithopter, or flying machine, that consisted of a lattice structure with two movable wings, operated by ropes and pulleys, and a windlass to be manipulated by the pilot lying prone inside the framework. Leonardo's flying machine, which looked much like modern hang-gliding gear, was one of several airborne inventions that were to be displayed from time to time at the Exploratorium.

Flying machines have long captivated the human imagination. They appeal to the creative fantasy of the artist and represent the lure of the unknown to the scientist. The Exploratorium has housed various examples of aeronautical enterprise inspired by the flight of birds. One of the first was the engineless glider flown by John Montgomery. But for the absence of its fabric wingsleeves, it would be flightworthy even now.[7] It hovered over the Exploratorium floor, suspended from the rafters, from the time that the museum opened until it closed for renovations ten years later. The reopening of the museum in 1980 was commemorated with the display of another historic flying machine, the *Gossamer Albatross,* a seventy-pound, man-powered airplane that resembles a giant dragonfly. The plane, "a combination of whimsy, expert workmanship and sophisticated materials" was pedaled by its pilot across the English Channel in 1979.[8]

The art and romance of space travel have been celebrated by the museum throughout its history. The *Apollo 11* moon landing occurred in the summer of 1969, just as the Exploratorium was opening, and exhibits borrowed from NASA commemorated that event. Later, in 1974, one of the museum's first artists in residence, George Bolling, arranged a dramatic presentation of the *Pioneer 11* Jupiter fly-by, bringing a direct video broadcast from the NASA monitoring center at Moffett Air Force Field into the Exploratorium. A piece of living theater, it was staged by Bolling to heighten the involvement of ordinary citizens in a moment of technological history. Nearly 25,000 people watched during the thirty-five hours as the spacecraft approached to within 27,000 miles of Jupiter (which is 400 million miles distant from the earth) and circled around it. The museum viewers shared in the dramatic buildup at the space center and in the tensions and uncertainties that accompanied the flight. The event was also a carefully prepared educational program. There were in-house seminars and lectures by eminent scientists in related fields. Reading materials were distributed, and pertinent exhibits from the Exploratorium collection were prominently displayed. The artist narrated the flight from the NASA control room with unglamorized descriptions—the flight was spectacular enough—displaying the actual communication as it occurred between the spacecraft and the earth station. This was no sterile newscast or simulated replay. When the spacecraft's orbit took it behind the planet, blocking all contact with the earth for more than forty minutes, the spectators waited tensely, and when *Pioneer* reemerged, they broke into applause. As a participant described the festive event: "Your coverage, which was informative, pretty to look at and intensely moving, was a triumph for the kind of thinking the Exploratorium represents. I read that as a commitment to make science an inclusive human experience instead of an esoteric exclusive specialty. The sense I had that night of all of us there bound together by events half a billion miles away . . . bound almost physically, I felt . . . was a justification and reward of all the work you have done."⁹ George Bolling went on to do video coverage of other planetary explorations, including the *Viking 1* landing on Mars, and the Exploratorium staged a similar presentation in 1978 of a fly-by of the planet Saturn.

Countless other natural phenomena and events provoke similar excitement among both artists and scientists. Many more could if they were better known. Other artists seeking to link art and science were working together at the Massachusetts Institute of Technology's Center for Visual Studies. Guided by the director of the center, Gyorgy Kepes, a group, which called itself the Multiple-Interaction Team (MIT), planned a collaborative exhibit of their work. Their aim was to illustrate the interaction of art with the environment and to show the identity of certain life processes with those of art. In his introduction to the catalog for the show Kepes wrote: "We begin to recognize that the world as a set of structural systems does not divide into two distinct territories, scientific knowledge and artistic or poetic vision. Rather, both our rational grasp and our grasp of sensibilities and feelings exist within a common structure of motivations, values and communications. Art and science complement each other: together they constitute the common structure of a richer life."¹⁰

On a visit to MIT, Oppenheimer met with Kepes and discussed the possibility of bringing the show to the Exploratorium and to other science museums. Together with the Chicago Museum of Science and Industry and the Franklin Institute of Science in Philadelphia, they obtained funding from the National Endowment for the Arts (NEA) for the MIT show to travel to major cities throughout the country. The grant marked the NEA's acknowledgment of the aesthetic dimension of science, and it enhanced the legitimacy of science centers as museums, a status that had not yet been accorded to them by the American Association of Museums. It would make collaboration between science museums and art museums easier, helping each to learn from the other, but the marriage was not an easy one. Collaboration between museums had to be individually negotiated, and the complex arrangements for the MIT tour were voluntarily set up by the contracting museums. The show was ambitious, including fifteen works—electronic pieces, programmed light displays, heat sculpture, sonic systems, and a variety of materials and complex constructions. Several of the works were audience interactive, as well as involving the interaction of different art forms. The pieces were fragile, some were cumbersome, and most posed serious problems of maintenance and repair. Some had to be radically reconstructed before they could even be exhibited.[11]

Some of the works had been created cooperatively. One of the most popular ones was designed by Kepes in collaboration with physicist William Walton, artist Mauricio Bueno, and a composer of electronic music, Paul Earls. Entitled "Flame Orchard," it was a sculpture constructed of aluminum tubes filled with propane gas. Music was played through the tubes, causing vibrations that forced the gas at varying pressures out of tiny openings on the surface of the tubes. When the gas was ignited it formed a fiery record of wave-shaped sound patterns. The sculpture was technically brilliant and aesthetically pleasing. It inspired the ambivalent comment by the *San Francisco Chronicle* art critic Alfred Frankenstein: "It is one of the few things in the show which is more beautiful than astonishing."[12]

Like "Cybernetic Serendipity," the MIT show forced some reassessments on the museum world and on the private viewer. Its use of scientific concepts and new technologies, some of which were unfamiliar even to the artists who used them, demanded extraordinary collaboration between artists and museum personnel. Simply to mount the MIT exhibit required technical expertise that is uncommon in art museums. The necessary skills and shop facilities were available at the Exploratorium but would have been prohibitively expensive in many other museums. Art museums typically provide only security and custodial care for visiting exhibits. The people who work there are historians, and they are not prepared to handle the technological demands of some of the newer installations. New techniques in art and the convergence of art and science exhibits will demand that art museums become more technologically sophisticated and that they learn to attend as carefully to repair and maintenance as they have to restoration and conservation. That will entail greater emphasis on material and practical skills, besides the traditional art historical expertise of the art museum curator. Today's art demands new syntheses in practice and conception that will necessarily shake the foundations of the museum world.

The Exploratorium found that the MIT artists depended on staff technicians to complete the works for them. The staff met with practical problems of engineering and design that had little to do with art or even aesthetics in a narrow sense. One biological sculpture, for example, featured the growth of an organic culture on a giant agar plate. Unwanted molds and other cultures kept appearing, however, resulting in a smelly mess that had to be thrown out. Exploratorium biologist Charles Carlson helped the artist devise a more nearly sterile medium to control the organic growth. Only science museums are likely to have a resident biologist on hand to help an artist out in such an emergency.

Although the MIT show was interesting, it was not an unqualified success. Some of the difficulties might have been avoided had it been less hastily assembled, but the problems were not exclusively practical. Critics had doubts about the artistic merit of the works and questioned whether some of them were works of art at all. Still, the show was a landmark for the Exploratorium. It was among the more ambitious traveling shows that visited the San Francisco museum, and it helped to cement bonds between museums and other teaching institutions.[13]

The circulation of traveling exhibits has become more routine since the founding of the Association of Science and Technology Centers, which now fabricates shows as well as distributing them.[14] It relieves museums of some of the business negotiations and burdens of transportation and can work more directly with artists on the installation of their pieces. The Exploratorium works most effectively with individual artists whose creations, if not produced explicitly for the Exploratorium, are at least filtered through an active involvement of the artist with the museum and its staff. That relationship between the artists and the museum gave rise to the artist-in-residence program, but at first the museum relied on an informal grapevine to find artists who could donate labor and works of art in exchange for workspace and technical assistance. The museum was happy to accommodate those whose style or interest coincided with its projects.

Perhaps the most important work that came to the Exploratorium by that informal route was the "Sun Painting," by Robert Miller. Many people think of it as the symbol that best expresses the character of the Exploratorium and conveys the unity of art and science. Miller began the work in a dark basement apartment in San Francisco. To brighten his dreary living space, he brought the light of the sun into his room with the help of a small mirror outside and some prisms set into the window. At the suggestion of a friend, Miller invited Oppenheimer, whom he did not know, to come and see his invention. As soon as Oppenheimer saw it and realized its source, he asked the artist to try it out at the Exploratorium. Miller experimented with ways to mount the prisms at different angles so that light would be refracted through at least one prism at all times of day, projecting vertical streaks of color into the room. Among other modifications, he varied the shape of the light patterns and scattered them by suspending tumbleweeds between the light source and the screen, and he made the screen of Mylar, a pliable plastic material that softened the hard edges of the color stripes and turned them into wispy streams of pure and intermingled color.

The construction that Bob Miller installed in the museum included a mirror placed outside the west entrance of the building to catch the sunlight. Explainers had to be sent out every few minutes to turn the mirror to follow the sun, and on winter afternoons, when a row of trees blocked the sun, the work was not visible at all. To improve on the design Miller contrived a device that would be synchronized with the earth's diurnal rotation and its seasonal tilt, so that the mirror would move automatically with the sun. The project of building a photoelectric sun-follower was funded by a grant from the NEA and several private donors. Eventually, with the advice of a University of California physicist, Miller and some of the Exploratorium staff members were able to construct a heliostat that used a revolving mirror to direct sunlight through a hole in the roof and bounce it onto a series of mirrors and prisms, finally breaking it into a mixture of pure color on the Mylar screen. Once the heliostat was installed, the "Sun Painting" became visible to spectators whenever the sun was shining, and explainers no longer had to run outside to "turn it on."

Although the idea for the "Sun Painting" was original to Bob Miller and his friend Kent Holloway, it is a truly collaborative work and could not have been realized at the Exploratorium without the help of several consultants and technical assistants. Even casual visitors contribute to its beauty by casting their moving shadows on the screen. And of course, without the cooperative presence of the sun, there is no "Sun Painting" at all.

Miller's fascination with light and shadow led him to study and experiment with images cast by the sun and eventually to come up with the novel theory that light is information. His "Image Walk" has become a museum tradition. It begins, on a fine day, at a sun-dappled spot under a shade tree outside the museum and takes the visitor inside to exhibits that show how light consists of overlapped images, in noisy profusion, while shadow is their blockage. Miller's walk represents a personalized depiction of the physical world, as do the many exhibits that he has created. It is difficult to classify them as either art or science, but visitors learn from them to see relationships among phenomena and to understand nature a little better.

Miller's exhibits reveal the artistry in nature. Ultimately it is the sun that makes and remakes the "Sun Painting." The devices that Miller has contrived to track and hold it are ingenious, but they can be reproduced, and a recipe for their construction appears in the *Cookbook*. The "Sun Painting" itself is irreproducible and is not man-made. A product of nature, it is always changing. It does not explain or describe anything; it presents it. Not a painting by or of the sun, it is the sun painting. As such, it underscores the ambiguity of art and science and is a fitting point of departure for a study of the nature of light. The "Sun Painting" graphically illustrates how light is dispersed and how rays of light can be recombined and superimposed to achieve subtle hues and nuances of color. Other Exploratorium exhibits refine and elaborate those themes, but the "Sun Painting" conveys the experience directly so that it is immediately grasped.

Inspired by the "Sun Painting," the poet Muriel Rukeyser, one of the most famous artists in residence at the Exploratorium, wrote a stirring tribute to its author—whoever that might be.

The Sun-Artist
FOR BOB MILLER

I

The opening of the doors. Dark.
The opening of the large doors.
Out of the daylight and the scent of trees
and that lake where generations of swans
no longer move among children. In a poisoned time.
But the bright-headed children move.
Dark, high, the beams of a huge building
exposed in the high dark air.
I see brightness with a shock of joy.

II

Past the darkness a lashing of color.
Not color, strands of light.
Not light but pure deep color beyond color,
like the pure fierce light I once knew, before

a minute of blindness. These colors are deeper;
the entire range in its millions,
twisting and brilliant traveling.

III
I stand in the strong sun before a bank of prisms.
On the screen in front of me, tangled colors of light,
                              twined, intertwined.
A sensitive web of light changing, for the sun moves, the
     air moves.
The perceiver moves.
                    I dance my slow dance.

IV
The deepest blue, green, not the streams of the sea,
the clear yellow of tellows, not California, more,
not Mediterranean, not the Judean steeps. Red beyond
                              blood over flame,
more even than visionary America. All light.
A man braced on the sun, where the sun enters
through the roof, where the sun-follower,
a man-made motor with a gentle motion
just countered the movement of the earth, holds this scene
in front of us on the man-made screen.
Light traveling, meets, leaps and becomes art.

V
Colors move on a screen. The doors open again.
They run in, the California children.
They run past the colors and the colors change.
The laughter of running. They cry out, bird voices,
ninety-seven children, Wow! Wow! How come?

VI
Another day. I stand before the screen,
Alone I move, selecting out my green,
choose out the red with my arm, I let the orange stand,
a web of yellow, the blue stays and shines.
I am part of the color, I am part of the sun.

VII
You have made an art in which the sun is standing.
It changes, goes dark, goes grey. The sun appears.
You have led me through eleven states of being.
You have invited us all. Allow the sunlight,
dance your dance.

VIII

Another day. No sun. The fog is down,
Doing its slow dance into the city,
It enters the Gate of my waking.
There will be no colors but the range of white.
Before the screen, I wait.

IX

Night. What do you know about the light?

X

Waiting. A good deal like real life.
Waiting before the sea for the fish to run
Waiting before the paper for the poem
Waiting for a man's life to be, to be.

XI

Break of light! Sun in his colors,
streaming into our lives.
This artist dreams of the sun, the sun, the children of the sun.

XII

Frail it is and can be intercepted.
Fragile, like ourselves. Mirrors and prisms, they
                          can be broken.
Children shattered by anything.
Strong, pouring strong, wild as the power of the
    great sun.
Not art, but light. In distance, in smiting winter,
the artist speaks: No art.
This is not art.
What is *an artist*? I hear the song of the sun.[15]

Is the "Sun Painting" art? Is Bob Miller a scientist because he is a
keen observer and found a way to help the public see the light? Miller
has the rare artist's gift to present phenomena concretely and evoca-
tively, but to do that well, he had to learn a great deal of science.
Similarly, people who came to the museum to build science exhibits
found themselves stretched to become artists.

Some years after the "Sun Painting" was completed, museum
staff members constructed another exhibit that used the same roof
opening and heliostat. It too was a sun painting, but in a different
medium. It too breaks up the sun's light into its constituent bands
of color, but it uses a spectroscope to do it. A spectroscope is an
optical device used to study the characteristic spectra produced by

the energy emitted by substances when they are excited. Pure elements can be visually identified by the light frequencies they emit when stimulated, much as people can be distinguished by their fingerprints. The spectroscope passes light from a glowing substance through a series of lenses and prisms that display a band of colors from which the composition of the substance may be inferred.

The Exploratorium exhibit "Fraunhofer Lines," so named after Joseph von Fraunhofer (1787-1826), the scientist who first observed and mapped these spectral patterns, displays the light frequencies emitted by the sun. The spectral color display also includes some dark lines, indicating frequencies that were absorbed by the elements at the sun's surface as the light produced by the sun escaped. The chemical composition of the sun's atmosphere can be inferred from those missing color bands. In effect, the exhibit simply projects the sun's spectral fingerprint on a screen inside the museum. Few people would be inclined to identify "Fraunhofer Lines" as a work of art, and yet it and "Sun Painting" are both displays of light directly transmitted from the sun. The exhibits invite further study of the nature of light, the one to clarify optics and the radiant behavior of light, the other to understand the emission, absorption, and storage of light and its behavior as particles. Additional Exploratorium exhibits are devoted to each of those subjects.

"Fraunhofer Lines" (also identified as "Solar Signature") is one of a series of exhibits on the capacity of substances to absorb, store, and release energy in the form of light, but something closer to ordinary experience seemed necessary to begin to explain such familiar but mysterious emission phenomena as fluorescent light bulbs, Day-Glo paints, and the "brighter than white" detergents that were fashionable at the time. Phosphorescent and fluorescent substances glow when their atoms are excited and their energy is released. But an artist's insight was needed to enliven that observation. A Swiss artist, Carl Bücher,[16] had coincidentally invented a phosphorescent vinyl material, which he used to produce light art. The Exploratorium readily accepted his offer to create an exhibit out of the same material.

"Shadow Box" is a three-sided, semi-enclosed wooden structure whose inside walls are lined with the phosphorescent vinyl. The exhibit has a ceremonial appeal like that of a Japanese shrine. Visitors remove their shoes before entering the space and place themselves in poses against the vinyl walls. At intervals a buzzer sounds, alerting them to hold their position as a bright strobe light flashes. The light excites the exposed phosphorescent material on the wall but not the areas covered by the people's bodies. As the people move away from the wall in normal light, their shadow images remain as a choreographed frieze, until the phosphorescent wall around the images is de-excited and stops glowing.

One critic complained that there was nothing to be learned from "Shadow Box"—it was just fun! Bücher's piece, however, paved the way to collateral exhibits on light emission and absorption. While experimenting with materials and lighting techniques that would heighten the shadow effect, the staff developed several other didactic exhibits that display related phenomena such as the effect of temperature on light storage and the variations in energy release, or glow, due to differences in the wavelength (color) of the illuminating light. Even if it were true that nothing could be learned directly from the artwork, it successfully draws visitors' attention to the behavior of light by delighting them with an exhilarating instance of it. In the optical light ray exhibits—those introduced by the "Sun Painting"—and the energy absorption and emission exhibits—those introduced by the "Fraunhofer Lines" and "Shadow Box"—the artist's presentation is an enticing first encounter that draws the museum visitor into a deeper analysis of light.

Another example of collaboration between an artist and the Exploratorium is the "Tactile Dome," in which the artist's desire to construct a tactile environment coincided with the museum's aim to develop exhibits that explore the sense of touch from a scientific perspective. The cooperative effort was initiated in 1970, when the NEA suggested that artist August Coppola discuss his kinaesthetic project with the director of the new museum in San Francisco. Coppola, a professor of comparative literature at California State College at Long Beach and the brother of moviemaker Francis Ford Coppola, was interested in environmental aesthetics and existentialist philosophy. Raised in a tradition of emotional expressiveness, he found the American environment coldly distant and sensuously impoverished. He regarded the predominantly visual character of American culture as physically incapacitating and spiritually confining, and he looked to art as a means of awakening tactile sensitivity and breaking down barriers of loneliness and isolation. Coppola, collaborating with designers Carol and Carl Day, had built a gallery at California State College where blindfolded visitors were guided through a variety of haptic sensations.[17] There were pressure and temperature changes, surfaces of different textures, vibrations from external sources, and also internal kinaesthetic adjustments. Coppola applied to the NEA for support to enlarge his project, which led to a joint proposal by the artist and the Exploratorium that was funded in 1971. That summer Coppola and a large crew of artists, craftspeople, technical designers, and volunteers constructed a geodesic dome inside the museum.[18]

The dome is thirty feet in diameter, and in it people crawl, slither, tumble, and climb in total darkness through labyrinthine passageways from one haptic experience to the next. There are rough surfaces and smooth ones, tight spots and open spaces, cold places and warm areas, networks of ropes to clamber on and tight tubes that contract and expand as bodies wriggle through them. At the midpoint of the journey, visitors emerge into a dimly lit ceremonial space at the top of the dome, where they can recline on couches of fur and corduroy before making the final descent through a chute, feet or head first, into a deep bed of birdseed and then out into the familiar world. Most people come out laughing and shaking the birdseed out of their hair and clothing. A few are afraid of the dark and find the experience unsettling, but most, especially the children, return at once for a second run-through.

The exhibit was an immediate success. Children's parties and groups of adults reserved the dome for special occasions. School groups made tactile maps of it, and people came from all around the country to try out the novel experience. It became necessary to restrict entry to scheduled groups and for limited periods to allow visitors to savor it fully. In the first three years of its operation at least 35,000 people went through the dome, and it was a particular favorite of blind visitors, who were at no disadvantage exploring its darkness. Many people come to the museum expressly to tour the dome. As they walk through the building, however, they are often distracted by other exhibits, and so they stay or come back to see more. Like the "Shadow Box," the "Tactile Dome" has become a springboard for other, more analytic exhibits. Some explore tactile discrimination, balance, and thermal sensitivity, and others compare human tactile sensitivity and its physiology with that of other organisms.

To accompany exhibits on the properties of sound, the museum has developed a whole collection of exhibits on the perception and theory of music. Some of them help visitors to understand how traditional acoustic music is made and what is new about electronic musical instruments. Visitors can listen to and produce different tones or alter their sound by adding harmonics and changing the timbre, and sometimes a group of visitors will strike up a jam session. The music section was begun by Leni Isaacs, a music teacher and morning explainer, who wanted to demystify music not just as applied physics but also as aesthetic experience. The music program that she coordinated presents music, musical instruments, and musicians as exhibits to be "explored and touched," as are all the museum exhibits.[19] Isaacs organized a series of concerts in the museum's theater and asked the performers to converse with the audience about the nature of their instruments and their music. Since then, the Exploratorium has improved its concert hall, and the "Speaking of Music" series has achieved a loyal following. Well-known and avantgarde artists play in the museum, and so do less famous experimentalists. The museum thus helps performing artists explore the unknown while educating the public to appreciate what they are doing.

The greatest obstacle to the encouragement of new art has always been the lack of financial support. Whenever possible, the Exploratorium pays artists for their work, but the museum is constantly raising money for other purposes as well. Artists are notoriously poor, and the materials they work with are often expensive. Oppenheimer was able to find public and private support for individual art projects, such as the "Sun Painting" and the "Tactile Dome," and was even able to persuade federal agencies such as the NEA to accommodate the unconventional proposals of a science museum. His ambition, however, was to find a more permanent base of support for the production of art pieces and to bring working artists into the museum as a regular interactive exhibit.

In 1973 Oppenheimer won NEA support and matching state and private funds for year-long artist residencies.[20] The artist-in-residence program would pay artists and provide them with time, space, and equipment for their creative work, along with access to the technical skills and material resources of the museum staff, which the Exploratorium hoped would promote innovation by the artists. The museum would be able to display the artists at work as an exhibit, much as the operations of the machine and woodworking shop were conceived as exhibits. Furthermore, the program stipulated that the work produced by the artists during their year of residence would be kept for permanent display at the museum. The artists, especially those who were young and unknown, would profit from the public exposure and promotion that the museum was able to give their work and from the critical reviews that it would receive. Still another anticipated benefit was the interaction between artists and staff, which could heighten the aesthetic sensitivity of the latter while strengthening the material competence of the former, once again a form of mutual enrichment and education. Finally, the museum saw the program as a chance to tap into the arts community by including local artists, art educators, and museum heads on the selection committee that evaluated projects submitted to the artist-in-residence program.[21]

It took some time to work out guidelines for selecting participants. In the first year too little money was distributed among too many artists. There were also political disagreements, for some of the funding agencies specified that awards be made on the basis of ethnic origin and cultural disadvantage. Many museum staff members shared the social concern implicit in those conditions, but others objected to the constraints. In the end the point was moot, since there were ample candidates, of all genders and genres, whose artistic orientation was consistent with the Exploratorium's rationale.

But the program still had its conflicts. The artists were expected to work in the museum in close interaction with the staff, who were to be available for technical assistance. Some staff members found that burdensome and resented the privilege extended to the artists, whom they saw as elite parasites. Artists in their turn were sometimes exploitative and imperious, demanding service while evincing contempt toward the utilitarian staff. Eventually a system was worked out under which each artist was assigned to the watchful care of a single and sympathetic staff mentor.

With successive funding renewals, the artist-in-residence program, like the explainer and SITE programs, became a permanent feature of the museum. A standard contractual arrangement between the artists and the museum was agreed on. Each residency, having begun with the acceptance of a proposal, proceeded to a "fiddling period," during which the artists were free for experimental play. The period gave the artists time to become acquainted with the museum, its shops, equipment, and staff, to learn skills and build models, and to reassess their original proposal in the light of concrete realities. Occasionally they abandoned ideas at that point, when it became evident that their realization would be unfeasible. The museum also held veto power over proposals but used it only rarely.[22] The exploratory period was followed by the artist's actual production of the work, and on its completion, there was a shakedown period of a month or longer during which the operation of the piece could be evaluated on the museum floor and, if necessary, modified. Final payment to the artist was not made until the testing period had been completed, which was supposed to insure that artists would not abandon incomplete works for the staff to finish and debug.

Even with that protection, the staff had to be prepared to maintain the artworks. Since they are integrated with other exhibits on the museum floor, the works are susceptible to injury by the public. The regular museum exhibits are routinely designed for ease of repair and maintenance, and they are constantly under review, but works of art tend to be one of a kind and are not normally expected to require repair. The personal immortality that artists proverbially strive for is seldom reflected in the durability of their creations. And so it often has fallen to the staff to restore or even reconstruct works of art. Sometimes they improve on them, within the restrictions that law and propriety impose.

Some of the artist-in-residence works are among the most popular exhibits in the museum. One of the first was the "Tactile Tree," made by Richard Register, an artist known locally for his marigold-filled "Vege-car." His tactile sculptures were related to his interest in the politics of ecology and alternative energy. Register had assisted in the construction of the "Tactile Dome," and "Tactile Tree" is, in a sense, a complement to the dome. Where the dome encloses the visitor in darkness and womblike seclusion, Register's tree is extroverted, presenting a variety of surfaces and textures to be visually as well as tactilely explored. Much of the shop staff collaborated on its construction; the hollow interior houses systems for refrigerating, heating, spraying, vibrating, and activating all the appendages at the surface of the tree. The mood of the piece is different from the dome's, and it evokes altogether different behavior on the part of visitors. A bizarre and unforbidden tree of life, it is generally bedecked with shrieking children and with fascinated, if less vocal, adults who pat, stroke, caress, and tug at its edges and extremities. Although it is unquestionably a public success, the project revealed how taxing the program could be on the staff and how it must be modified to work effectively.

Several works by another artist, William Parker, probe the ambiguous space between art and science. Parker was a member of the MIT Center for Visual Studies, and one of his works was included in the MIT traveling exhibit. Educated as a physicist and trained as a glassblower, Parker proposed an interactive glass plasma sculpture as a residency project. He completed several pieces for the museum but was never able to work the bugs out of the one originally proposed. His sculptures all explore the remarkable colors and forms that occur when high-frequency electric discharges pass through low-pressure gases.

To get the full experience of Parker's works, the viewer must interact directly with them. One piece, "Quiet Lightning," uses the visitor's body to complete an electric circuit. A charge passes from electrodes at the center of a transparent glass sphere, through tubes of neon and argon gases that radiate from the center of the sphere, and out through the hands of the visitor holding the sphere. Visitors feel only the pleasantly smooth, warm surface of the glass, but their hands become part of the electrostatic field, acquiring alternate positive and negative charge, and their fingers look weirdly skeletal in the pink glow of the sphere. A second sculpture by Parker, called "A.M. Lightning," is similar in style. It is a large horizontal glass sculpture in which high-frequency radio waves pass through xenon and helium gases in a tube. The excited gases emit a purple glow that separates into discrete beads, stringing like a poodle tail across the tube. Visitors can pass their hands over the surface of the sculpture and deflect the stream of beads so that they squeeze together, merge, spread, and bend. Parker's works have an eerie beauty that makes them appealing to the public, and they also involve an appreciation of plasma physics. As exhibits, they are conceptually continuous with some of the didactic exhibits, and they can serve as a point of departure for the study of electromagnetic waves, stored light, lasers, and radiation. Parker has since made a commercial success of his plasma sculptures, especially those that are operated by preprogrammed microprocessors.

Quite a few of the artists who made their debut with the residency program went on to win recognition in the art world. "Forms in Motion," a smoke sculpture well loved by everyone at the museum, launched the art career of young Dianne Stockler, who was experimenting with animated films while making a meager living driving a delivery truck. Her sculpture was composed of geometric images inscribed on film and projected into a transparent container filled with ammonium chloride vapor. The images appear suspended there as three-dimensional figures, moving, swelling, billowing, changing shape, and becoming involuted and falling back on themselves. Visitors find in the serenely metamorphosing forms a moment of tranquillity, and many take time out from the bustling confusion of the museum to sit before the sculpture and gaze quietly into its darkness.

The piece again called for the collective expertise of the Exploratorium staff, to construct an airtight and unbreakable glass tank, to fill it with smoke that would not darken the glass, to find a film sturdy enough, and to produce a practical film loop projection system that could run safely and unattended for long stretches of time. The finished work has become one of the most popular of the museum's exhibits, and the artist has become internationally known for her film animation.

Many of the artists have kept up a long-term affiliation with the museum. Some constructed additional exhibits for the museum even after completing their year's residence, working on commission or as adjunct staff members. Some just continued to hang around because they had formed friendships among the staff or needed advice on new enterprises. Many became ensnared in the dynamic of their residence project, lured on, as by a scientific research program, to follow an initial work of art with the further explorations that it seemed to demand. That continuity in the artistic enterprise itself became a subject that Oppenheimer, in particular, sought to find a way to display.

Aesthetic problems, like the conundrums of physics, are nested within one another and have a way of enticing artists, much as scientists are drawn, with a seductive force from one problem to the next. The public, aware of only a final product and ordinarily acquainted with only a few samples of an artist's work, is generally ignorant of the dynamic that moves an artist onward. And the coherence that marks an artist's style tends to spring from a private discipline that few besides the artist can observe.[23] The process of art is less documented and less public than that of science but no less grounded in problems encountered and in their tentative solutions. Scientific inquiry is ordinarily carried out in research laboratories and classrooms, as well as in group meetings and seminars and on the pages of scholarly publications and proposals submitted for peer review. Artistic exploration, by contrast, is more often confined to the studio or to private coffeeshop conversation. It may be entrusted to a diary or journal but is only rarely given public exposure as a process that might be undergone collectively or whose logic might be understood. The Exploratorium sought to shed light on such aesthetic rumination and to present that quest as a museum exhibit.

A sequence of works by sculptor Douglas Hollis turned out to be a good illustration of an artist's research. Hollis had been exploring the quality of materials not only as occupants of space but also as containers of space. He had worked with inflatable environments that included the movement of spectators as a sculptural event. He had also created a movable environment in which people were transported. Using the principle of the camera obscura to produce a moving cinema obscura, he made a giant, mobile pinhole camera out of an ordinary van. As Hollis drove his optical van about the city, his passengers, seated inside the dark enclosed space, watched the passing San Francisco cityscape projected as an inverted image on the inside wall of his truck. Many of the Exploratorium staff members recall bumping somewhat nauseously through delightful city tours and cinematic crossings of Bay-area bridges.

Hollis had also played with the sculptural effect of sound in space. His "Nocturnal Aviation Wind Ensemble" was a performance in sound and light. Huge, light-bearing kites were launched on a windy night, filling the air with swirling patterns of light as the wind currents seized them and blew them in different directions. A natural music accompanied their flight as the sound of the wind whistling through the kite strings was amplified. Hollis became fascinated by the idea of bouncing sound off a resonant surface in space and began studying texts on the construction of musical instruments. Recalling the Homeric tale of Aeolus' cave of the winds, whose sound Odysseus and his men heard on their journey home from Troy, Hollis decided to build an Aeolian harp that would resound to the natural strumming of the wind.[24] He experimented by placing objects of different shapes and materials in his window and recording the sound of the wind playing through them. Just as Bob Miller had splintered and bent the light of the sun and drawn it into the museum, so now Doug Hollis proposed to sculpt and tame the sound of the wind and bring it indoors. Like Miller, he was warmly received when he brought his proposal to the Exploratorium. Staff members helped him design the instrument, trying out variations in its composition.

In its final form the harp resembles a huge futuristic sculpture consisting of three stainless steel scoops, strung vertically with eighteen strings. The structure was mounted on the roof over the north entrance of the Exploratorium, where it continues to resound with an erratic and sometimes plaintive song. Most of the time it hums a soft accompaniment to the rustling of the surrounding eucalyptus trees. Although all of the strings are tuned to a low E, the sound of the harp varies in complex ways with the direction and turbulence of the wind. Different harmonics resound irregularly, and sometimes all the strings are unexpectedly silent even though there are

are violent gusts of wind. Below a certain wind velocity no sound is produced, but then it may emerge suddenly out of the still of darkness. Like the "Sun Painting," this work of musical art can be simply enjoyed. But for those who choose to encounter it as a question, it may be taken as the first of a series of exhibits on the physics of sound and of musical instruments. Hollis continued to develop ideas for sound sculptures that had been suggested by his experimentation with the wind harp. In the Aeolian harp the sound is the effect of the wind circulating about and vibrating the strings. Hollis moved conceptually from that shaping of sound to the more abstract idea of vortical motion.

He proposed a second artist-in-residence project that would display the shape of water in motion as an immense vortical whirlpool. The whirlpool generated a host of unanticipated engineering difficulties and taxed the creative energy of the museum staff to its limit. The result, after a long trial period during which the museum floor was often flooded, was a dramatic human-sized water funnel, visible in a clear glass cylinder and activated by the visitor who opens a valve that sets the whirlpool in motion. Visitors who watch the huge funnel of water slowly take shape and rotate and finally elongate downward to the bottom of the vat feel like a tiny Alice in Wonderland pulling the plug in a giant bathtub. Hollis's "Water Vortex" is a beautiful and provocative work that like other resident pieces, hovers at the edge of art and science, defying categorization as either. It can be viewed in conjunction with other playful water sculptures constructed in the museum. Most visitors are pleased to sit or stand at its base and gaze at the awesome water funnel or at their companions, seen skewed and distorted through the massive water lens.

Each year brings more new artists to the museum. They have explored new media and old technologies and have applied new technologies to old subjects. They have modernized traditional art forms such as stained-glass window design and painting and have also invented new art forms. Many of the proposals are site-specific. Some artworks take the visitor outside the museum, into the columns of the rotunda to listen to sound reverberations, or into the adjoining park to look at the flora and fauna there, or to the nearby Pacific Ocean to make a record of its ecology or its music. Not all projects that were proposed have been completed. One that remains to be realized would make a work of art out of the ever-present San Francisco fog, and at least one airborne project was supposed to capture the movements of the bay on videotape. Artworks have been proposed to concentrate on animals and plant life, including their social habits. Some suggestions are politically motivated, and others reflect philosophical concerns or psychological interests. Some have had moral implications. Most have a way of transforming the accepted realities of nature and experience so that we confront them anew and find novel configurations of meaning in them.

Not all the works produced under the Exploratorium's artist-in-residence program are great works of art. Although the promise of aesthetic quality is surely one reason for their selection, it is not the only one. Just as the museum is not there to celebrate the genius of great science, neither is it determined to glorify great art. Rather, the aim of the Exploratorium is to bring both art and science into the common ground of human experience where its veneration consists less in distanced reverence than in appreciative use. We use works of art, just as we use scientific theories and technical inventions to help us identify and understand the processes of nature. The validity of art, like that of science, lies in its capacity to enlarge our experience of the world and enhance our comprehension of it. The production of art, like that of science, requires a great deal of random and apparently aimless experimentation. But some of that experimentation will bear fruit in works that synthesize and recombine our perceptions in a revelatory fashion. When that occurs we have the aesthetic equivalent to what Oppenheimer called "the right answer."[25] The search for the right answer is not the mission of a select few, and it is not confined to science. It is a human responsibility and a human pleasure, not the only worthwhile human enterprise but one to be cherished and propagated.

The Exploratorium does not defend the precept that all patterns are of equal merit—there are criteria for the identification of good art, just as there are tests of valid scientific beliefs. No single approach to understanding the universe is invariably right or demonstrably legitimate, and no one group of seers has a privileged insight. Science is often glorified as a collective body of truth that is to be authoritatively imparted by cultural institutions such as schools and science museums. The presence of works of art in a science museum thus has a leavening and somewhat disruptive effect. Scattered among the analytic exhibits at the Exploratorium, the irreverent and apparently frivolous objects may take people unawares and inspire them with confidence in their ability to perceive the world as artists and as scientists.

The Exploratorium has established a reputation as a science museum. Although that commits it to displaying the findings of science and the techniques and instruments that make them possible, it does not prohibit exposure of uncertainty and doubt. It also does not preclude showing the complementary perceptual discoveries and the intellectual and imaginative creations that artists, using different tools and methods, continue to reveal. A poll of visitors would probably show no discrimination on their part between those exhibits that are officially designated as artworks and those that are meant to illustrate particular concepts of science. And afterward, when visitors are asked what they remember of the museum, it is frequently the artworks that spring to mind when most of the didactic exhibits are long forgotten.

Chapter 7

Funding the Museum

I n 1984 the Exploratorium celebrated its fifteenth anniversary with a gala dinner attended by more than six hundred people.
The honoree was one of the museum's most
loyal benefactors, William R. Hewlett, cofound-
er of the Hewlett-Packard Company and an international leader in the field of electronic instrumentation. Hewlett's support had been
influential in winning the museum its initial
grant of $50,000 from the San Francisco Founda-
tion. Since then a total of $20 million had been
raised and expended mostly on programs, exhibits, and capital improvements. The annual operating budget had risen to more than $3.5 million.
Frank Oppenheimer died a few months after the
dinner. Although his presence would be missed,
there was little doubt that his long, hard struggle
had been vindicated. The museum had achieved
stability and would survive even without his direction.

People tend to assume that the Exploratorium
was founded with public funds or with the help
of massive philanthropic donations. But it was
more like a family business, begun by Frank and
Jackie Oppenheimer and their son, Michael,
with the goodwill of a few friends and no endowment whatsoever. The institutional growth
of the museum can be divided into two phases.
The first period, dominated by the crusading ef-

171

forts of Frank Oppenheimer and his friends, was devoted to building the contents, establishing the idea of the museum, and winning financial support for it. The second phase began with the arrival of Virginia C. Rubin. Her creation of a development department stabilized the museum's structure at a time when it had achieved some maturity as a cultural institution. The history of the Exploratorium is in part a familiar tale of institutional growth that has much in common with other successful contemporary American institutions and commercial enterprises. But it is also a story of an unorthodox enterprise that has left an indelible impression on museums and science centers throughout the world. The Exploratorium's struggle for economic security is inseparable from its campaign to gain credibility as an educational institution for itself and museums in general. Those endeavors combined to make a model of the museum that has inspired emulation.

When the Oppenheimers arrived in San Francisco in 1967, they did not find much interest in science museums. Unlike the ballet or the opera or even art museums, which are commonly the beneficiaries of philanthropic support, science centers did not have a ready-made following. The aquarium, planetarium, and museum of natural history seemed to provide about as much coverage of science as the city thought it needed. The Oppenheimers therefore had to convince those prominent families and business executives who were mainstays of the arts and culture that another kind of science museum would make a worthwhile contribution to the Bay area.[1] Frank Oppenheimer had the endorsement of eminent scientists the world over, but they could not make the museum financially operative. To win support from the local business community, the museum had to demonstrate its practical viability. It had to prove itself a good investment.

A trail of personal connections led Oppenheimer to John May, executive director of the San Francisco Foundation, a community trust organization that combines several smaller family fortunes, including that of the Hewletts. Its initial grant[2] in May 1969 was the breakthrough that permitted the museum to open its doors to the public on August 20, 1969. That expression of confidence by the San Francisco Foundation paved the way to other funding sources, and the museum attracted a small but increasing stream of income during its first year of operation. Donations from private individuals accounted for nearly a third of the initial year's operating funds.[3] Some fund-raising events were organized by members of the Palace of Fine

Arts League and by the board of directors, but Oppenheimer himself was invariably the persuasive force. The board saw itself as auxiliary to Oppenheimer's leadership and left most of the promotion as well as the management and day-to-day operation of the museum to him.[4] Oppenheimer's time was taken up in negotiations with civic leaders and city officials and in obtaining materials for exhibits, but by the end of the first year after the museum's opening his relentless scavenging had raised $145,000. Most of that was individual donations and small foundation grants, and $105,000 was dispersed at once to pay salaries, including those of the explainers, to purchase the most essential machinery and shop supplies, and to make the most pressing building repairs. Exhibits were necessarily built on a shoestring. Fund-raising never ceased to be a burden. According to Oppenheimer's estimate based on the value of the dollar in 1969, the annual cost of building and maintaining the museum would stabilize at $750,000, and he projected that $6.5 million would be needed over a ten-year period to pay for capital improvement and construction of new facilities—a library, auditorium, television and video studio, shops, and a refreshment area.[5] His calculations proved to be remarkably accurate given the rate of inflation over the next decade.

The biggest hurdle was to change the way museums were perceived and to obtain for them the large-scale, on-going support that educational institutions are in the habit of receiving. As a seasoned academic grantsman, Oppenheimer was familiar with the federal funding agencies that support scientific research. It seemed reasonable to go to those same agencies for what he considered an extension of his research. But his appeals to the National Science Foundation (NSF) and other agencies met with a disappointing response. As far as the government agencies were concerned, only certifying institutions were authentically educational. Informal education dispensed to the general public did not qualify for support, and museums were not eligible even to apply for funds. The major private foundations reacted similarly. They too were interested in educational reform but restricted their support of it to degree-granting, teaching institutions. Furthermore, they regarded the San Francisco museum as essentially a local institution with limited regional outreach. Through prolonged and persuasive efforts, Oppenheimer was able to change the attitudes of the government agencies and some of the foundations and ultimately to win their support.

One of Oppenheimer's first applications for grant support was to the NSF's Division of Education. The NSF had funded the Library of Experiments that Oppenheimer constructed at the University of Colorado. The Exploratorium was, he thought, a similar enterprise on a larger scale. He hoped that endorsement by the NSF would give the museum a national reputation and would draw the attention of the academic world and the scientific establishment to it as an alternative educational resource. National status would make the museum independent of purely regional political and economic constraints. It would also weaken intellectual parochialism. In Oppenheimer's mind the situation of the museum in San Francisco was incidental to its universal subject matter. Science, he believed, has no location. The museum offered a new way of teaching science.

But the NSF turned the application down. Although it had recently opened a new division for the support of the "public understanding of science," no NSF programs existed for the support of science museums.[6] Oppenheimer was advised to apply to the National Endowment for the Arts (NEA) for museum assistance. That was bad advice, for only museums that possessed permanent collections of value—a condition that excluded most science centers—were even accredited as museums by the American Association of Museums. Until the formation of the Association of Science and Technology Centers, there was no advocacy organization for science centers at all, and they had little legitimacy within the museum profession, let alone the educational establishment.

At last in 1971, after two years of frustration, Oppenheimer applied successfully to the NSF Pre-College Education in Science Division. To suit the agency's guidelines, he carefully formulated the proposal not for the construction of exhibits but for the training of high school students as shop apprentices.[7] That program had the endorsement of local high school counselors and shop teachers, and with the award the Exploratorium was able to hire additional personnel as well as to purchase expendable materials. Most important, it broke the NSF's resistance to funding museums, and the first grant of $35,640 was followed in 1972 with another grant of $70,000, now explicitly given for exhibit construction as a part of curriculum development. From there the NSF became one of the Exploratorium's chief supporters. It subsequently funded exhibit curricula in the life sciences and on electricity, including not merely the development of new exhibits and programs but also their periodic reassessment and reconstruction. In 1979, ten years after rejecting Oppenheimer's first appeal, the NSF Program for the Public Understanding of Science granted a two-year award of $366,000 to the Exploratorium for the development of an exhibit section on language that was to include the physics of speech production, the biology and evolution of language, the psychology of the perception of meaning and its expression through language, and the use of language as an art form and a model of thought. By 1980 the NSF had become the museum's largest single source of funding, having awarded nearly $1.5 million. The Exploratorium's educational legitimacy was no longer in question.[8]

Winning support from the National Endowment for the Arts was likewise an uphill struggle that required creative adaptation to the guidelines set by that agency. The NEA, like the NSF, revealed remarkable flexibility and respect for the integrity of its applicants. Under the early chairmanship of Nancy Hanks, the NEA held to a policy of supporting innovative projects rather than continuing operating and maintenance costs. Hanks believed that maintaining museums was primarily the responsibility of local and state agencies, government and private, and that the federal government should interfere with that process as little as possible.[9] Before the passage of the Museum Services Act in 1976, which created the Institute of Museum Services, whatever federal support was given to museums was restricted to specific projects, and there was little help available for the day-to-day business of survival.[10]

Nevertheless, the NEA listened with interest to Oppenheimer's proposals. The Exploratorium had a champion in Barbara Newsom, the museum program study director of the Council on Museum Education in New York and a staff associate of the Rockefeller Brothers Fund. She and Oppenheimer had met in 1971 as participants on a panel on the arts,[11] and she subsequently visited the San Francisco museum while gathering data for her book *The Art Museum as Educator*.[12] She encouraged Oppenheimer to apply to the NEA for a grant and wrote an enthusiastic letter endorsing his appeal.[13] Although the endowment had rejected Oppenheimer's earlier request for funding to build exhibits on depth and pattern perception, in 1974 it awarded $25,000 for support of the explainer program under the agency's new Wider Availability of Museums Program, aimed at bringing new audiences into museums.[14]

The NEA also supported some of the more conventionally art-related projects, including the performance series "Speaking of Music," the construction of the "Tactile Dome," the completion of the "Sun Painting," and the assembly of the Steinberg exhibit. An unusual award, made collectively to the Exploratorium, the Chicago

Museum of Science and Industry, and the Franklin Institute in Philadelphia, enabled those three science museums to mount and circulate the MIT show produced by Gyorgy Kepes and the artists at the Center for Visual Studies.[15]

The NEA subsequently funded dissemination of Exploratorium exhibit ideas and designs by means of a catalog and the *Cookbook*. It also paid for a film, *Exploratorium* by Jon Boorstin, a project that was at the same time a promotional venture and a work of art. The NEA agreed to fund it jointly with the NSF, requiring the film to meet the aesthetic standards of the one agency and the educational conditions of the other in order to receive the $28,500 contributed by each agency.[16]

Another matching grant, this one designed to elicit support for the arts from state and regional sources, was awarded to the museum in 1974 for the artist-in-residence program. To obtain the $18,000 given by the federal agency, the museum had to build connections with the California arts establishment and enlist its collaboration. Consistent with Nancy Hanks's goals, the NEA expected state and local agencies to take over the projects once the federal government had given them a start. Like the NSF, the NEA discovered that it could fill its priorities—to stimulate artistic creativity and to encourage new constituencies for the arts and their support—while satisfying the needs of the museum. Local support to meet the NEA challenge was generated from the California Arts Commission and from the Mary A. Crocker Foundation, a private family fund. The NEA continued to support various Exploratorium projects and had contributed $340,000 to the museum by the end of its first decade of operation. It was no longer necessary for the museum to legitimate itself as an institution that serves the arts, but it was still perceived as predominantly a science museum. The collaborative and matching grants awarded to the Exploratorium imply that there are close ties between science and art and that the institutions that house and promote the one are entirely compatible with those that advance the other and may in fact work together on joint objectives. Their administrative segregation has been an obstacle not only to endeavors to unite them in concrete projects such as those of the Exploratorium but, more generally, to their conceptualization as part of a single human enterprise.

Another federal agency that helped the Exploratorium bridge cultural and political gaps was the National Endowment for the Humanities (NEH). Often defensive of its nonpractical and nonvocational orientation, the NEH is mandated to preserve and honor a beleaguered historical tradition. The function of the humanities is not well understood in America, but it is ordinarily distinguished from the practice of the sciences and the arts.[17] Oppenheimer argued that science is a humanistic subject rather than a vocational one, but the received view is that it is primarily practical. The study of its history and philosophy is not widely taken as integral to the understanding of scientific ideas. Indeed, the scientific past is routinely discarded as superceded by the present. According to NEH guidelines, only historical, critical, or theoretical studies of the arts and sciences are eligible for NEH funding, and so a science center seemed an unlikely grant recipient. Awardees are drawn chiefly from the academies of higher education, although a recent change in NEH guidelines favors increased emphasis on public programs and outreach. That shift has brought grants to secondary teaching institutions, libraries, community service organizations, research institutes, and even museums, but that was not the case during the Exploratorium's early years.

The first NEH grant awarded to the Exploratorium, in the summer of 1974, was $20,300 for a typically academic project—the production of interpretive essays, a series of short pamphlets to be distributed for teaching purposes, which described some of the museum exhibits and related them to real-world phenomena. Humanists were hired to write the essays, and a series was produced, but there was no mechanism for their dissemination and they were not well integrated with the teaching program. Marketing and distribution were not yet among the museum's strengths.

The museum made a more ambitious and less traditional appeal to the NEH in 1976. Beginning with a planning grant and followed by a two-year implementation award of $231,000, the project was to create an exhibit section on the development of ideas about the nature of heat and the measurement of temperature. The subject matter was obviously consistent with the perceptual theme described in the Exploratorium's rationale, but the manner of presentation had to be made consistent with the NEH mandate. The NEH would not have funded the construction of exhibits on the basis of their scientific subject matter alone, but casting the exhibit curriculum in terms of the history of an idea and its elaboration reconciled the Exploratorium's aims with the conditions of the NEH.

The "Heat and Temperature" exhibit curriculum does embody the conviction that the appreciation of science is a truly humanistic study that takes us from body heat to the inferred temperature of distant stars. Although the exhibits are not all examples of instruments that measure temperature, they reveal how people's understanding of heat has changed with the technology of measurement and, correspondingly, how theoretical concepts of heat have drastically affected human cultural development. The signs mounted with the exhibits include, besides the usual explanations under "To do and notice" and "What's going on," an additional description under "So what?" that places the exhibits in a historic context.

Two years later, in 1979, in celebration of the centennial of Albert Einstein's birth, the NEH supported another series of historical exhibits. They illuminated Einstein's accomplishment by setting it in the framework of what was believed and understood by the scientists of his generation. The exhibits were to trace the development of the theory of electromagnetism, culminating in Einstein's affirmation of the particle theory of light and the banishment of the ether. The exhibits and accompanying reading material emphasized Einstein's revolutionary role in changing a worldview. The historical theme of the series, as Oppenheimer characterized it, was "The Triumphs and Puzzles of Physics That Were Dumped Into Einstein's Lap."[18] The NEH grant was supplemented by an award from the IBM Corporation through the Institute for Advanced Studies at Princeton, where Einstein spent his later years.[19] The grant also covered the publication of a separate catalog, essentially a booklet of historical essays on the state of physics at the turn of the present century.[20]

Oppenheimer solicited help from state and city agencies as well as from federal sources for the promotion of museum projects. The California Arts Council underwrote a series of evening concerts and contributed $10,000 to the artist-in-residence program. But major state support did not come until 1979, when the Exploratorium qualified under a new "prominent organizations" category for a large grant of $67,400, which was nearly doubled the following year. That award represented another breakdown of stereotypes, for previously only major arts organizations such as the opera, ballet, and symphony would have been classified as "prominent" cultural institutions.

Municipal support, likewise, was almost unobtainable in the beginning, despite enthusiastic endorsements of the museum by the mayor, the superintendent of schools, several members of the chamber of commerce, and city officials.[21] Oppenheimer's requests for support under the city's hotel-tax program were repeatedly turned down, until a small allocation of $3000 was granted in 1973. By 1976, however, the museum's local status had risen, and well-placed supporters were able to apply pressure to the city to raise the tax allocation by a third and soon to double it. In 1981, the Exploratorium received $100,000 from the hotel-tax fund, and 12 percent of the museum's entire income was derived from city agencies or city-administered funds.[22]

Apart from a minimal per capita payment for school field trips, funding from the San Francisco Unified School District was negligible. The district was barely able to meet even the in-kind commitments that it had made to the museum, and it was left to the individual schools to work out payment contracts with the Exploratorium on an instance-by-instance basis for services rendered. The early SITE courses were generally paid for through voluntary donations by the parent-teacher organizations. Most of the later school-related programs were teacher training workshops, and they were generally funded either by client institutions or by major foundation grants.

Oppenheimer's quest for foundation funds followed much the same dynamic as the search for government support. The first step was usually a brash and general overture by Oppenheimer that would be met by a cautiously skeptical, but not final, refusal. The museum would then submit a tempered request, modestly tailored to the priorities that the foundation had set for itself, and negotiations would begin. A list of early and discouraging rejections includes the Ford Foundation, the Alfred P. Sloan Foundation, the James Irvine Foundation, the Mary A. Crocker Foundation, and the Bank of America Foundation, not to mention those that did not respond at all. Many of those foundations were eventually swayed by Oppenheimer's persistence and came through with some type of support.[23]

Some wealthy individuals immediately appreciated the idea of the museum and gave it their personal support. Martha Gerbode, heiress to a Hawaiian sugar fortune and the wife of a prominent heart surgeon, was a frequent visitor and a continuous encouragement. She arranged meetings, held benefits, and personally made an initial gift of $10,000. After her death in 1972, the museum received additional grants from the Gerbode Foundation. Another crucial connection was with Ruth and Scott Newhall, both members of prominent California families with journalistic and cultural influence, who helped the museum achieve a political and social foothold in the city. Their foundation provided the initial $5000 for a machine and woodworking shop in the museum, and Ruth Newhall's intercession enabled Oppenheimer to present his $4 million proposal for the use of the Palace.[24]

The first large, national foundation to give its support to the Exploratorium was the Alfred P. Sloan Foundation. It funds scientific research and technology, but like the state agencies, it tends to make awards to established academic and research centers. Oppenheimer sent a bold and overoptimistic request for $1 million "to support the costs of planning, development and installation of exhibits and the supporting facilities of the museum." The foundation rejected his appeal but encouraged him to make one that was more restrained and specific. Oppenheimer responded with a revised proposal that stressed the relationship between research and pedagogy: "Although we are not engaged in research with a capital R, my own experience has been that any attempt to develop non-trivial pedagogical material has invariably involved an important element of questioning and of subsequent discovery. I am certain that our efforts here will inevitably make some contribution to new knowledge."[25] That appeal won the museum the initial grant of $15,000 that launched the vision section. The grant provided for materials and consultation fees, and with that stimulus, the construction program got under way. The Sloan Foundation supplemented its award with $125,000 the following year ($25,000 for the explainer program), and for the next twelve years it funded assorted museum projects, including the writing of this history. Many years later it again provided funds for the reassessment of the vision section.[26]

The Rockefeller Brothers Fund and Ford Foundation gave grant support to the Exploratorium school outreach program, although both had reservations about subsidizing programs outside New York City. According to the Rockefellers' policy, "the majority of ongoing or sustaining support [must] come from local foundations and municipal and school contributions."[27] At the time of the award the Exploratorium was still perceived as a regional institution, and the national foundations insisted that it redouble its efforts to obtain regular local funding.[28] The Ford Foundation, moreover, had to be convinced that museums are educational institutions. A voluminous correspondence over a period of years finally persuaded the foundation to make a three-year grant of $225,000 to the School in the Exploratorium program. The grant stipulated that the museum receive material support from the local educational establishment. Because of its severe economic crisis, however, the school district was able to make only a nominal contribution, and the program appeared to be in jeopardy. The foundation agreed to renew the grant with another $100,000 for an additional two years, and during that time the museum was expected to create a base of local support sufficient to sustain its educational program.[29]

Although private foundations and individual donors continued to sustain the museum, they were no more willing than the government agencies to function as its primary lifeline. Some were glad to give start-up funds, but like the government agencies, the foundations sometimes imposed formidable conditions that had to be negotiated with diplomacy. They were not inflexible, however, and some were sufficiently impressed with Oppenheimer personally and with the Exploratorium's accomplishments to reconsider and modify their guidelines. Many were willing to cooperate with the museum to find some part of its program that could be funded within the terms of their charters and without promotional strings attached. Thus, the Reader's Digest Foundation justified support of the explainer program under the heading "leadership development," and the Miranda Lux and James Irvine foundations saw their way to funding the machine shop as a vocational training center for local youths.[30] For its part, the Exploratorium, without sacrifice of its own goals, was able to accommodate some of its programs to the objectives of the funding agencies. School-related services, for example, were altered to increase emphasis on teacher training and curriculum design and to reduce the direct teaching of children. Similarly, the biology section's concentration on neurobiological exhibits, which certainly reflected the perceptual focus of the museum, was also to some degree a consequence of the interests and support of the Grass Instruments Company and family foundation.[31] In that mutually conciliatory way, the Exploratorium and the private and public granting agencies affected and educated one another's vision.

In 1976, seven years after their move into the Palace of Fine Arts, Oppenheimer issued an in-house statement, "Where We Are and Where Do We Go From Here." In it he pointed out that the museum had accumulated four hundred exhibit pieces and had received $3 million in gifts and grants during that period. Half a million people visited the museum annually, and it had achieved an excellent local and national reputation. The exhibit style was evolving and had become an example to other museums. The Exploratorium's funding pattern, however, remained unpredictable and dependent on Oppenheimer's charismatic appeal. It was as opportunistic as the exhibit philosophy. Now that the museum had taken root, had built a collection, and had a place in the cultural life of the community, it was time to develop a more rational fiscal management plan and to create a reliable base of support.

The exhibit collection was by no means complete, but there was no longer a pressing need to fill the museum floor, and the staff could direct its energy to the structural and programmatic aspects of the museum that had been postponed in the first rush to create its contents. The overall plan of the museum was only about half realized, and the projected capital improvements were barely begun. A soundproof classroom and meeting edifice with an upper deck of 2400 square feet had been built at great expense with combined city and private funds. The original design for a second floor turned out to be too expensive and infeasible, but a new plan, for a mezzanine that would add 30,000 square feet of exhibit space to the 90,000 square feet available on the ground floor, was conceived by architect James Ream. The design also included space for improved public and staff areas.

In an application to the NEH for a building-renovation grant, Oppenheimer described the museum's shift of focus:

It is clear that the Exploratorium must now increasingly turn its attention to those aspects of a museum that most institutions are concerned with at the outset, namely developing predictable ongoing sources of general operational funding and renovation of the space and facilities within the Palace of Fine Arts. We are concerned with the rough, ugly and dirt producing floor (two acres), the leaky roof, the decaying doors that allow the wind to blow through the building, the inadequate storage space, the disorganized and not up-to-code shop facility area and the lack of sound proofing of concert and film showing areas and of adequate facilities for efficient function of the staff or effective utilization by the general public, such as rest areas, reading areas and orienting entrance areas. We believe that the renovation of the space and facilities are essential to the future function of the Exploratorium. In addition, and perhaps crucially, such renovation will immensely improve our ability to attract long term commitments from prospective donors. There is a suggestion of impermanence to the unrenovated space that we now occupy, which, though less than it did five years ago, contributes to the unwillingness of some donors to make the required ongoing commitments, bequests and endowments.[32]

At the same time, Oppenheimer applied to the NEA for a restructuring grant, to consolidate the museum's management and personnel program. Within a few months of each other, the Exploratorium received a $50,000 challenge grant from the NEA and a $100,000 challenge grant from the NEH. The first was for the improvement of administrative capability and fund-raising, and the second was for physical reconstruction. Challenge grants require the recipient to raise matching funds—$3 to every $1 pledged by the awarding agency. They are meant to stimulate new revenue sources and so to help institutions develop the internal means to become self-supporting. Before the creation of the Institute of Museum Services, the somewhat indirect route of the challenge grant was the chief means by which the federal government offered operating support to cultural institutions.[33]

In 1977, soon after the Exploratorium received the challenge grants, the Institute of Museum Services (IMS) was founded as a new agency within the Department of Health, Education, and Welfare. Its creation was largely the result of the efforts of John Brademas, majority whip and a Democratic congressman from Indiana. The IMS was deliberately separated from the arts and humanities endowments and was mandated to treat museums as educational organizations. It was the first federal agency empowered to subsidize at least a part of museum operating costs, and museum supporters throughout the country hailed the government for its long-awaited recognition of the educational importance of museums and of its responsibility to promote them. The first IMS director, appointed by President Carter at a rank equivalent to that of the heads of the two endowments, was Lee Kimche, former assistant director for special projects at the American Association of Museums and, since 1974, the executive director of the Association of Science and Technology Centers.

Kimche was obviously sympathetic to museums in general and was a good friend to science centers and the Exploratorium in particular.[34] The IMS did not have a large endowment, beginning with only $3.7 million to distribute in its first year, but it grew rapidly, rising to $10.4 million in 1980. Its elimination was threatened under the Reagan administration but did not occur. IMS grants are restricted in size but unrestricted in purpose, and so they can be used for operational costs, filling the gap that had been left mainly to state and local agencies. The Exploratorium was given a maximum initial grant for 1978 and has regularly received IMS funds since then.

As the Exploratorium looked toward stability, it was evident that fund-raising and development could not continue to be left to the director alone. A public relations officer was appointed, and in 1975 Oppenheimer hired Signa Dodge, a former NEH staff member, to become the Exploratorium's first official fund-raiser. Dodge worked with the board of directors, whose chairman then was W. Parmer Fuller III, vice president of the western region of Pittsburgh Plate and Glass Company and a trustee of Stanford University. A finance subcommittee of the board was formed to enlist the business community's active involvement in the museum. Dodge also staged public fund-raising events, worked with museum volunteers, and looked for expanded corporate support. The activities that she encouraged are conventional in the world of art museums and other cultural institutions, but they marked a significant social and stylistic turn for the Exploratorium.[35] The image of the back-yard mechanic creating exhibits out of yard-sale remnants was definitely eroding as the Exploratorium moved into a new and more respectable maturity. Some of the early staff members resented the change, and the resulting conflict and rejection convinced Dodge that fund-raising was not her métier. She resigned after a year, when the grant that paid her salary came to an end, but maintained an amicable informal connection with the museum. Her professional successor at the museum remained only long enough to introduce a system of corporate research and to organize the Oppenheimer Associates, a group of donors of large sums whose continued munificence he hoped to stimulate.

In August 1976 Oppenheimer placed an advertisement in the *Wall Street Journal* that attracted Virginia C. Rubin, and she became the museum's executive associate and director of development. Oppenheimer's leadership continued to give the museum its distinctive flavor, but Rubin's arrival marked a shift in the museum's future as an institution.

Rubin had worked for several educational and nonprofit organizations on the East Coast.[36] In San Francisco she served as program director and associate publisher with the Foundation for National Progress/*Mother Jones* magazine and also as part-time program and development director for the Mexican American Legal Defense and Educational Fund. Although unacquainted with science museums, she had written a master's thesis on the development of government patronage of the arts and humanities in the United States, with particular attention to the legislation that created the Council for the Arts and Humanities, the parent organization of the national endowments. An experienced fund-raiser and administrator, she transformed the Exploratorium executive structure from a comparatively small operation with an annual budget of $625,000 to a $5 million program with annual earnings of more than $4 million. Beginning with one assistant, she quickly set up an ambitious development plan with subordinate programs for membership, public relations, volunteer service, merchandise and exhibit sales, fund-raising, and earned-income activities.

Rubin's funding objectives represented a departure from Oppenheimer's survival techniques. She favored a clear fiscal policy that emphasized reliable continuity (in the form of modest but regular corporate and individual donations and internally generated revenues) on the one hand and the pursuit of major special funding for restricted purposes on the other. In addition, she proposed to lobby persistently at the state and local levels to establish the museum's reputation not merely as a physics museum but also as an important cultural resource. With that several-faceted approach, she began a fund-raising and publicity campaign that had almost immediate effects.

Museums often use membership programs to build a local following, but the Exploratorium had few special favors to offer potential members. Even admission was free to all. Among other incentives, Rubin proposed that a magazine be mailed every two months to members and friends. The first issue appeared in July 1977, and since then the quality of the magazine, *The Exploratorium,* has continuously improved. Because of high publication costs, it was reduced to a quarterly schedule, but its format was increased in size. Each issue contains a cluster of articles exploring a single topic—junk, illusions, flying things, bridges, baseball, among others. They are usually written by staff members or guest authors, and they generally bear on some group of exhibits found in the museum. The magazine has been well received. The fall 1983 issue, "Thinking About Maps," won an award from the National Council for Geographic Education as "the best collection of geographic education articles in a non-geographic publication," and a survey conducted by the Mellon Foundation cited the magazine as an example of professional excellence in the field of museum publications. The magazine has since been supplemented by a monthly newsletter.

An annual dinner was another donor benefit that Rubin introduced in 1977 to increase the museum's social visibility and to raise funds. The first $125-a-plate affair, which honored Frederick Terman for his "outstanding contribution to science education and the public understanding of science," was enormously successful. Terman, Stanford Professor of Electrical Engineering and former vice president and provost of Stanford, had taught William Hewlett and David Packard at Stanford and then served on the board of directors of the Hewlett-Packard Company. William Hewlett was invited to be honorary chairman of the dinner and to present the award to Terman. Guests roamed the Exploratorium before and after dinner, socializing as they played with the exhibits. The awards dinner was quickly taken up into the San Francisco social calendar as an acknowledged annual benefit. In the first year, it netted the Exploratorium a profit of $23,700. Eight years later, when William Hewlett himself was honored and Oppenheimer was the chief speaker, the dinner raised $225,000.

In subsequent years the museum honored a list of notable figures including Russel V. Lee, M.D., founder of the first comprehensive group medical practice clinic in the United States; Wolfgang Panofsky, director of the Stanford Linear Accelerator Center, recipient of the Enrico Fermi Award in nuclear physics, and one of the Exploratorium's original board members; and Donald H. McLaughlin, a former regent of the University of California and dean of its Colleges of Mining and Engineering and the Exploratorium's first chairman of the board. Speakers at the events have included Donald Kennedy, vice president and provost of Stanford University (subsequently to become president of the university) and a former commissioner of the U.S. Food and Drug Administration; Luis W. Alvarez, Nobel laureate, professor emeritus of physics at the University of California, and one of the first members of the Exploratorium board; Lewis Thomas, president of the Memorial Sloan-Kettering Cancer Center in New York and author of the National Book Award winner *The Lives of a Cell;* and Philip Morrison, professor of astrophysics at MIT, book editor of the *Scientific American,* and also one of the Exploratorium's most devoted supporters. In addition to the major awards, special commendations for science writing were given to David Perlman of the *San Francisco Chronicle;* Victor Cohn, medical and biological science editor of the *Washington Post;* Lewis Thomas; and K. C. Cole, science columnist for *Discover* magazine and author of *Sympathetic Vibrations: Reflections on Physics as a Way of Life.* The awards dinners have served not only as fund-raisers but also as a means for the museum to express gratitude to its many friends and benefactors.

Following out the second facet of her plan, to locate specialized support for major museum projects, Rubin turned to the Department of Health, Education, and Welfare (HEW), which had previously refused even to consider applications from museums. On a hunch she appealed to the Fund for the Improvement of Post Secondary Education, an HEW subsidiary, for support of a two-pronged dissemination strategy. One part was the production of written descriptive and interpretive materials, the other an internship program that would bring resident interns from campuses, museums, and community centers to the Exploratorium to study its exhibit-based educational philosophy.[37] The grant was to subsidize the interns' travel and stay at the Exploratorium and also to pay for staff follow-up visits and consultations at the interns' home institutions. The agency came through with an award of $123,220 that provided for, among other things, supervisory staff, enabling the Exploratorium to hire Robert Semper, a young physicist who also turned out to be an excellent administrator; he eventually became an associate director of the museum.[38] The program was enlarged in its second year and extended with minor modifications, thanks to a similar program funded by the Michigan-based W. K. Kellogg Foundation. That foundation had a policy of supporting applied education, particularly in the areas of agriculture and health care. In the nearly fifty years of its existence, the Kellogg Foundation had never funded a museum, but its officers were intrigued by the Exploratorium's slightly audacious appeal. The museum initially requested support for an adult program of health-care teaching, in line with the interests of the foundation. In considering that proposal, however, the foundation became interested in the broader question of how museums might contribute to public education, and the original proposal was revised. In October 1979 the Kellogg Foundation awarded $566,400 (over five years) to "establish a national fellowship/internship program for museum curators and directors to strengthen the educative impact of museums."[39]

The agency programs and the Kellogg program were vital to the dissemination of the idea of the Exploratorium. They enabled the museum to explain to people what it was doing, to show them how it was done, and to publish its programs and policies. The volume of written material describing the museum increased vastly, as did the imitators and the requests for *Cookbook* recipes and replicas of Exploratorium exhibits. In the twelve years between 1970 and 1982, the museum devoted at least 10 percent of its funds to the dissemination of its theory and practice. The Kellogg Foundation was evidently convinced of the educational capacity of museums, for it became a major contributor to museum education throughout the

United States, donating large sums to the Smithsonian Institution, the Field Museum of Natural History in Chicago, and other museums.[40]

Capital improvement was another long-term goal for Rubin. The decision to open the Palace of Fine Arts to the public as soon as the Exploratorium took possession of it had focused all the museum's energy on building exhibits and programs, and improvement of the premises had been deferred. By 1977 the floor was crowded with nearly 450 exhibits, and housekeeping repairs could no longer be put off. It was time to expand the exhibit space and to provide some comforts for the public and the staff that had been neglected for the sake of exhibit development.

The Kresge Foundation of Troy, Michigan, which offers grants for construction and capital improvement projects to institutions of higher education or health care, seemed a natural benefactor for the Exploratorium. Oppenheimer had applied to the foundation in 1974 but received a polite refusal. In December 1977 he and Rubin traveled to Michigan to appeal directly to the foundation's president, Alfred H. Taylor, for funds to build a mezzanine inside the Exploratorium. Despite Taylor's quaint advice "that your expectations be restrained, your dreams temperate and your hopes controlled," the president was obviously impressed, and in July 1978 the foundation awarded the museum a challenge grant of $250,000.[41] The museum was obligated to raise an additional $325,000 by June 15 of the following year. The deadline had to be extended by three months, but the museum met the challenge, raising $945,900, and construction began in the fall of 1979. The building project was divided into separately fundable stages, the first at an estimated cost of $715,000, and the second at $320,000.

The closing of the museum during the construction represented a rite of passage for many long-term staff members, and they marked the event with a rowdy celebration of destruction. Field trips and SITE classes were discontinued, exhibits dismantled and stored, and some of the makeshift quarters that by then had acquired a psychic permanence were torn down. Since the Exploratorium's relationship with the Palace of Fine Arts League had deteriorated over the years, the hope of sharing the theater at the south end of the building was finally abandoned. Consequently, the construction design included plans for a small theater within the undisputed Exploratorium space. There were a few delays and mishaps along the way, including the inevitable floods caused by punctured water mains, but the mezzanine was erected, and with its completion the museum seemed to leave its adolescence for a stable and autonomous maturity. The reopening of the museum, which also marked its tenth anniversary, was celebrated in May 1980. A huge social event honored the occasion, however saddened by the recent death of Jackie Oppenheimer, who had given so much to the Exploratorium.

It is often remarked that success breeds success and that the appearance of prosperity invites additional wealth. There is no doubt that the Exploratorium began to attract larger grants and that Frank Oppenheimer no longer needed to extract them with such excruciating feats of persuasive demonstration. People had heard of the Exploratorium, and indeed, there were emulators everywhere. But they were now competing for the same financial resources, and even though the awards that came were larger, it was necessary to explain to prospective granting agencies that the Exploratorium had not outgrown its need for help. Indeed, its expanded commitments had made continued support all the more necessary, for it remained difficult to raise funds to cover operational expenses—the mundane business of paying staff and maintaining the building and exhibits.

The museum received large, long-term grants for various restricted purposes. In 1981 the Andrew W. Mellon Foundation, having surveyed the needs of the museum world, gave a three-year grant of $250,000 to the Exploratorium for its publication program. And the NSF, after giving $366,000 for the development of an entire section of exhibits on language, awarded another three-year grant of $329,000 for a series on electricity, "to enhance the public understanding of electricity and show its unity with all natural phenomena." In 1982 the Buck Family Foundation of Marin County offered a large, long-term grant of $675,000, which brought the School in the Exploratorium program back to its original location across the Golden Gate Bridge to provide teacher-training workshops in Marin County. Two years later the San Francisco Foundation made a similar grant of $500,000 to the San Rafael City Schools for SITE teacher training workshops to improve science instruction in the public schools there. Those grants enabled the Exploratorium to improve its services to schools beyond the city of San Francisco and to develop its exhibit-based curricula. The programs never were absorbed into the public educational systems as Oppenheimer had hoped, but in 1984 the California Assembly did pass a bill designating the museum a science education resource to be funded for its High School Teacher Institute.[42]

An unrestricted grant in 1981 from the John D. and Catherine T. MacArthur Foundation was an enormous benefit to the museum's well-being. Best known for its "genius" grants to individuals, the foundation also gives institutional support, and it awarded $1 million to be delivered over four years to the Exploratorium.[43] The grant was doubly welcome for its open-endedness, for the Exploratorium's annual expenditures were outrunning its income. During the first nine years of its existence, the museum had balanced its general fund income against general fund expenses, although that sometimes required temporary borrowings from restricted funds. But in 1979, despite its unquestionable success, the museum prepared itself to cut back on programs in the expectation that federal funds would be reduced. For fiscal year 1982 the annual cost of running the museum, exclusive of specially funded programs, was $1.7 million, and the museum faced a projected debt of $228,000. At the expected growth rate, the estimated budget for the following year would nearly double.[44] (In fact, the 1984 annual budget, including capital projects, exceeded $6 million.) The MacArthur grant therefore came at a critical time. It freed the director and staff to concentrate on their educational and cultural mission. A great morale booster, it bought time to make important improvements in the museum's internal self-support system.

In general, foundations and government agencies, with the exception of IMS, still donate funds only for specific and preferably innovative projects, but the rising cost of operation makes ad hoc funding hazardous for museums. The problem is that the museums must maintain their buildings in all seasons, pay staff, and keep exhibits in repair regardless of the spectacular events to which they play host. That is why museums are sometimes reluctant to accept highly publicized, blockbuster shows, which frequently cost more than they earn and generally fail to pay for roof repairs and heating bills. The bigger the event, the more excessive the overhead costs. Thus museums are often forced to skimp on costs that are hidden to the public but nevertheless essential to the quality of the institution.[45]

Corporate and individual donations tend to be more reliable, albeit less extravagant, than the earmarked grants by foundations and government. Once a corporation has made a commitment to a particular funding project, it can be counted on, barring wild market fluctuations, to sustain that support. Until recently, the structure of the United States income tax laws, as well as the corporations' interest in being an enlightened presence in the community, have worked to the advantage of cultural institutions. Corporate contributions are less likely than foundation grants to be tied to special programs or products and are generally not directly reflective of self-interest. Corporations are concerned with the quality and tone of their environment and have an interest in the educational well-being of their employees. They do not perceive museum exhibits as a form of advertisement, although they are unlikely to support a show that is flagrantly contradictory to their interests.

With the hope of winning a corporate foothold for the Exploratorium, Rubin organized a systematic development campaign to cultivate regular corporate funding and also generate an endowment. Despite the increased competition for private funds that followed the passage of Proposition 13 (limiting property taxes in California), Rubin's aggressive new program did bear fruit. Annual corporate and individual gift-giving to the museum doubled between 1978 and 1980. By 1984 corporate funding was approximately $250,000 annually, and nearly a third of the museum's operating cost was underwritten by corporate support. Although the competition with other institutions was keen, Proposition 13 tended to increase rather than diminish corporate giving.

The building of an endowment was high on Rubin's list of priorities, since it was sure to enhance the museum's prestige and its stability. That recognition was achieved in 1979, when the Exploratorium's old friend John May once again came to the museum's assistance. May had first been impressed by the Exploratorium at a 1968 meeting, where Oppenheimer made an impassioned appeal for support from the San Francisco Foundation. Later, as executive secretary of the Hewlett Foundation, May again helped the Exploratorium by interceding on its behalf for municipal funding. After becoming associated with the San Francisco-based Columbia Foundation, May continued to look out for the welfare of the museum by helping it become financially independent.[46] The Columbia Foundation pledged $250,000 for an endowment fund, which was to be matched three to one over four years, thus yielding $1 million at the end of that time and an expected $10 million in ten years. The grant represented, in the words of the foundation's executive secretary Susan Silk, the "recognition of the Exploratorium's emergence, over the past ten years, into one of the major science museums in the world and of the clear necessity of developing an endowment to insure the continuity and excellence of its programs."[47] The income from the Columbia grant, calculated at 10 percent interest, could be expected to cover the recurrently troubling shortfall in the museum's annual operating expenses.

The endowment proclaimed the museum's coming of age. It promised stability, but to fulfill that promise the Exploratorium had to raise $750,000 over four years. It had to generate a core of committed donors willing to give large sums with no immediate or visible recompense. Contributions to an endowment fund are essentially expressions of faith in the future of an institution. One of the fruits of the endowment award was a critical reassessment, by a professional evaluator, of the role of the board of directors. As a result of his recommendations, the board was reorganized into working committees active in the support and management of the museum. Donations from the board itself increased after the reconstitution: six board members pledged $100,000 each toward the endowment, and a seventh pledged $25,000, a drastic change from the board's previous, cumulative total of $123,000. With the help of an enlarged development department and a board subcommittee, $1.2 million of the $5 million goal was raised by the summer of 1984.

The endowment gave hope of a secure future, but the present remained problematic. The prospect for federal funding looked dim as the Reagan administration threatened budget cuts (which ultimately did not occur) that would all but eliminate support for science education, the arts, and culture. Funds from federal sources dropped from a high of 39 percent of the museum's income in 1978-79 to 12 percent in 1979-80. Although federal funding was up to 22 percent again the following year, it continued to decline, reaching 6 percent in 1983. In the same period, state funding rose to 6 percent of the museum's income. The state figure reflected a large increase and a turnaround in the attitude toward the museum, which was all the more remarkable in light of the reduction of state aid to many human services and cultural agencies after passage of Proposition 13. Still, it was nowhere near the level of support that Oppenheimer had originally anticipated. In 1968 Oppenheimer had projected that a fifth to a sixth of the museum's annual budget, especially the school-related portions and the teacher training programs, would come from state and city sources, but in 1979 the combined state and city support amounted to only 7 percent, and even the school-related programs continued to be funded largely by private foundations. Proposition 13 forced the school districts to cut their subsidy to museum programs. Nevertheless, the museum did receive support from the city through increased hotel-tax funds, additional municipally administered CETA funds, and less tangible services and emoluments.

It was clear that the museum had made its mark on the city and was perceived as a touristic and cultural asset. The city continued to lease the Palace of Fine Arts building to the museum for $1 a year and to maintain the park area around the building. After nine years of holding a sublease under a master lease negotiated between the San Francisco Parks and Recreation Commission and the Palace of Fine Arts League, the Exploratorium finally won a direct lease from the city in 1980, guaranteeing its continued occupancy of its present space and the perpetuation of its rent-free terms. The city also paid a portion of utility costs, although the Exploratorium provides its own janitorial service, telephone equipment, security system, and insurance under its general operating budget. Major repairs were undertaken jointly with the cooperation of the Palace of Fine Arts League, the city, and the Exploratorium. In 1984 the city allocated $2 million for the repair of the roof of the building. Thanks to that contribution and to additional grants from the Hewlett, Wells Fargo, and Herbst foundations, the crumbling concrete roof panels that dated back to the original 1915 construction were at last replaced with steel decking.

It is unlikely now that the Exploratorium will be relieved of the burden of fund-raising, although city and state governments have responded to the museum's appeals with much greater generosity than in the past. The State of California has continued to fund the museum through the California Arts Council, and in 1984, 62 percent of the museum's total public and private funding was raised within the state. Much of that support came from corporations, as well as from the individuals and small family foundations that were a mainstay of the museum from the beginning.

The business community is inclined to respect sound fiscal planning and good management policies. Its contributions are often contingent at least as much on the evidence of the viability of an enterprise as on the nobility and originality of its mission. William Hewlett was personally supportive of the Exploratorium since its founding, but he also restrained the corporation's giving until the museum showed promise of survival. As early as 1973 the Hewlett-Packard Company began making regular and increasing donations. In 1975 the William and Flora Hewlett Foundation made a two-year pledge of $50,000 to the museum, and that was subsequently supplemented by a three-year grant of $165,000. One of the paramount objectives of the directors of the foundation was to help make the museum self-sufficient. The 1978 annual report expresses the purpose of the foundation, "To make ours an effective democratic society, a society whose institutions work." The report sharply criticizes the organizational deficiencies of many not-for-profit agencies, including "lack of clarity about the purposes of the organization; inadequate definition of the role of the lay board; ambiguous relations between board and staff; poor personnel practices; inadequate long range planning, both programmatic and financial; ineffective fundraising efforts; inexperienced management."[48] Not all of those faults applied to the Exploratorium, but there undoubtedly were organizational problems and a need to restructure the fund-raising base. The three-year grant from the Hewlett Foundation was explicitly designated for a managerial overhaul, which included the hiring of a deputy director.

Oppenheimer's absolute authority over the operations of the museum, along with his advancing age and delicate health, was causing concern in some quarters about the hierarchical succession. Oppenheimer himself had tried on several occasions to diminish his administrative burden by employing a second-in-command who could inherit the mantle of power, but invariably there were personality conflicts and failures of understanding, and the deputies' tenures were brief. In 1984 the new chairman of the board, F. Van Kasper of Van Kasper and Associates, and some of the board members strongly urged the appointment of a second-in-command to relieve Oppenheimer. A management consultant hired by the board proposed the reorganization of the museum administration with a distinct chain of command. As an interim measure, an executive council was formed, consisting of six Exploratorium staff members and Oppenheimer. Each council member assumed responsibility for a cluster of related museum operations. The group met regularly until after Oppenheimer's death, providing a centralized source of decisions while decentralizing the museum's management and the order of accountability.

As long as Oppenheimer lived, the matter of his succession remained moot. It was evident that the best strategy for the interim was to strengthen the internal structure of the museum. The day-to-day operations were well within the competence of the existing staff, many of whom were extremely skilled and had thoroughly absorbed the Exploratorium's philosophy. They could be relied on to maintain the museum and to steer it along the course that Oppenheimer had ordained, which is what they did for two years after Oppenheimer's death. Virginia Rubin was appointed acting director at that time, and Robert Semper deputy director, while a search committee composed of board members, staff, and science advisers looked for a new director. Their task was completed in 1987 with the appointment of Robert L. White, professor of electrical engineering and materials science engineering and former chairman of the Department of Electrical Engineering at Stanford University.[49]

The museum remained on a fairly even keel after Oppenheimer's death. Under the management of the acting director, the board, and the executive council, it continued as before to receive large, special-purpose grants and to move ahead with measures to produce income internally. Most of those measures, such as the adult admission charge imposed in May 1981, the snack bar and pretzel concessions, and the contracts to build Exploratorium exhibits for other museums, had been initiated before Oppenheimer's death. The museum's development department—now grown to a staff of ten, including persons in charge of membership, public relations, and special events—continues to solicit corporate and individual support on a regular basis.

No museums are self-sustaining. They cannot expect to support themselves entirely out of internally generated or earned income, although some raise as much as a third of their revenue from restaurants, gift stores, and even parking garages. To make earnings of such magnitude the Exploratorium would have to expand its capital investment greatly. A grant of $100,000 from the Henry J. Kaiser Family Foundation for the express purpose of developing earned income enabled the museum to contemplate such improvements. The museum gift store, originally set up by Jackie Oppenheimer in a small, transparent geodesic dome in the middle of the museum floor, was refurbished and reorganized and enlarged. When the mezzanine was built, it was moved to new quarters with space for a much larger inventory. A change in management in 1981 also markedly affected sales revenues, and the store began making money for the museum. Other improvements still to be realized include an income-producing restaurant and an adequate lounge. They were part of the initial plan for the museum as Oppenheimer presented it to the Palace of Fine Arts League, but they could not proceed until phase three of the building program. In the meantime, a concession that serves hot dogs and soft drinks and a pretzel pushcart on the museum floor have provided relief for tired visitors and brought in some revenue.[50]

The campaign to augment earned income raised the museum's internally generated revenues dramatically, from 11 percent of the museum's intake in 1975 to 45 percent in 1982-83. Income was produced from interest accrued on the endowment, memberships, rental of the museum for outside use, concert series tickets, weekend film programs, and increased admission to the ever-popular "Tactile Dome," as well as from the admission fee, now up to $5 for visitors over sixteen, and the increasingly profitable sale of exhibits to other museums. A negligible profit is also earned from summer classes, which serve somewhat as loss leaders, that make the museum visible in the community and attract attendance.

Cultural institutions are always financially at risk. Especially in the United States, where there is ambivalence as to who should assume responsibility for their support, museums have a mendicant existence. The story of the Exploratorium, however, illustrates that the sprawling public and philanthropic system can be cultivated and is responsive to intelligent appeal. As a productive academic scientist, Oppenheimer was familiar with the rituals of the research grant, but he had yet to learn the greater complexities of the cultural establishment that preserves the arts and humanities. Determined to display science as a humanistic study and an art form, he was undaunted by the artifice of their bureaucratic separation, and he argued persuasively enough to win a hearing from the guardians of the segregated dispensing agencies. That success has opened doors for museums and cultural institutions everywhere and broken down a few of the disciplinary barriers that fragment modern society.

Oppenheimer's unwavering determination and charismatic leadership were crucial to the success of the Exploratorium. His knowledge, inventiveness, absolute self-confidence, and clear-sighted opportunism kept the museum afloat in the darkest times. Though unafraid of conflict, he did not welcome opposition, and he clung relentlessly to control. Others were persuaded by his eloquence and charm but above all by his indubitable intelligence. He was not universally admired, but he easily won disciples who became loyal proponents of his ideals. Many of them remain on the Exploratorium staff and in its entourage.

Nonetheless, even before his death, Oppenheimer's influence had diminished. The Exploratorium's reputation and stature no longer depended on the person of its founder, and the operation of the museum had become less personal. New staff members with different and more specialized professional commitments came forward, and their presence has affected the museum's style. The board of directors, too, has assumed a more active role in the museum's management. More of the museum's efforts are directed toward marketing exhibits, and proportionately less innovative exhibit development is taking place.

The Exploratorium's success as a museum has burdened it with the classic responsibilities of management, financial stability, and community accountability that are faced by all institutions of any magnitude. The museum's responses to those challenges are not original, but they have been effective. Although its future is in no way assured, there is good reason to anticipate that the Exploratorium and other museums like it will continue to be attended by a public that has come to appreciate their educational function and their value as entertainment.

Chapter 8

Conclusion and Prospect

Today, many of the ideals with which the Oppenheimers began the museum remain intact, and many of their envisaged projects have been accomplished. Some had to be abandoned or modified, and a few have given way to more current preoccupations.

The staff have achieved a high level of professional maturity, in many instances parallel to their personal growth as they came of age with the museum. Most of the early staff were young and inexperienced when they came. The field they were entering was similarly untried. As the museum matured, later staff members were more likely to arrive with the skills and competencies that the modern world of business demands. They tended not to have their predecessors' omnivorous interest in all things relating to the museum, and they sometimes lacked the playful experimentalism that had given the Exploratorium its unconventional start. But perhaps the abilities they do have are better suited to the maintenance of an institution that has come of age and to an era that prizes efficiency and professionalism.

Frank Oppenheimer's health had been failing, and his death in 1985 was not unexpected, but it initiated a period of suspended animation at the Exploratorium. The daily operations of the museum went on as before—exhibits continued to be designed and built, surprisingly, at about the same rate. Grants were applied for, and projects executed. In-house and external workshops proceeded uninterrupted, and visitors came in ever-increasing numbers. Most of the older staff members had so thoroughly incorporated Oppenheimer's style and ideas that it was as if his voice remained among them and the familiar figure was still peering inquisitively over their shoulders or wandering among exhibits on the floor. Nevertheless, the prolonged search for his successor gave the staff ample opportunity to forge a new collective image of itself, and individual staff members experienced an intense moment of reflection and self-appraisal. Almost no one of the regular staff resigned. New generations of explainers came and went with each school semester, and a few new faces appeared among the shop staff, but by and large it was a time of waiting as the search committee pondered its task.

That period marked a shift in the centers of responsibility. Staff members found a sense of their own authority as they were forced to make decisions that would formerly have been deferred to Oppenheimer. Meanwhile, new voices were beginning to be heard and to affect the museum's orientation. After a year of waiting people were impatient for resolution and wanted a clear line of direction. It was not authority they were seeking but clarity and definition. A new generation had arisen in the public as well as the museum worlds. Less eccentric and more systematic, these people were educated and confident. They wanted goals and procedures and were undeterred either by exciting distractions or by lofty ideals. Their influence could be discerned even among the original members of the museum staff.

During the interim without a leader the operation of the museum was overseen by a committee of staff members, headed by Virginia C. Rubin, who was appointed acting director. Ultimately decisions rested with her, but the board of directors, under the chairmanship of F. Van Kasper, became more involved than ever before with the routine functioning of the museum. Chiefly a back-up group as long as Oppenheimer was alive, it now became a typical working board that set policy for the museum and participated in general planning. The board members continued to have little to do with the content of the museum or with its programs, but they took an interest in the presentation of the museum to the world, particularly through income-generating operations such as the store. Fiscal security and sound management were primary concerns, and while they looked for a scientist and teacher to be the new director, they hoped to find someone who could make the museum financially self-supporting.

As the staff carried on, two perspectives on the future of the museum could be distinguished among them. Their difference was largely conceptual and pedagogic, but each embodied a notion of the public good. The newer staff members, who had come to the museum with specific professional skills, believed in a model of efficiency based on the clarification of educational objectives and their well-articulated presentation to the public. The older group had gravitated to Oppenheimer in the formative years of the museum and had absorbed his philosophy almost as an article of faith. They adhered to an ideal of learning as undirected and self-initiated discovery, occasioned by the experience of stimuli and advanced by opportunistic use of material and conceptual resources. They put a premium on the visitor's individual experience and saw the museum as an aid to the enrichment of that experience. They were less concerned with achieving a preordained set of educational goals than with inculcating an attitude of inquiry and a zest for exploration. Ironically, the second generation propagated the Exploratorium message more zealously, while the older staff was at once more critical and more easily distracted by other concerns.

Some of the early staff had been attracted to the museum and had stayed there because of its educational philosophy, a blend of optimistic individualism and social radicalism that flourished in the sixties. They had grown up in the 1964 Free Speech and student protest movements, defending civil rights and opposing public wrongs, and they believed that their example would demonstrate that people could liberate themselves from the constraints of ignorance and conventional oppression. They joyously took part in the creation of a protected environment in which museumgoers could indulge their curiosity and play with limits, and they expected people to transport that introduction to critical inquiry from the shelter of the museum into the world outside. Although few would have described it as such, they conceived the museum as a political training ground, and their effort to make it work was an act of political idealism as well as an intellectual commitment.

It is hard to recall or to reconstitute the faith of that moment. In retrospect, a museum seems an unlikely political frontier, and yet the general instability of the time allowed even this stodgiest of institutions to undergo transformation. Seemingly outside the fray, museums have generally been regarded as harmless reservoirs of scholarly memorabilia and safe centers for family recreation. They did not appear to harbor conservative political principles;[1] neither did they seem to be a staging ground for self-liberating guerrilla action. But in the heady sixties, the idea of resistance to the dead weight of convention was so tantalizing that even a museum that professed only to reverse modest institutional constraints on experiential learning conveyed a sense of self-determination and discovery. Oppenheimer was part of a movement; his ideas were in the air. Others were also promoting a move away from traditional, hands-off museums, toward informal and interactive experimental institutions that would help people understand, among other things, science and technology.

The Exploratorium did speak a liberatory language, and Oppenheimer's personal style created an atmosphere in which people, including staff members, could enjoy maximum intellectual freedom and exploratory space. There was too little money to pay more than subsistence wages, and so they volunteered their labor. The small paid staff had to be involved in almost every facet of the museum's operation. Specialization was out of the question, but neither did it seem desirable, for traditional categories were viewed with suspicion. The most enterprising people came with a vocation but no profession, and they would have refused the security of classifications had they been available. They made up in natural intelligence, youthful energy, and enthusiasm for whatever they lacked in experience and professional training. Confident of their ability to change an imperfect world, they did not need titles to do it. Workers at the Exploratorium had to create their own niches and at the same time be involved with the project as a whole. It was no place for people who needed instruction. Job applicants never knew exactly why they had been hired. Oppenheimer assigned tasks to them, but he expected them to design their own work program, and he ignored them while they figured out what needed to be done. The model was the academic research laboratory, not the commercial workplace. It left no doubt as to the locus of authority, but it gave considerable responsibility to subordinates, and not the least of its objectives was to help them achieve competence and autonomy. It clearly distinguished those who relished the freedom to frame their own enterprises from those who were overwhelmed by uncertainty and needed the comfort of certified conclusions. Oppenheimer was impatient with the latter and not always charitable toward them. He demanded loyalty to his ideas but at the same time relished controversy. He was willing to take a chance with people. Sometimes he risked and lost, but there were notable successes.

People are a significant product of the Exploratorium, as much a component of it as its exhibits and programs. The staff who created the Exploratorium and who carried its influence elsewhere were both students and teachers. Ultimately they would interpret Oppenheimer's message and transmit the philosophy of the museum to the world. They would teach the teachers, build the exhibits, and design the programs, and they would spread the news to other museums and educational centers. There is no measure of the influence that the Exploratorium may have had on millions of visitors who have passed through since its opening, but some record of those most intimately associated with it is available and can be cited here in illustration.

One person whose life was profoundly touched by the museum was Sheila Grinell. In December 1969 she had graduated from Radcliffe College and moved to Berkeley to attend graduate school. But having earned a master's degree in sociology, she was disenchanted with academic life and hungry for adventure. A friend happened to mention a job opening at the new museum in San Francisco, and she went to look into it. She had no premonitions whatsoever about a museum career but was merely curious. Walking among the first few exhibits, she and Oppenheimer found an instant rapport, and over rum at his and Jackie's Lombard Street home, he invited her to join the staff, which then consisted of four people.

Grinell was fascinated with the subject of inquiry and, correlatively, with the creation of values. A technically skilled communicator, she believed herself equipped with the tools to build a new society, and she eagerly allied herself with an institution that promised to strive for similar goals. She was enchanted by the rationale that Oppenheimer had written for the museum and shared his zeal to make connections between phenomena and events and realms of discourse that had previously been discontinuous and segregated. Oppenheimer assigned her the task of initiating the explainer program.

The rest was up to her. She called local schools, selected and hired students, and taught them the science they needed to know to explain the exhibits. She was young and casual enough to feel at ease with the streetwise adolescents, who called their clean-living mentor "Grunchy Granola" but respected her abilities. Grinell became a museum spokesperson, indispensable as an interpreter inside the museum among the staff and outside as a representative to the public.

Where Oppenheimer sometimes appeared as an eccentric, woolly-headed, and slightly suspicious intellectual, Grinell had a youthful directness that put people at ease. Called to mediate between the public and the museum, she learned to evaluate the effectiveness of exhibits, to recommend modifications where needed, and to suggest new exhibits to make a concept clear. Eventually she began designing exhibits, and Oppenheimer relied on her as a touchstone for exhibit ideas.

At twenty-seven years of age Grinell introduced the museum's outreach and educational programs. She took responsibility for the school-related component as well as the explainer program and was working with Oppenheimer in a general administrative capacity. He appointed her codirector for exhibits and programs, and with Oppenheimer and other staff members she conceived and oversaw the production of exhibits. Still pursuing her interpretive bent, she composed descriptive graphics to accompany and explain the exhibits and subsequently wrote a catalog to amplify the explanations and relate the exhibits to one another. By that time she had hired someone to replace herself as explainer supervisor and several teachers to carry on the classroom program as she continued to devise new jobs to be done.

For five years Grinell shared in the exhilarating expansion of the museum, taking a leading part in its transformation from a family shop to an institution that attracted half a million visitors annually to play with a collection of exhibits that had multiplied tenfold, in numbers and in technical sophistication. Ambitious to take on new challenges, she left the museum to go to Japan, where she worked with a publishing firm, and next joined a New York publisher to produce a newspaper for children.

But museum work had become her calling. Even while employed otherwise, she continued consulting with new children's museums, science centers, and museums of technology. In October 1978 the Association of Science and Technology Centers (ASTC) invited her to become the coordinator of the its Traveling Exhibits Service, and in that position she arranged for a national tour of Exploratorium exhibits on optics and light. She also conceived and supervised the fabrication of a major ASTC exhibition on the cultural impact of computer technology, and that show had its national opening at the Exploratorium in 1984. In 1980 Grinell became the executive director of ASTC, which included 150 science museums and centers. She was responsible to them as advocate, and for planning and implementation of policy, programs, and financial management. Then, rounding another turn of her career cycle, she was appointed associate director of the New York Hall of Science, together with Alan J. Friedman, a Berkeley colleague whose museum career had begun at the Lawrence Hall of Science. The New York museum, on the Flushing Meadows World's Fair site, had been empty for several years before it was selected to house the Hall of Science. When it opened two years later, with the "Seeing the Light" exhibition that the Exploratorium had constructed for the New York IBM show, the state-subsidized Hall of Science had a $3 million operating budget, a working staff of forty full-time and forty part-time employees, and an ambitious exhibit development program. The director of exhibits was Michael Oppenheimer, who had also chosen, after a hiatus of more than ten years, to return to the museum world, specifically to the building of science exhibits. Grinell and Oppenheimer, children of the Exploratorium and now with young children of their own, were building the next generation of science centers that would carry on Frank Oppenheimer's tradition infused by their contemporary vision.

Grinell has, by now, achieved a prominent place in the museum world in which she travels widely, and she often returns to the Exploratorium. She still feels rooted there and indebted to Oppenheimer for his inspiration and the opportunities that he made available to her. She feels strongly, moreover, that her ideas helped shape the Exploratorium and are embodied there. As other institutions emulate the Exploratorium, they also absorb a part of her, which is transmitted and reincarnated in many fashions. She has the satisfaction not merely of titular success but also of concrete creative input, a gratification shared by numerous early Exploratorium staff members. They felt they were listened to, their thoughts taken seriously, and they saw their ideas realized. It was Oppenheimer's great merit that he imparted a sense of possibility and stood by to let it happen.[2]

That passive power of enablement is what the early staff members—and a few later ones—remember of Oppenheimer, and that is the heritage they hope to pass on. There is an apparent paradox in designating Oppenheimer's energetic resourcefulness as passive, yet it was that withholding, an almost perverse refusal to be definitive or to make final pronouncements, that gave the museum its peculiar cast. The same fluidity, so elusive and so difficult to imitate, is wholly consistent with the opportunism of the natural world, a deliberate and explicitly cited inspiration for the museum's philosophy. The young people who left their mark there and were themselves shaped by the Exploratorium were exquisite opportunists who profited from the creative tension of that environment and used it productively. Grinell is but one example of that adaptive success.

Another is Peter Richards, a member of the executive council and the director of the artist-in-residence program. Richards was a friend of Michael Oppenheimer's while they were growing up in Pagosa Springs. Richards subsequently studied sculpture at the Baltimore Arts Institute in Maryland and was living in San Francisco when the Exploratorium opened. He asked Frank Oppenheimer if he might use the museum facilities as a sculpture studio. In exchange he maintained and then built exhibits. Together with Michael he designed a giant checkerboard whose pieces are moved from a distance by polarized light beams. Undertaken as a playful diversion, "Checkerboard" is also a light sculpture and an instructive exhibit on polarization.

Richards entered his artworks in juried shows and exhibited locally, and he brought artists to the Exploratorium. Gradually Oppenheimer entrusted him with the task of soliciting and organizing displays of art in the Exploratorium. Richards mounted the early traveling exhibits, and when in 1974 the artist-in-residence program was instituted, he was the obvious choice to take charge of it. He became an intermediary between the artists and the museum staff and helped the artists create projects that were specific to the Exploratorium but also faithful to their personal style.

As Richards came to understand it, the museum was shaping a new type of public art that was site-specific and collaboratively produced and that fostered environmental awareness. Public art, he thought, is not simply a private expression in an open space or a privately inspired work that commemorates an event of public note; it should be, like our experience of nature, a collectively engendered artifact that is genuinely shared. Public art is thus preeminently a counterpart to science, requiring the intermediation of individuals to bring out values that are collectively held. Many of the works that he selected for the artist-in-residence program reflect that perspective. They are not modernist subjective expression but rather explorations that highlight natural processes and forms. His own work, likewise, tends to underline the natural and common and not to be aggressively innovative.

Richards promoted the idea that the museum should be a resource and research center for artists, much as institutional research centers serve scientists, where they can work with new materials, perfect skills, and explore novel ideas. Such a project was not realized within Oppenheimer's lifetime, although a few artists did use the museum informally in that fashion. Oppenheimer's view of art was more individualistic and closer to the stereotype, that the artist expresses feelings and conveys a sense of the natural universe by directly communicating a personal experience of it. But Oppenheimer did agree with Richards that art presents perceived truths about the world, consistent with those of science though differently discovered. And like scientific hypotheses, those of art are shareable and testable.[3]

Although Oppenheimer's aesthetic judgment undoubtedly determined the initial selection of artwork to be displayed in the museum, he let himself be influenced, and it was Richards who molded an environment where artists could work and blend their aesthetic insight with the museum's educational aims and utilitarian concerns. As a result, science and art are genuinely integrated at the Exploratorium. They are offered without comment as complementary probings of the natural world, displaying it with analytic articulation and with delight, and appealing to museum visitors to partake of the same pleasurable exploration.

Richards revealed a second and unsuspected set of talents, namely the ability to plan and oversee construction projects. Oppenheimer came to rely on him as curator of the physical plant, and each new building program—the classroom, the mezzanine, the roof replacement—ended as Richards' responsibility. As chief liaison between the museum, the architects, contractors, and city officials, Richards was drawn into local political negotiations as well as physical plant management. With the receipt of major grants for capital improvement the pressures on him as foreman increased, and a greater proportion of his energy was devoted to negotiating the museum's interests in the system of commerce, industry, and municipal government. His artwork reflected the change. Along with the play of the wind and waves or the sights and sounds of the nearby sea found in his previous environmental and impressionistic pieces, his work began to incorporate managerial references to private industry and local bureaucracy as conceptual components of a new and larger-scale dissemination of culture. The man-made world has obtruded itself on the environment in a manner that cannot be ignored and echoes likewise in his art. A work that he conceived and whose construction he supervised has attracted popular notice in San Francisco. "Wave Organ" (1986) is a sound garden and amphitheater built on public land near the Marina Yacht Harbor. A created landscape that required private and public funding and much collaborative labor, it seems to have grown naturally. Those who happen on it now hardly think of it as deliberately planned when they discover a restful park in which to contemplate and listen to the urban seascape.

Since Oppenheimer's death Richards has remained at the Exploratorium. He continues to promote it as a place that interprets our culture to ourselves and that invites the public to join in a radically participatory scientific-aesthetic experience. His vision of the science-art center of the future is more institutional than Oppenheimer's original idea. It lacks the authorial imprint of the visionary creator but substitutes an authentic openness to collaborative enterprise. His "museum of the future" remains within the general spirit of Oppenheimer's intentions, but its anonymous collectivism and pluralism depart markedly from the pronounced sense of personal mission and pedagogic direction with which Oppenheimer launched the Exploratorium.

That same democratic pluralism places Richards somewhat at odds with the product orientation of the second generation of staff members. Not everyone is as enthused as he is over the proposal for an artists' center for research and development, which would have no specific output but would be an artist's equivalent to a think tank. Some people are offended by the apparently aimless playfulness that Oppenheimer cherished and that Richards now advocates for artists. Opponents see it as a waste of goodwill and donated funds. To them the support of objectless exploration is simply irresponsible academic self-indulgence. They believe the museum has a public trust and is obligated to articulate well-formulated goals that can be met. Professing to be a teaching institution, it has a duty to perfect marketable pedagogic techniques and demonstrate their worth by their success. Just as exhibits are reproduced and sold to other museums, so, the critics believe, the ideas that distinguish the Exploratorium should also be packaged and marketed. A good example of that approach is the prepared series of "Pathways," which are now distributed to teachers in advance of class trips to the museum. They provide alternative digests of exhibit curricula, which are then supplemented during the visit by correspondingly prepared morning explainers who guide the student tours.

Staff members who have reservations about retailing even excellent ideas are beginning to find themselves in a minority. Lacking the crusading vision of Frank Oppenheimer, they also lack the rhetoric to defend the nebulous benefits of maintaining fallow ground for inconclusive exploration and uncertain discovery. In an era of "object clarification," when the absence of well-defined goals is generally held suspect, there is lessening support for the idealistic opportunism with which the Exploratorium was inaugurated—even among staff members who profited most from that "dreaminess."

One staff member who came to the museum unformed and unaware of her capacities is Sally Duensing. In 1973 she was a certified and inexperienced teacher, looking for employment. Though no stranger to museums, she had not planned a museum career for herself and took a job as a morning field trip guide temporarily while continuing to hunt for a teaching position. As luck would have it, the Exploratorium school program was funded soon afterward, and so she was hired to teach in the fledgling SITE program. There she developed exhibit-based curricula that required her to learn new subject areas—particularly physics and perceptual psychology—and to become familiar with the museum exhibits. Along with the still small museum staff, Duensing was involved with most facets of the museum's operation and felt herself to be part of a family enterprise. Oppenheimer encouraged her to follow up on independent interests, even where they appeared to distract from the immediate demands of teaching. Looking back, she recognizes that such implicit support of staff initiative was itself an element of Oppenheimer's pedagogic philosophy and that it served strategically to bring out unknown talents in staff members. Her educational formation was profoundly affected by that permission to subordinate task orientation to free and "unproductive" indulgence of curiosity.

Since staff members were not made to feel that their explorations were a waste of time, she and Bob Miller set out unhindered to satisfy their curiosity about stereoscopic vision. Their research led to the construction of a new exhibit, "Cheshire Cat."[4] From the perspective of staff development, the experience gave Duensing hands-on knowledge of exhibit-making, including the posing of a problem and its intellectual solution, as well as dealing with the material practicalities of construction. It also enhanced her appreciation of what museums can and cannot be expected to do, and that understanding in turn infused the curricula she developed and the teaching techniques that were incorporated into the SITE program. Their effectiveness depended on their site specificity, their programmatic use of exhibits. Later, Duensing discovered that many museums overlook their own material resources while preparing educational syllabi for protracted classroom use. Direct practical exposure to exhibit conception and making helped Duensing become a better teacher.

Conversely, her teaching experience was a tool for exhibit development. When Duensing and Lynn Rankin, another SITE teacher, decided to build a light table exhibit, they employed all the educational devices and schemes they had used in classroom and teacher workshops. The "Light Island" exhibit was a gap-filling solution to some of the problems the SITE teachers had encountered in trying to convey optical notions in the abstract. By creating a concrete exhibit they also gave the students in their teaching workshops a hands-on demonstration that could easily be transferred from the museum into the school classroom.

It was clear to Duensing that convertibility and noncompartmentalization on the part of the staff are at the essence of Exploratorium philosophy. She has tried to impart those ideas to the many visitors and interns from other museums who come to the Exploratorium in search of exhibit models and programmatic inspiration, but they often fail to grasp the point. Duensing's fluid transition between making the museum and talking about it led her naturally into the next stage of her museum career.

As the fame of the Exploratorium grew, Duensing often served as an informal guide for visitors from other museums and especially from foreign countries where governments were contemplating the institution of science museums. Official visitors from China, Singapore, Argentina, and Australia all remember Sally, an attractive young woman with flowing blond hair, who charmed them while she escorted them from exhibit to exhibit. Many were surprised that she was also knowledgeable about the exhibits. Because she knew the museum well and could talk about it, Duensing was an apt explainer, and she saw that role as continuous with her previous teaching experience. When the Kellogg grant for the internship program was received, Duensing asked to be its coordinator. Oppenheimer had no difficulty with that transition, but the Kellogg officers had to be convinced that a teacher from the SITE program was adequately equipped for the task. To their credit, they accepted her appointment and quickly agreed that it had been a good one.

Not long after assuming the internship position, Duensing made another employment shift, this time at Oppenheimer's suggestion. He asked her to take charge of developing an entire exhibit section on language that had recently been funded but not yet implemented. She hesitated to plunge herself into a whole new area of research and consultation, but she was also flattered by Oppenheimer's confidence in her and tempted by the opportunity to stretch her capacities once again. It would mean setting aside her involvement in the SITE program, which was by then amply staffed and operational, and splitting her time between the internship and language programs. That proved to be a good balance, for it enabled her to keep a hand in the day-to-day building of the museum while continuing to teach others the principles and pragmatics of the museum as a whole.

Duensing's environment shifted from the school world to the museum world, although her commitment to teaching remained constant. She was drawn into the international network of museum professionals, attending conventions, presenting papers, and often maintaining informal ties with former interns at their home museums. Without setting out to do so she had become an ambassador for the Exploratorium, known throughout the world by museum people who had corresponded with her directly or indirectly. As coordinator of the Kellogg program she became a catalyst for communication between the Exploratorium and its visitors and also among the visitors themselves. She was the link that brought museum people together. Although she remained at the Exploratorium, she was no longer parochially identified with it. Like Grinell and others who had been drawn into Oppenheimer's circle, she was ready to take her place in the museum world. A onetime Oppenheimer protégé who had repeated his opinions with schoolgirlish admiration, Duensing is now confident in her ability to oversee museum programs and to make exhibit decisions. She tries to avoid dogmatism but is firmly convinced that the Exploratorium has a pedagogic message of empowerment and that other museums stand to benefit from adopting the philosophy as well as the technical and programmatic plan of the Exploratorium. Her career is persuasive evidence of the museum's successful and unorthodox staff development program.

Duensing believes that the spirit of Frank Oppenheimer is being maintained and that the development of the staff is in line with his principles. Like the exhibits, she says, staff members are never complete—there is always room for growth, and if channels are left open, others can travel the same route of self-discovery that she followed. At the same time, she recognizes that the close familial environment that bound the early staff together in a spirit of concerted effort is gone forever. It is not possible for the entire staff to be familiar with the more than six hundred exhibits. Floorwalks must be a formal and mandatory condition of employment if employees are to know the museum well. And since new staff members are hired to fill distinct job specifications, there is not much room anymore for the merely imaginative generalist.

In the area of future museum directions, Duensing, like Richards, hopes for a greater emphasis on research and collaboration. She proposes that scientific researchers use the museum as a sabbatical site where they can pursue their research interests and, when possible, use the museum resources and public as a part of their inquiry.[5] The museum could display the performance of scientific research as an interactive museum exhibit, permitting the public to ask questions of researchers, to understand their purposes and methods, and sometimes to become part of a research program. Duensing would like to see people moved to ask questions about how science is done, and also about why. She suggests that exposing the motivation for particular research projects to public scrutiny will make their creators more answerable to the public.[6] Obviously not all scientists would choose to make public exhibits of themselves or their work, but some might welcome the opportunity to achieve more widespread understanding of their enterprise. It remains to be seen whether it is feasible to display science as a sort of performance. And how like is this goal to Oppenheimer's intention of teaching the performance of science to the nonscientist?

No one any longer questions the pedagogic mission of the Exploratorium or challenges its credentials. However, like many revolutionary ideas, this one risks erosion by its own success. As more and more institutions adopt the hands-on trappings of the Exploratorium without grasping the essential idea of interactive exhibitry, its impact will be attenuated. An even greater risk is the devaluation of commitment on the part of the Exploratorium staff as Oppenheimer's vision is displaced by a misguided zeal to preserve and perpetuate whatever has worked before. Assured by learned opinion, by public response, and by hard-won official confirmation of the educational effectiveness of its exhibit policy and programs, the museum is now under less pressure to forge and refine them and has turned instead to their distribution. The new generation of managers has not followed the circuitous life path of Oppenheimer and his friends. Less disposed to impart their own substantive values, their chief measure of the merit of a product is the volume of its success. Since that has now been proven by public acclaim, their objective is to maintain and augment it, and so there has been concerted effort to package exhibits more attractively, to improve public services—lounges, restaurants, rest rooms—those features that make museum visits more recreationally enjoyable, and to upgrade revenue-generating programs such as the store and the exhibit replica business. There is, to be sure, nothing wrong with making the museum prosper, but that should be a secondary goal and not the chief objective.

Everyone at the museum agrees that improving the physical facilities is a necessity. Few are as impervious to personal discomfort as Oppenheimer was, and the increase in staff and exhibits has made working conditions intolerable. But some would retain the rough edges that Oppenheimer loved so well, while others see little merit in historic clumsiness and have no attachment to an aesthetic of disorder.

Oppenheimer considered himself the first of the exhibit users, and he openly confessed to constructing exhibits to please himself and his friends. The current staff assess exhibit performance impersonally by appraising visitor reaction, and their deviation from Oppenheimer's standard of measurement is as significant politically as it is educationally.[7] Where Oppenheimer would take visitor indifference or the failure to grasp an exhibit as an indication of the need for public enlightenment, his successors point to a feedback mechanism that shows what the public wants and guide their action accordingly. Their aim is to satisfy customers; his was to transform them. Both objectives may be seen as public service, but they are different in kind and motivation. Oppenheimer certainly wanted to please people, but he was not interested in entertainment as such. He had no doubt that what the museum offered was of value to the public, and he relied on no other measure of the museum's effectiveness than his own judgment and that of a few colleagues. He had little use for conventionalized evaluative techniques and was openly disdainful toward visitor surveys. Some staff members and many museum professionals criticized his intolerance of so-called objective evaluative instruments. Generally his response was the same, namely that no mechanical survey or blind questionnaire could measure or predict the discoveries and revelatory insights that people often experience in their interaction with exhibits. A canned question would elicit a canned response but would not bring out the quality of experience that the museum meant to foster and would, if anything, destroy it. Clocking time spent in front of an exhibit or asking visitors direct questions about what they remember as they depart only reinforces preconceived ideas of what visitors ought to be apprehending, and Oppenheimer insisted that the real learning was qualitative and imponderable. His favorite and often-repeated success story was of the woman who went home after visiting the museum and repaired a floor lamp—not because there was anything in the museum that taught her how but because she had gained the confidence to figure out how to do it. No questionnaire could have elicited that story.

Oppenheimer's successors in the museum are at once more modest and more authoritarian. They do not claim to know what makes an exhibit successful, and so they accept a perceived public consensus. But having observed what that is, they rely on professional skills to assure its uniform delivery. Many of them are contemptuous of the academic self-indulgence and narcissism of aimless exploration. They share with Oppenheimer the desire to make scientific knowledge accessible to the public, but they believe that is best accomplished by a direct transferral of skills. Insofar as museums derive their support from public resources, they are also accountable to them, and in the view of this generation of museum professionals, it is the duty of museums to dispense to as wide an audience as possible those cultural commodities that have heretofore been the possessions of a selected few. They would accomplish that by perfecting learning techniques and promoting their distribution.

People evidently do go to museums for a variety of reasons—for reverential contemplation, for entertainment, for social communion, and for education. But they do not always experience what they set out to find. No single set of evaluative procedures could apply to the entire spectrum of interests that are stimulated and satisfied by the museum.[8] Furthermore, evaluative studies tend to assess the educational experience of the visitors either relative to goals that must be reconstructed after the fact or in terms of standards that are predetermined by someone other than the visitors. There is no necessary connection between what visitors go in search of in a museum and what they actually find, and they may even come away with something that was never put there.

The inclusion of museums among educational institutions is a welcome recognition of their capacity to teach, but it should not desensitize us to important distinctions. Museums are not schools, and their patrons are neither matriculated nor tested. They are not required to cover a specified body of material. We must trust them to pick out what appeals to them, or even let them come out empty-handed. Oppenheimer's "walk in the woods" analogy is appropriate, because no one ever takes in all there is to experience. That is why repeat visits are rewarding and why going with a companion who has different perceptions can enrich one's own experience. It is unfortunate that, albeit for the best of ecological motives, even walks in the woods are being turned into guided tours, roped off with designated objects marked for attention. Admittedly that helps some people see more than they otherwise might, but it also means that everyone sees roughly the same, and many will experience less. There is certainly less likelihood that anyone will make the delightful discovery of something that no one intended them to see.

Oppenheimer believed that those who gain the most from museums are not the visitors but the people who work in the museum—the staff, the explainers, the volunteers, and those who keep a continuing connection. He often remarked that the Exploratorium was not designed for first or one-time users but for the repeat visitor. Field trips were really meant as a preview. Those who were interested would come back. Staff members sometimes applied a workhorse image to the museum, and one of the interns observed, "The Exploratorium is wholesale, not retail. It exists for other science museums and science educators."[9] Oppenheimer did not think it necessary that everyone agree on the goals and objectives of the Exploratorium. It pleased him that so many persons from so many walks of life appeared to find something meaningful there to take away with them. It did not have to be the same thing, and it did not have to be previously identified. Indeed, those museums that are most inspired by the Exploratorium are often entirely unlike it except in spirit, while others that appear to be clones of it actually fail to understand its principles altogether.

Central among those principles is an appreciation of impermanence. Much as Frank Oppenheimer deserves credit and would wish to be remembered, it would dishonor his memory to make the Exploratorium a shrine to him. Though he would undoubtedly oppose specific innovations made by any successor, the greatest tribute that could be paid to Oppenheimer's ideals would be a museum constantly refreshed by dynamic and controversial new visions.

Many people love and understand the Exploratorium, but it is not for everyone. Some are disoriented by the surfeit of sensory stimuli and find the museum threatening. They feel alienated and unsure when they come in the door and do not know where to turn. For them the museum is not liberating but simply disorderly. Others are challenged by that same disorder. Some people walk right through it unperturbed and find a favorite exhibit or discover a new one that wholly absorbs them. For some people the pleasure is in creating pathways that represent a new order, effectively making the world in their own image. A few are at home in the clutter without requiring any regularity at all.

All of those responses to the Exploratorium are legitimate. There is no single right way to experience it, and many more possible ways than anyone has thought of. That open-endedness is controversial and may now be in jeopardy. I have tried to show that it is neither random nor out of control, but that it arises out of principled choices that Oppenheimer made. His successors may choose not to follow his principles. There is no compulsion to follow them and a good deal of pressure to depart from them. I for one would hate to see those principles abandoned, especially in a misguided endeavor to implant them more firmly. In the hope of preserving those principles, I have tried to enunciate them, and I conclude this book with the hope that curiosity, risk-taking, and, above all, the taste for uncertainty will remain among us.

A Rationale for a Science Museum

There is an increasing need to develop public understanding of science and technology. The fruits of science and the products of technology continue to shape the nature of our society and to influence events which have a world-wide significance. Yet the gulf between the daily lives and experience of most people and the complexity of science and technology is widening. Remarkably few individuals are familiar with the details of the industrial processes involved in their food, their medicine, their entertainment or their clothing. The phenomena of basic science which have become the raw material of invention are not easily accessible by the direct and unaided observation of nature yet they are natural phenomena which have, for one segment of society, become as intriguing and as beautiful as a butterfly or a flower.

There have been many attempts to bridge the gap between the experts and the laymen. The attempts have involved books, magazine articles, television programs and general science courses in schools. But such attempts, although valuable, are at a disadvantage because they lack props; they require apparatus which people can see and handle and which display phenomena which people can turn on and off and vary at will. Explaining science and technology without

217

props can resemble an attempt to tell what it is like to swim without ever letting a person near the water. For many people science is incomprehensible and technology frightening. They perceive these as separate worlds that are harsh, fantastic and hostile to humanity.

There is thus a growing need for an environment in which people can become familiar with the details of science and technology and begin to gain some understanding by controlling and watching the behavior of laboratory apparatus and machinery; such a place can arouse their latent curiosity and can provide at least partial answers. The laboratory atmosphere of such an "exploratorium" could then be supplemented with historical displays showing the development of both science and technology and its roots in the past.

The purpose of a science museum and exploration center would be to satisfy this need. It could be valuable and entertaining for the general public and would serve as a resource for schools and existing adult education programs.

The demonstrations and exhibits of the museum should have an aesthetic appeal as well as pedagogical purpose and they should be designed to make things clearer rather than to cultivate obscurantism or science fiction. The museum cannot be a mere hodge-podge of exhibits but should be conceived with some basic rationale that can provide a flexible frame work.

A Possible Form of Organization for Such a Science Museum

A form of organization which could help fulfill the underlying purpose of the museum would involve introducing the various areas of science and technology with sections dealing with the psychology of perception and the artistry associated with the various areas of perception. One might, for example, have five main sections based respectively on hearing, on vision, on taste and smell, on the tactile sensations (including perception of hot and cold) and on propriosensitive controls which form the basis of balance, locomotion and manipulation.

The section on hearing might be introduced with a collection of musical instruments. The tonal qualities of the instruments could be demonstrated or reproduced. There could be a section on various musical scales, followed by a section on everyday sounds and noises which could make people aware of the problems of sound recognition and memory. The details of auditory perception could then be explored with experiments on the frequency and loudness response range and on the determination of sound direction, etc. The thread could then divide in two. One part would explore the physics of sound, that is the study of vibrations, oscillations, resonance, interference and reflections. The other part would be the physiology and histology of the ear and the associated central nervous system. The final section would then elucidate the technology and the industrial techniques involved in sound reproduction, (thus introducing electronics) speaker and microphone construction, the acoustics of auditoriums and various devices such as hearing aids, telephones, radio, sonar, and the like.

With the sense of vision one might start with painting and introduce the ideas of perspective and the effects involved on op-art and moiré patterns. One would move to experiments in the psychology of visual perception and then branch to the physics of light on the one hand and to the biology of the eye on the other. These would each then lead to technology. The technology might include pigment manufacture, optical instruments, glass manufacture, television and photography, lighting, infrared and ultraviolet devices and lasers. It might even be appropriate to demonstrate the use of high energy radiation on biological tissue and other aspects of medical technology.

One would proceed in a similar fashion with taste and smell starting with food and perfume, then developing some aspects of chemistry and ending with the vast and mysterious technology of the food and cosmetic industries. The fourth section would start with clothing and housing, pass through a section on perception of hot and cold and roughness, and then develop the physics of heat and lead to the section on industrial production of fibers and building materials.

Finally, the section on control would involve dancing and athletics and various skills such as balancing rods on one's fingers or riding a bicycle. It would demonstrate the proprio-sensitive mechanisms of the body and would then branch to the mathematics of feedback mechanisms and the physiology of muscles and nerves and the semicircular canals, etc. and end up with the sophisticated technology of control mechanisms in industry and technology.

This form of organization is but one of many possible plans for a museum. I believe it would capture the interest of many people and might provide a pattern which museums might wish to follow. However, although it seems essential that the museum be structured according to some underlying plan such as the one suggested above, it is also important that the people who use the museum not be forced to follow some preconceived pattern. In the proposed organization some people might be interested in following the domain of perception from one area to another. Some might remain rooted in just one area such as in the physics of sound or in food technology, whereas others may want to wander around the halls at random.

Immediate Programs

The design and building of elegant, clear and reasonably public-proof experiments and exhibits will proceed slowly. It might easily take many years to complete the type of displays for the program outlined above. There are, however, some programs which could be initiated within a short time and which should be continuing features of the museum. These are outlined below.

1) School science fairs have become established institutions. At present, however, the projects are displayed for only two or three days and are then dismantled or returned to some storage place. They could well be displayed for much longer periods and the students who have built them could occasionally be on hand to explain them to the public. In the future, the talent and effort involved in these projects might well be marshalled to make more integrated displays for the museum.

2) The apparatus used in educational television science programs could be displayed in the museum after the television program had been shown. With competent supervision, this apparatus could be demonstrated again, and in at least some cases, the public might be able to work with it. In time, a television studio could be incorporated into the museum and a symbiotic relation between the museum and educational television could be developed.

3) There is a need for a central location in which to display the laboratory apparatus which has been developed for use in schools and colleges. This apparatus could be displayed in such a fashion that teachers and their pupils could work with it. Support for this activity might come both from the manufacturers of this apparatus and from the National Science Foundation which have invested heavily in its development.

4) There are many objects of industry and science which are themselves quite beautiful even when displayed with no pedagogical motive. The art department at Stanford University recently put to-

gether an exhibit using instrumentation for the Stanford Linear accelerator. Such exhibits would be worth displaying and would fit quite naturally with a practice of having displays of sculpture in the gardens and buildings which are adjacent to the museum building.

A museum should not be a substitute for a school or a classroom but it should be a place where people come both to teach and to learn. Visitors should be able to find it refreshing and stimulating. Above all it should be honest and thus convey the understanding that science and technology have a role which is deeply rooted in human values and aspirations.

Frank Oppenheimer
Department of Physics
University of Colorado

Exhibits on Visual Perception Proposed by an Exploratorium Advisory Committee

We have attempted to illustrate the type of exhibit and demonstration material that is envisaged for the Exploratorium in the following pages. We have limited the list of exhibits to those that involve the domain of visual perception. Even this list, long as it is, leaves out some of the medical and physiological exhibits that will be included. The experiments that are listed are based on the phenomena with which the director is already familiar that concern the eye and how it registers and interprets the world of light. We have set up a committee of Bay Area scientists who are primarily concerned with vision. Some of the material listed below may be omitted in the final exhibit arrangement and a great deal more will certainly be included.

Some of the demonstrations are designed primarily to arouse curiosity; others are meant to be explanatory. Some of the exhibits will be large and can be viewed by many people at once; others will be arranged in cubicles or on table tops and will be designed to be viewed in some logical sequence. The large ones will be displayed on the main floor of the Palace hall; the smaller ones may be arranged in specially designed spaces which will direct the flow of the visitors. An introductory area will include interesting and sometimes startling visual effects and so-called "illusions." For example:

1. The Eames distorted room. A room which appears to be square when one looks into it. The viewer looks into this room and sees a square room with two window frames on the opposite wall. In actuality, the room is not square; the far wall recedes sharply from the viewer, and the two window frames which appear to be the same size are in fact very different. If a friend of the viewer peers through one window his head will appear small whereas through the other window it will appear huge.
2. A hallway with painted steps to which the visitor reacts as though they were real steps.
3. Strobe lights with variable frequencies. The effects of "flicker."
4. A room in which one can wander wearing glasses which interchange left and right or which make everything appear upside down.
5. A room in which one wears a dark glass over one eye. The brain-eye system reacts more slowly to dim light than to bright light. A swinging pendulum appears to move in a circle under these conditions.
6. A hall of real images. The "objects" in the room are the images of hidden objects and cannot be touched or felt.
7. A holography exhibit. One looks through a photographic plate with no apparent pattern on it and perceives a three-dimensional view of a scene.
8. Random dot stereoscopy. One views two pictures, neither of which has any discernible pattern with one eye alone. The pattern emerges only when viewed with both eyes.

The eye

1. Observation of one's own eyes.
   One can observe the way the pupil changes size as the light intensity varies by looking into a magnifying mirror and controlling the light intensity.
   One can hold up a narrow beam of light to the cornea and observe the pattern of blood vessels on the retina.
   One can hold a blue light up to the pupil and observe the moving sparkles which are due to the red blood cells in the capillaries of the retina.
   One can observe the "yellow spot," a pigmented area around the region of most-sensitive vision.

2. A large model (walk through) of the eye.
3. Eye models with a ground glass screen in place of the retina.
   Effect of an iris diaphragm in front of the model.
   The effect of eye glasses.
   The appearance of an astigmatic image on the ground glass of the model.
   A model of the eye with a focusable (cylindrical geometry) lens.
4. The range of distinct and peripheral vision.
5. The closest distance of distinct vision with different intensities of light.
6. The pin-hole magnifier . . . vision through a very small aperture.

If they can be developed for public use there will be devices which enable one visitor to look into another's eyes.

Models, photographs, and specimens of the eyes of other animals and insects.

Size and distance judgments

1. Experiments in which one attempts to "thread a needle" with remote manual control of the "needle" and the "thread."
   a. Using one eye.
   b. Using both eyes.
   c. Using the image of the needle and thread on a ground glass screen.
2. Experiments using two model eyes with ground glass screens acting as the retinas of the models.
   a. Can the visitor judge by the way these model eyes have to point to "see" the objects in the scene?
   b. Can he judge distance by moving the model eye back and forth?
   c. Can he judge distance by focusing the model eyes?
   d. The effect of a hazy atmosphere on distance judgments.
3. Stereoscopic vision.
   a. Illustration of the fact that each eye "sees" a different picture of nearby objects.
   b. What kind of images can and cannot be fused? The uncomfortable feeling which results when the images cannot be fused as in some Vari-Vue pictures.
   c. Two television cameras plus a computer which sees stereoscopically.

  d. Diagrams which illustrate the logic of stereoscopic vision.
  e. The reverse distance perception that occurs when a scene is viewed through prisms that interchange left and right.
  f. Illustrations of the way in which a judgment as to the size of an object is dependent on a distance judgment, e.g., the fact that the moon appears larger on the horizon than in mid-sky.
  g. Examples of stereoscopic vision. Aerial photographs, stereo-photos of the moon, contour maps.

Color vision

1. Spinning color wheels.
2. Mixing of colored lights.
3. The observance of normal colors through colored eye glasses.
4. Colors produced by black and white patterns that are in motion.
5. The after-image colors produced by eye fatigue and bright lights.
6. The Land demonstrations on color: Two projectors and a color filter on only one of the projectors. The difference between pictures taken with red and blue filters.
7. Color blindness tests.

Visual effects used by artists in painting

1. The history of perspective, the Egyptians to Leonardo da Vinci.
2. The use of color and colored boundaries to indicate distance.
3. Size and shape distortions that are required to reproduce a scene, e.g., a comparison of photographs and paintings of the same scene. These comparisons have been made, for example, of many of Cézanne's paintings.
4. Op-art, kinetic art and flashing-light art.
5. Oscilloscope and television art. These can be displayed on a color oscilloscope that is computer controlled.
6. Motion picture art.

The effects of light on matter

1. Some effects of light on plants and animals.
   The bending of plants toward light.

The production of carbon dioxide as shown by bubbles in an aquarium (using light of different colors).

The reaction of single-celled animals to light.

2. Some effects which show the connection between light and electricity.
   a. The ejection of electric charges from metals.
   b. Electro-optical shutters for polarized light.
   c. Soft-X-ray production and fluorescence.
   d. Light from electric discharges.
   e. Light-activated batteries.
   f. Sodium iodide light counters and photo-multipliers.
   g. Light from beams of electrons hitting various substances, e.g. television tubes, phosphores.
   h. Photographs of light from the electric currents in high energy accelerators.

(The exhibits and demonstrations in this group are envisaged as a series of many small displays without too much explanation which will provide a survey of the many ways in which electrical phenomena produce light and in which light can induce electrical phenomena.)

3. Some chemical effects of light.
   a. The chemistry of photographic processes.
   b. Solutions which reversibly change color when acted on by light.
   c. Glass which darkens when exposed to light.

Optical instruments

1. Large plastic lenses, prisms, and mirrors which the visitor can place in beams of light that are produced by low-power lasers. He will be able to move the lenses and turn them and observe their effect on the path of the light beams.
2. Lenses mounted on a track. There will be a lamp filament and a movable screen; the visitor will be able to produce images of the filament by moving the lenses and the screen.
3. Lenses arranged (without mounting tubes) which illustrate the principles of telescopes, microscopes, projectors, cameras, etc.
4. A demonstration entitled "What is an image?" A point of light with a movable aperture in front of it. When the aperture is moved an image of this point of light will remain stationary.

5. An exhibit on the techniques used in light shows.
6. Special optical instruments: fish-eye lenses, Schmidt telescopes, infra-red cameras and telescopes, television, x-ray cameras, image intensifiers, light pipes and fiber optics, etc.

Light waves

(This section should be closely connected with demonstrations relating to sound waves, water waves, radio waves, etc.)
1. A point source viewed through holes of varying diameter.
2. A line source (lamp filament) viewed through slits of varying width. These demonstrations will show beautiful light and dark rings or bands.
3. An apparatus which can measure the distance between the crests of a light wave.
4. A laser beam which travels from one end of the Palace to the other with appropriate optics to demonstrate the prodigious speed of light.
5. The origin of the color in soap films, butterfly wings and opals, etc.
6. The reduction of light loss in camera lenses by using thin coatings.
7. Polarized light: polarization by scattering, by reflection, by crystals, and by Polaroid sheets.

The technology of light

There are many possibilities for exhibits and demonstrations in this area. We give a few examples of such possibilities.
1. The manufacture of incandescent light bulbs.
   a. The mining, refining, and drawing of tungsten filaments.
   b. The manufacture of the glass bulbs and the glass support structure for the tungsten. This display would involve motion picture films of the industrial production and a prototype of the equipment used for blowing glass bulbs.
2. An illustration of the factors which determine the life of a light bulb.
3. A display of different types of light bulbs and their history.
4. Some additional areas of interest would be the industrial process

involved in the manufacture of such products as: Polaroid sheets, photographic film, fluorescent lights, mercury arcs and cadmium vapor street lights, glass and lenses (including trifocals), color television screens, pigment and dye, industrial mirrors, special types of glass (heat resistant, bullet proof, photo-sensitive, etc.), photographic flash bulbs, photo-electric cells, solar batteries, fluorescent screens, etc.

5. The manufacture and properties of the industrial products currently available to artists: plastics, epoxy-resins, acrylic paints, adhesives, phosphores, etc.

Tactile substitutes for vision

1. Braille and cane.
2. Photo-electric sensors which produce word "images" on the finger tip.
3. Television cameras which imprint a tactile "image" on the small of the back.

Eye care

1. Radiations which injure the eye.
2. Eye defects and their tests and correction.
3. Eye surgery (films and TV tapes).
4. Genetic variations in vision.

Distance and size perception of the very large and the very small

1. Exhibits on the measurement of astronomical distances.
2. Exhibits on the measurement of the size of atoms and atomic nuclei.

Exhibits Related to Vision Completed During the Tenure of the Sloan Foundation Grant, 1970–71

Collateral optical exhibits

Real images in space seen by both eyes (no projection screen)
> Real images from spherical mirrors (two)
> Real image from low-f-number lens (large optical bench)

Lenses and prisms
> Giant hanging plastic lenses.
> Lenticular and cylindrical lenses.
> Light paths through smoky light pipes and lenses using laser beam (demonstration).
> Bathroom window optics (patterns produced by various prismatic windows).
> Fiber optics exhibit.
> Sun paintings.

Mirrors
> Dodecahedron with inside mirrors.
> Multiple images in two variable angle plane mirrors (shadow kaleidoscope).
> Parabolic mirror with plane mirror in focal plane (see your head on someone else's shoulders).
> Sound mirror in the rotunda (multiple echoes).

Interference and diffraction
> Interference using laser beams (demonstration).

Thin film interference using sodium vapor light.

Thin film interference in soap films.

Diffraction patterns from the eye of a needle, from a grating, and from the lens of the eye.

Ripple tank.

Polarization

Polarization colors in stressed cellophane tape (using overhead projector).

Polarization by reflection—Pin Ball Machine by Ben Hazzard.

Polarization by reflection—didactics exhibit with string analogue.

Polarization of microwaves.

Miscellaneous

Moiré patterns.

Diomoirekineses—a kinetic art moiré pattern.

Kinetic fluorescent light pipe exhibit—showing stroboscopic effects and moiré patterns.

Laser demonstration.

Pin-hole magnifier.

Slit camera images of rotunda columns.

In process of development:

Fluorescence and phosphorescence.

Exhibits on the eye and seeing

Eye chart and eye model

Stereo-vision

Threading a "needle" with one eye and two.

Retina disparity exhibit—two vertical rods.

Artificial distance perception—polarized red and green slits.

Reversed distance perception—vertical rods with dove prisms.

Random-dot stereoscopy—Bela Julesz.

Lenticular lens stereoscopy, horizontal and vertical cylindrical lenses.

Stereo-viewer with separate picture to examine retinal disparities.

3-D images from large colored shadows.

Size and distance

Trees on a roadway illusion.

Arrow illusions.

Trapezoidal window.

Escher prints.

Three-dimensional "Escher," Sue Orlof.

About the eye

Macula shadow on a purple field.

Red blood corpuscles in the retinal capillaries.

Eye jitter poster.

Visual field discrimination—Russell Valois.

Eye track—eye movements while reading.

After-images in white light (strobe flash).

Blind-spot chart.

Color

Colored after-images.

Simultaneous contrast—colored dots on various backgrounds.

Simultaneous contrast—colored shadows.

Color table—color filters, reflectors, and color-blindness charts.

Primary and complementary colors—movable lens with colored filters.

Monochromatic light—sodium vapor lamp.

Chromatic aberration of the eye.

Miscellaneous

Standard line drawing illusions.

Rotating rings.

Figure reversal with drawings and with shadows.

Independent images from each eye—looking through a cardboard tube.

Summation from each eye—looking through two cardboard tubes with overlapping fields of view.

Strobe light effects—the Overloaded Eye.

Planned for the immediate future
    Ames room.
    Two-dimensional eye track.
    Light-dark adaptation with wide-range photometer.
    Logarithmic response curve with wide-range photometer.
    Pupil dilation demonstration.
    Viewer with six-inch retinal disparity.
    Short-term exhibits of tactile-visual simulator devices.
    More eye-brain models and charts.
    Eye dominance exhibit.
    The optics of eye glasses.
    Time-Life film on visual perception.

Statement of Broad Purposes

The Exploratorium in the Palace of Arts and Science was conceived to accomplish educational objectives that are difficult, if not impossible, to achieve in school classrooms or through books, films and television programs.

The Exploratorium provides exhibits, centering around the theme of perception, which are designed to be manipulated and appreciated at a variety of levels by both children and adults. The exhibits that explore and interact with the senses are fascinating in themselves; they also provide a genuine basis for inter-relating science and art. Furthermore, understanding the mechanisms of sensory perception leads to a flow of exhibits about beautiful and basic natural phenomena. By illustrating the re-occurrence of natural processes in a multiplicity of contexts, we convey a sense of unity among such processes and counteract any overly fragmented view of nature and culture.

In the Exploratorium, the visitors achieve the satisfaction of individual discovery. We do not want people to leave the Palace with the implied feeling: "Isn't somebody else clever." Our exhibits are honest and simple so that no one feels they must be on guard against being fooled or misled. We are not polemic nor do we alarm. On the contrary, we believe that people are more sensible when not frightened of each other or of nature. The serious intent but nevertheless somewhat playful atmosphere of the Exploratorium allows teacher and pupil, child and parent, scientist and non-scientist, all to feel both comfortable with and enlightened by the exhibits.

September 27, 1971

Notes

Except where otherwise indicated, correspondence cited is found in the files of the Exploratorium.

Introduction

1. The Lawrence Hall of Science was founded in the spring of 1968 by the regents of the University of California in honor of its first Nobel laureate, Ernest Orlando Lawrence. It is an organized research unit of the Berkeley campus. See *Program Report, 1978-79,* Lawrence Hall of Science, University of California, Berkeley. The Ontario Science Centre, conceived in 1963 in honor of the Canadian centennial, underwent "a gestation period rivalling that of six elephants." Built with federal and provincial funds, it opened officially on September 26, 1969. See *First 10 Years: Ontario Science Centre,* J. Tuzo Wilson.

Chapter 1: Roots and Soil of the Exploratorium

1. Since the definition of a science museum is a matter of dispute, it is difficult to assign a date to the first one. Some people credit the international exhibitions of the nineteenth century with their origin. See Eugene S. Ferguson, "Technical Museums and International Exhibitions," *Technology and Culture* 6(1965). Others trace their history to seventeenth- and eighteenth-century cabinets of mechanical models and natural objects. See Victor J. Danilov, *Science and Technology Centers* (Cambridge: MIT Press, 1982). In the United States, the Charleston Museum, which collected natural history materials, was founded in 1773. See Laura M. Bragg, "The Birth of the Museum Idea in America," *Charleston Museum Quarterly* 1(1923). Following the example of European societies for promoting industry and invention, the American So-

ciety for Promoting and Propagating Useful Knowledge was founded in 1766 with the backing of Benjamin Franklin. It subsequently merged with the American Philosophical Society, and one of its activities was the organization of a collection of models (Danilov, *op. cit.*, p. 16). The Franklin Institute of the State of Pennsylvania for the Promotion of the Mechanic Arts was established in 1824, offering classes, public lectures, and the American Manufactures Exhibition. See Bruce Sinclair, *Philadelphia's Philosopher Mechanics: A History of the Franklin Institute, 1824-1865* (Baltimore: Johns Hopkins University Press, 1974). The bequest of James Smithson to the United States for "an establishment for the increase and diffusion of knowledge among men" was not made until 1835. See Walter Karp, *The Smithsonian: An Establishment for the Increase and Diffusion of Knowledge Among Men* (Washington, D.C.: Smithsonian Institution Press, 1965); Geoffrey T. Hellman, *The Smithsonian: Octopus on the Mall* (Philadelphia: J. B. Lippincott Co., 1967).

2. Edward P. Alexander, *Museums in Motion: An Introduction to the History and Functions of Museums* (Nashville: American Association for State and Local History, 1979).

3. *Ibid.*, p. 63.

4. *Ibid.*, p. 65.

5. The Franklin Institute Science Museum and Planetarium, an outgrowth of the nineteenth-century institute, was founded in Philadelphia in 1934, followed in 1939 by the Buhl Planetarium and Institute of Popular Science in Pittsburgh. Some natural history museums broadened their emphasis to include the natural sciences and technology. The Boston Museum of Science developed after World War II out of the Boston Society of Natural History, which had been founded in 1830. Similarly, on the west coast, the Oregon Museum of Science and Industry in Portland took its present form in 1957 after fitful earlier starts as a natural history museum. In Seattle, the Pacific Science Center opened in the U.S. Science Pavilion after the closing of the 1962 World's Fair. Science museums of a more specialized nature, some addressed primarily to children, could also be found in Dallas, Columbus, Brooklyn, Indianapolis, Cleveland, Oak Ridge, Albuquerque, Mexico City, Huntsville (Alabama), and Jackson (Michigan). More than twenty new science centers opened during the sixties and seventies in the U.S. and around the world. See Danilov, *Science and Technology Centers*, pp. 27-36.

6. Private communication from Lee Oppenheimer and Louise Oppenheimer Singer.

7. Letter from Julius Oppenheimer to Frank, March 11, 1930, cited in Alice K. Smith and Charles Weiner, eds. *Robert Oppenheimer: Letters and Recollections,* (Cambridge, Mass.: Harvard University Press, 1980), p. 95.

8. *Ibid.*, p. 154.

9. There are many ecstatic accounts of the moment, which has been described as resembling the state of the universe after its first primordial explosion. Robert Oppenheimer turned to the Bhagavad Gita for the image that was used as the title of the book by Robert Jungk, *Brighter Than a Thousand Suns* (New York: L. Gollancz, 1958). See also Richard Rhodes, *The Making of the Atomic Bomb* (New York: Simon and Schuster, 1986).

10. *The ESS Reader* (Newton, Mass.: Education Development Center, 1970).

11. John Cairns, Gunther S. Stent, and James D. Watson, eds., *Phage and the Origins of Molecular Biology* (New York: Cold Spring Harbor Laboratory of Quantitative Biology, 1966).

12. Frank Oppenheimer, "The Sentimental Fruits of Science," *Durango Herald* May 1959; "Science and Fear," *Centennial Review* 5(1961):396; "The Character of a University," *Colorado Quarterly* Spring 1964; "The Mathematics of Destruction," editorial in *The Saturday Review* Dec. 1965; "The Role of Creative Pedagogy in Developing

Countries," paper delivered to International Conference of Science in Developing Countries, published in *The Scientific World* 4(1966); "A War in the Shadow of the H-Bomb," *Bulletin of the Atomic Scientists* May 1968; "Science and Invention," *The Scientific Worker*.

13. Frank Oppenheimer, "A Library of Experiments," with M. Correll, *American Journal of Physics* 32(1964):220.

14. Frank Oppenheimer, "The Role of Science Museums," published in *Conference Report* (Washington, D.C.: Smithsonian Institution Press, 1968).

15. Frank Oppenheimer, letter to David Saltonstall, program director, Andrew W. Mellon Foundation, New York, June 24, 1981.

16. *San Francisco Chronicle* Aug. 1967. An article by Richard Harcourt about the Palace of Fine Arts was published in the San Francisco Chamber of Commerce magazine and mentioned the possibility of a museum there. It was called to Oppenheimer's attention in a letter from Hans U. Gerson, Nov. 8, 1967.

17. See interview with C. Weiner, May 21, 1973, archives of the Niels Bohr Library, American Institute of Physics, New York. See also Exploratorium memo by Frank Oppenheimer, "The Relationship Between the Exploratorium in the Palace of Arts and Science and Other Museums in the Bay Area" (n.d.).

18. Exploratorium memo by Frank Oppenheimer, "A Proposal for a Palace of Arts and Science in the San Francisco Palace of Fine Arts" (n.d.).

19. Exploratorium memo by Frank Oppenheimer, "A MOSAIC in the Palace of Arts and Science" (n.d.).

20. Exploratorium memo by Frank Oppenheimer, "An Exploratorium of Perception, Science and Technology in the San Francisco Palace of Fine Arts," May 1968 or 1969?

21. There was even a warmly personal letter of support from Lieutenant General Leslie R. Groves, who had been the Army commander in charge of the entire Atomic Bomb Project, offering "to assist you in any inactive way that I could, provided this did not entail travel." Letter to Frank Oppenheimer, Oct. 2, 1969.

22. Frank Oppenheimer, letter to David E. Nelson, San Francisco Maritime Museum, Sept. 24, 1967.

23. Berkeley: Howell North Books, 1967.

24. Palace of Arts and Science Foundation Board of Directors, March 26, 1969: William Coblentz (attorney, regent Univ. of California), Edward U. Condon (Dept. of Physics and Astrophysics, Univ. of Colorado), Louis Goldblatt (secretary-treasurer ILWU), Lorenz Eitner (art department chairman, Stanford Univ.), Martha Gerbode, Donald Glaser (Nobel laureate, Virus Laboratory, Univ. of California), Z. L. Goosby (member San Francisco School Board), Mrs. Randolph Hearst (regent Univ. of California), Arthur Jampolsky (director Smith-Kettlewell Institute of Visual Sciences), Chauncey Leake (Univ. of California Medical School), Joshua Lederberg (Nobel laureate, Stanford Univ. Medical School), Donald McLaughlin (Homestake Mining Company), Edwin McMillan (Nobel laureate, director Lawrence Radiation Laboratory), Einar Mohn (president Western Conference of Teamsters), George Moscone (California state senator), Scott Newhall (executive editor *San Francisco Chronicle*), Elliott Owens (vice president and general manager Owens Illinois Glass Company), Wolfgang Panofsky (director Stanford Linear Accelerator Center), J. B. de C. M. Saunders (Univ. of California Medical School), Louis S. Simon (area vice president KPIX-Channel 5), George Wheelwright (Green Gulch Ranch, Marin County), Richard Harcourt (head of transportation for Greater San Francisco Chamber of Commerce), Walter S. Johnson (honorary chairman). Officers of the board: Donald McLaughlin (president), William Coblentz (vice president), J. B. de C. M. Saunders (vice president), Elliott Owens (treasurer), Louis Goldblatt (secretary). Ex officio:

Frank Oppenheimer (director of the museum), Esther Pike (secretary to the board).

25. Act of Incorporation, Nov. 4, 1968 (Gayle Campbell, secretary), San Francisco, Calif.

Chapter 2. Creating the Museum: Design and Serendipity Meet

1. Frank Oppenheimer, "A Rationale for a Science Museum," *Curator* 11(Nov. 1968):206.

2. *Ibid.*

3. *Ibid.*

4. *Ibid.* p. 209.

5. See Chapter 6.

6. See Chapter 4.

7. Exploratorium memo by Frank Oppenheimer, "Status of the Project," June 25, 1969. The art committee included two additional members of the Stanford art department and representatives of Experiments in Art and Technology, Inc. The Committee on Visual Perception Demonstrations was headed by Merton Flom, of the Department of Optometry, University of California, and included Drs. Bliss and Cornsweet of the Stanford Research Institute.

8. *Ibid.* Mrs. Ruth Snow had organized a health fair that took place in San Francisco's Brooks Hall in the fall of 1968 and had organized the Bay Area Diabetes Detection Program.

9. See Chapter 3.

10. Exploratorium memo by Frank Oppenheimer, "Exhibit Planning," March 12, 1971. In this summary of the exhibit program Oppenheimer elaborates upon the criteria that exhibits are to fulfill "at a variety of levels ranging from relatively superficial sightseeing through a broad and deep understanding." He also states the intention that exhibits "will form a multiply interconnected web of thematic threads or 'curricula.'"

11. Condon wrote letters to Corning Glassware, Bell Telephone Laboratories, Ford Motor Company, General Motors, IBM, RCA; the federal departments of Agriculture, Commerce, the Interior, HEW; federal regulatory agencies such as the Atomic Energy Commission, the Maritime Commission, the FCC, and the Power Commission; and academic research institutions such as the Scripps Institute of Oceanography. Some did not respond, but many were moved by the specific and personal nature of his request. In a representative letter to Glenn T. Seaborg, chairman of the Atomic Energy Commission, Condon asks for the loan of exhibit material, commenting on the appropriateness of the location of the Exploratorium at the site of the Panama-Pacific International Exposition, where, as an adolescent boy, he had spent the summer of 1915 and had "pinched some carnotite ore from the Colorado exhibit there and got started in physics by making gamma ray shadow pictures with it." Letter from Edward U. Condon, July 16, 1969.

12. "Museum of Art, Science," *San Francisco Chronicle* Oct. 16, 1969.

13. The exhibit section that honors Einstein is an interesting example of the museum's opportunistic philosophy. Conceived to coincide with the celebration of the centennial of Einstein's birth, when funds for such presentations were available, the exhibits in the section are only remotely connected with the museum's theme of human perception. Nevertheless, they help explain how Einstein "set the stage not only for his own further work that was concerned with the uniformity and symmetry of the almost infinitely large; but also laid the groundwork for our understanding of the infinitely small through the quantum aspects of nature and the need for a duality

in our descriptions of atomic and subatomic interactions of light and matter." Frank Oppenheimer, Introduction to Bruce R. Wheaton, *The Rise and Fall of the Aether: Einstein in Context* (San Francisco: Exploratorium, 1981).

14. *San Francisco Chronicle* Oct. 16 and *Chronicle Datebook* Oct. 19, 1969.

15. Jasia Reichardt, *Cybernetic Serendipity: The Computer and the Arts* (New York: Frederick A. Praeger, 1968), p. 5.

16. The public understood that distinction well, for they wrote to the museum asking for explicit instructions and circuit designs to help them replicate the exhibits they enjoyed (e.g., letter from Gary B. Hoffman, Provo, Utah). It is not likely that a similar request for assistance in replicating a celebrated work of art would be made to a museum of fine art.

17. Letter from Mary Morain, executor of the Frances Dewing Foundation, to Frank Oppenheimer, 1970.

18. Jack Burnham, "Systems Esthetics," *Art Forum* Sept. 1968.

19. Frank Oppenheimer, "Initiation," *The Exploratorium* Aug.-Sept. 1978.

Chapter 3. Shops and Tools: Making Is a Way of Learning

1. Frank Oppenheimer, grant request submitted to the James Irvine Foundation, San Francisco, Calif., Feb. 1970.

2. Frank Oppenheimer, letter to Commander M. Edwards, Hunters Point Naval Radiological Defense Laboratory, June 29, 1969.

3. Frank Oppenheimer, letters to Representative Phillip Burton, Representative William Maillard, and Senator Alan Cranston, June 5, 1969; letter to Charles Blitzer, Smithsonian Institution, Nov. 10, 1969.

4. Charles Blitzer, letter to Frank Oppenheimer, Dec. 1, 1969.

5. The Miranda Lux Foundation supports "promising proposals for preschool through high school programs in the fields of prevocational and vocational education and training." The James Irvine Foundation awards "grants for higher education, health, youth services, community services and cultural projects" as listed in the U.S. Foundation Guide. See also Oppenheimer's grant reports to the James Irvine Foundation and the Miranda Lux Foundation, both dated Aug. 1970.

6. Frank Oppenheimer, letter to Lawrence Kramer, Miranda Lux Foundation, Dec. 2, 1976.

7. *Hardware Retailer* Dec. 14, 1970:74.

8. Esther Pike, letter to Mrs. James R. Saunders, Junior League secretary, May 12, 1971.

9. Signa I. Dodge, letter to Lawrence I. Kramer, Jr., Dec. 8, 1975.

10. Interview with Ralph Scott, member of SYMBAS, Nov. 1979. The structure, based on Buckminster Fuller's principle of tensegrity, was an extended geodesic dome. It was constructed of steel tubing with vinyl joints and cables at the corners. It yielded, then righted itself, when touched, and so worked both as an exhibit and as a perimeter, defining the space of the entire collection.

11. Frank Oppenheimer, letter to L. A. White, San Francisco Foundation, Aug. 27, 1975.

12. Frank Oppenheimer, letter to L. A. White, May 26, 1976.

13. This convention was introduced with the award of a grant from the National Endowment for the Humanities (NEH) in June 1977 for a series of exhibits called "The Measurement of Heat and Temperature: A History of the Concepts of Heat." In accordance with NEH guidelines, the exhibits interwove the details of technological and scientific history with social and intellectual history.

14. *Light Sight Sound Hearing* (San Francisco: The Exploratorium, 1974).

15. *Sound. Hearing. Resonance: A Guide to the Exploratorium Exhibits* (San Francisco: The Exploratorium, 1977).

16. "The Art of Discovery in San Francisco—Exploratorium," Oct. 14, 1972.

17. K. C. Cole, *Vision: In the Eye of the Beholder* (1978), *Facets of Light* (1980), *Order in the Universe* (1986).

18. New York: William Morrow and Co., 1985.

19. Raymond Bruman, *Cookbook I: A Construction Manual for Exploratorium Exhibits,* 3rd ed. (San Francisco: The Exploratorium, 1987). Volumes II and III were produced by Ron Hipschman in 1980 and 1987 respectively. The *Cookbook* gives detailed, quantitative instructions on which materials to use, how to obtain them, and how to construct the exhibits. It includes suggestions for modifying recipes to achieve different effects and ranks each recipe according to difficulty of construction. Potential builders can determine at a glance whether the proposed exhibit can be built as a classroom exercise or assigned to an apprentice, or whether it requires expert proficiency. Some recipes include anecdotes about ideas the Exploratorium has tried and discarded. Each recipe entry is cross referenced with a list of other exhibit recipes pertaining to related topics.

20. Editor Francy Balcomb, Sharon Stein Studio, Oakland, Calif. After several issues, the entire production was taken over by the museum's graphics staff.

21. Saul Steinberg, letter to the NEA, April 1974.

Chapter 4. Contents of the Museum: Creating and Experiencing Exhibits

1. New York: McGraw-Hill, 1970.

2. Alfred P. Sloan Foundation grant, March 17, 1970, to the Palace of Arts and Science Foundation.

3. Richard L. Gregory, *The Intelligent Eye* (New York: McGraw-Hill, 1970), p. 13.

4. *Ibid.,* p. 60.

5. *Ibid.,* p. 174.

6. Marshall H. Segall, Donald T. Campbell, and Melville J. Herskovitz, *The Influence of Culture on Visual Perception* (Indianapolis: Bobbs-Merrill, 1966). For a brief and intelligent discussion of the objectification of perception—"phenomenal absolutism," as these authors call it—see also Michael Kirby, "The Aesthetics of the Avant-Garde," in *The Art of Time* (New York: Dutton, 1969).

7. Another museum exhibit enables visitors to explore the phenomenon of persistence of vision in isolation, while others reveal its operation in various perceptual contexts. A familiar common experience of persistence of vision is our ability to see a succession of images projected onto a movie screen as a single moving picture.

8. Letters from Frank Oppenheimer to Bela Julesz, July 1970. Bela Julesz, "Computers, Patterns and Depth Perception," *Bell Laboratories Record* Sept. 1966:260–266; "Texture and Visual Perception, *Scientific American* Feb. 1965. B. Julesz and S. C. Johnson, "Stereograms Portraying Ambiguously Perceivable Surfaces," *Proceedings of the National Academy of Sciences* 61(Oct. 1968).

9. Sally Duensing and Robert Miller, "The Cheshire Cat Effect," *Perception* 8(Spring 1979):269.

10. No funding had been obtained specifically for biological exhibits, although some diversion of the Sloan Foundation award for the vision section could be justified, and the first NSF grant also permitted payments for staff to develop exhibits in the life sciences. Oppenheimer appealed without success to the Transamerica Corpora-

tion. See letter to Newell T. Schwin, Transamerica Community Relations, June 20, 1972. Apart from small private grants, the animal behavior section had to be built largely out of the museum's operating budget.

11. Interview with Dr. Evelyn Shaw, Jan. 1980.

12. *Ibid.* See also Evelyn Shaw, "The Exploratorium," *Curator* 15(1972):39–52.

13. Interview with Josh Callman, Jan. 1980. Callman began working at the museum as a high school explainer in 1975, then returned as a laboratory assistant. He later went to the University of California, Davis, to study neurophysiology.

14. Carlson consulted with several academic researchers at this point. Gunther Stent, Carlson's former professor at the University of California, Berkeley, was a physicist turned neurophysiologist, and he referred Carlson to Bill Kristan, a postdoctoral fellow, for practical advice. Kristan in turn led Carlson into a fruitful association with the Grass Instruments Company. Other important consultants were Dr. Kenneth Nakayama of the Smith-Kettlewell Institute; George Mpitsos of the Hopkins Marine Station; John Nichols and Donald Kennedy of Stanford University; Hugh Rowell, Ronald Calabreze, Jerry Westheimer, and William Hietler of University of California, Berkeley; Keith Nelson of San Francisco State University; Alan Gelprin from Princeton and Bell Laboratories; Michael O'Shea of Cambridge University; and William Davis of Santa Cruz.

15. Mary G. Grass, letter to Charles Carlson, June 17, 1975.

16. Mary G. Grass, letter to Charles Carlson, Aug. 18, 1975.

17. The suggestion to use *Pleurobranchia,* a large sea slug that has brightly pigmented and visible nerve fibers, was made by Dr. George Mpitsos, of the Hopkins Marine Station. The Exploratorium staff also visited the laboratory of Dr. Earl Mayeri, at the University of California, San Francisco, to learn the necessary recording technique, and one of Mayeri's graduate students, Dale Brenton, came to the museum to teach the staff how to implant micro-electrodes into single nerve cells.

18. Charles Carlson, Wayne LaRochelle, Susan Schwartzenburg, Sept. 22, 1977, report to the Grass Foundation on the development of three exhibits ("Grasshopper Leg Twitch," "EMG," and "Nerve Impulse") from Aug. 1975 to July 1977.

19. Mary G. Grass, letter to Charles Carlson, Aug. 18, 1975.

20. Nelson H. H. Graburn, "The Museum and the Visitor Experience," address to American Association of Museums annual meeting, Philadelphia, 1982. See Linda Draper, ed., *The Visitor and the Museum* (Washington, D.C.: American Association of Museums, Education Committee, 1977).

21. Jacob Bronowski, *The Ascent of Man,* cited in K. C. Cole, *Sympathetic Vibrations* (New York: William Morrow and Co., 1985), p. 29.

22. Exploratorium proposal to National Science Foundation for two-year grant, 1980, "to develop a broadly ranging collection of exhibits that will enhance the public understanding of electricity."

23. This exhibit was eventually constructed by Tom Tompkins and others in the machine shop.

24. Although an exhibit of this nature was suggested by the participants in the electricity conference that met in Nov. 1983, there was opposition to it by some of the museum staff members, who considered the analogy misleading and inauthentic.

25. One area that the Exploratorium sought funding for was the development of "electric currents with the wires removed." In one demonstration an electron beam was made visible by passing it through low-pressure helium. The beam could be deflected and made to produce effects such as heating a metal foil to a red glow. The exhibit was intriguing but still experimental. (See NSF proposal, 1980.)

26. The three electricity tours with Exploratorium staff members were taped by the author in July 1983.

Chapter 5. Teaching Without Schooling, Learning Without Experts

1. Frank Oppenheimer, "The Unique Educational Role of Museums," paper prepared for the Belmont Conference, "The Opportunities for Extending Museum Contributions to Pre-College Science Education," sponsored by the National Science Foundation and the Smithsonian Institution, Jan. 1969.

2. Bryant Lane, director Occupational Preparation, San Francisco Unified School District, letter to the Rosenberg Foundation, May 6, 1970 (cc Frank Oppenheimer).

3. See discussion in Chapter 3 on machine shop apprenticeship programs.

4. Interview with Martha Van Genderen, former volunteer worker and school program coordinator at the Exploratorium (Jan. 1980); interviews with Sheila Grinell, explainer supervisor (Dec. 12, 1979, and April 1987).

5. Bartlett H. Hayes, "A Study of the Relation of Museum Art Exhibitions to Education," and Scarvia Anderson, "Noseprints on the Glass, or How Do We Evaluate Museum Programs?" both in *Museums and Education,* Eric Larrabee, ed. (Washington, D.C.: Smithsonian Institution Press, 1968).

6. Interviews with Leni Isaacs, Jan. 1980; Sheila Grinell, Dec. 12, 1979; Nancy Garrity (Exploratorium teacher), Aug. 1986; Terry Lorant (Exploratorium teacher), Jan. 1980.

7. See discussion in Chapter 3 on machine shop apprenticeship programs. Interview with Martha Van Genderen, former volunteer worker and school program coordinator at the Exploratorium (Jan. 1980); interviews with Sheila Grinell, explainer supervisor (Dec. 12, 1979, and April 1987).

8. Lane E. DeLara, associate superintendent, Operations and Instruction, San Francisco Unified School District, letter to Harold Snedcof, the Rockefeller Brothers Foundation, May 29, 1973. This letter points out the benefit of direct experience to students but also emphasizes the value of the program for staff development.

9. Interviews with Exploratorium staff teachers Sally Duensing, Jenefer Merrill, Lynn Rankin, Cathy Joseph (1980).

10. Exploratorium memo, "School in the Exploratorium Follow-Up Activities," May 1974.

11. *Ibid.* See also letter to Frank Oppenheimer from teachers at Rooftop School, San Francisco, May 2, 1973: "At the Exploratorium itself, we saw advanced students being challenged at their level, and many reluctant learners developing interests and attitudes about learning that carried back to the classroom."

12. College credit in education was granted through extension programs at St. Mary's College and the University of California at Davis in 1973. In subsequent years UC Berkeley, the College of Marin, and San Francisco State University also gave education credit to students enrolled in the Exploratorium teaching workshops.

13. Lynn Rankin, Exploratorium program evaluation report, 1975.

14. Interview with Ron Hipschman, Nov. 3, 1979. There were mirror kits, color kits, lens kits, sound kits, strobe kits, and replicas of museum exhibits, packed in lightweight cardboard carrying cases for easy transport.

15. Funds allocated to the Exploratorium at a June 1974 meeting of the San Francisco Board of Education had become unavailable by October of that year, and even the 75 cents per student donated by the Unified School District to subsidize field trips had to be discontinued. See the Exploratorium in-house report "Background on Ten-Year Effort in Developing Exhibit-Based Teaching/Learning Programs at the Exploratorium."

16. The passage in 1977 of state Proposition 13, limiting the use of public funds, affected such hidden variables as the availability of transportation to bus the children

from schools, as well as curtailing the direct allocation of funds to the museum.

17. Leo T. McCarthy, letter to Wilson Riles, June 29, 1977.

18. California State Assembly Bill 4034, amended April 23, 1984, states that "the Legislature intends to provide ongoing funding to support regional science resource centers, in partnership with nonprofit agencies which have demonstrated success in attaining private and governmental support for similar activities on a regional level"—California legislature, 1983-84 regular session, amendment to Part 25 of the Education Code. Unfortunately the efficacy of this law depends on year-to-year allocation of funds by the legislature and the governor.

19. Exploratorium report "School in the Exploratorium: Middle School Workshops, 1983-84," Christopher de Latour and Lynn Rankin, project coordinators.

20. See note 18.

21. In 1977 the San Francisco Unified School District listed its enrollments by ethnic groups as follows: Black 19,000, Caucasian 15,000, Asian 13,000, Spanish-speaking 9,000, Filipino 6,000 (from Exploratorium report "Background on Ten-Year Effort in Developing Exhibit-Based Teaching/Learning Programs at the Exploratorium").

22. Interview with explainer supervisors Sheila Grinell and Steven Stoft (Jan. 1980), Darlene Librero (July 1983).

23. Interviews with former explainers Phil Lim and Granford Andrews and high school apprentice Steven Dunn.

24. Barbara Y. Newsom and Adele Z. Silver, eds., "Two Exploratorium Programs: The Explainer Program and S.I.T.E.," in *The Art Museum as Educator* (Berkeley: University of California Press, 1978).

25. Letter from former morning explainer Sally Moore, June 4, 1981.

26. Interviews with former morning explainer supervisors Stephen Bailey, Cathy Joseph, and Stephen Herrick. See also working paper for Exploratorium grant application, by Stephen Herrick, "Museum Field Trips: Programs Which Offer a New Resource for CETA-Eligible Youth," 1981.

27. "Inside the Puzzle Children: An Experiential Workshop for Adults," report from Garden Sullivan Workshop, March 21 to April 27, 1979. Interview with Susan Sherman, Exploratorium staff teacher and organizer of workshop.

28. The Fund for the Improvement of Post-Secondary Education, a unit of the Department of Health, Education, and Welfare, awarded a two-year grant of $123,220, which was later extended for a third year, for the purpose of museum dissemination, to include internship training and travel and also the preparation of written materials. Two years later (Sept. 1979) the Kellogg Foundation made its first-ever grant to a museum, awarding the Exploratorium $566,400 over five years to train museum personnel, publish, and organize conferences. By the end of 1982, those dissemination activities were funded by well over $1 million, representing over 10% of the museum's expenditure. See Exploratorium memo by Frank Oppenheimer, "Where We Are and Where Do We Go From Here—II," Nov. 1982.

29. Interviews with summer interns, July 1980, Richard Griego (director) and Jeff Nathanson (media specialist), Southwest Resource for Science and Engineering, University of New Mexico; Rita Sway, Office of Education, Humboldt County, Eureka, Calif.; Michael Gore (executive director), Questacon Project, ANU, Canberra, Australia; Elsa Feher (coordinator and exhibit developer), Reuben H. Fleet Science Center, San Diego, Calif.

30. Manuscript by K. C. Cole, "The Exploratorium Science Media Conference: One View," San Francisco, Feb. 13-14, 1981.

31. *Nova* 908, originally broadcast on PBS on March 7, 1982 (copyright 1982 WGBH Educational Foundation).

32. Frank Oppenheimer, "Let the Teachers Teach and the Learners Learn," paper

presented at a conference on evaluation sponsored by the Far West Lab, Redwood City, Calif., 1977.

33. Kenneth Starr, director of the Milwaukee Public Museum, "Exploration and Culture: Oppenheimer Receives Distinguished Service Award," *Museum News* 36(Nov./Dec. 1982):36.

Chapter 6. The Mutual Enrichment of Art and Science

1. Frank Oppenheimer, "The Exploratorium: A Playful Museum Combines Perception and Art in Science Education," *American Journal of Physics* 40(July 1972):978.

2. Art historian Samuel Y. Edgerton has argued that Galileo, educated in a family of artists and acquainted with the three-dimensional effect of chiaroscuro, recognized the dark spots on the moon that he viewed through his telescope as shadows and inferred the presence of mountains, while others were merely puzzled by the strange variegated surface. See "Renaissance Pictorial Imagination and Galileo's Universe," paper presented May 27, 1983, AAAS, Detroit, Mich.

3. One of the young artists who started in this way, Douglas Hollis, was appointed to the Exploratorium Board of Directors in 1987.

4. As this book was nearing completion, a controversy erupted over the physical appearance of a restaurant concession that was about to open in the museum. Some staff members were offended by its sleek, postmodernist look that others found attractive, and once again dispute centered on the graphics department and the image that the museum wanted to present to the public. (See Chapter 3.)

5. Frank Oppenheimer, interview with Ruth Newhall in *San Francisco Chronicle Datebook* Oct. 19, 1969.

6. *San Francisco Examiner* Jan. 12, 1972.

7. John J. Montgomery made mankind's first successful flight with a controlled and safe landing in a heavier-than-air craft, at Otay Mesa, San Diego County, Calif., on August 28, 1883 (long before the Wright brothers' flight in 1906). The later model of the Montgomery glider displayed at the Exploratorium was flown in 1911. According to its curator at Santa Clara University, "Had the ribs been enclosed in the fabric sleeves, the plane could have been flown" (letter to Frank Oppenheimer from Arthur Dunning Spearman, S.J., August 1, 1969).

8. On June 12, 1979, Bryan Allen made the twenty-three mile crossing from England to France in two hours and forty-nine minutes. The plane's inventor, Dr. Paul MacCready, himself a glider pilot and president of the AeroVironment Company in Pasadena, Calif., spoke at the Exploratorium during the craft's installation there. See *The Exploratorium* 4(April–May 1980).

9. Letter from Don Stanely, executive editor of *The Pacific Sun,* to Bill Baker, Exploratorium public relations officer, Dec. 26, 1974.

10. Traveling exhibit catalog, *Multiple Interaction Team* (Cambridge, Mass.: MIT, 1971).

11. Alexander Fried, "The Rise of the Technologies," *This World, San Francisco Chronicle-Examiner* Feb. 25, 1973.

12. "The Merging of Science and Conceptual Art," *San Francisco Chronicle* Feb. 11, 1973. In his somewhat critical review of the MIT show, Frankenstein pronounced that the difference between technology and art is that technology gets its grants from business corporations and art gets its support from foundations.

13. In a letter to Oppenheimer dated May 28, 1975, Victor J. Danilov, director of the Chicago Museum of Science and Industry, dispatches final business of their

collaboration and expresses his discontent with the endeavor: "I am glad that the project is finally over. The exhibit itself never lived up to expectations, and the headaches hardly justified the time, effort and funds. I hope ASTC has better luck on its cooperative traveling exhibits." At the same time, the project did increase political solidarity among the museums, no doubt contributing to their success in gaining greater government and public support. See letter from Danilov to Congressman John Brademas, chairman of the House Select Education Committee, June 10, 1975.

14. Association of Science-Technology Centers, *A Profile of Science and Technology Centers* (Washington, D.C., 1975).

15. Originally published in *The Gates* (New York: McGraw-Hill, 1977).

16. He is also known as Carl Lander, a name that he assumed at an exhibit of his environmental work "Landings," at the Los Angeles County Museum in 1973. He later reverted to his original name, Bücher.

17. *San Francisco Examiner* interview, Sept. 12, 1971. See also Keith Power, "Keeping You in Touch," *San Francisco Chronicle* Sept. 10, 1971.

18. The NEA awarded $3000 as a matching grant for the construction of the dome. It was built in a warehouse of the American Zoetrope Company, owned by Francis Ford Coppola. Among the volunteers who worked for food and lodging on the project was C. P. Hall, who had invented the water bed in a furniture design course as a student at UC Davis. The original plan for the dome included a water bed, but that turned out to be infeasible.

19. Leni Isaacs, "You Can Sing a Note and See the Pitch Light Up," *San Francisco Chronicle Datebook* Jan. 6, 1974. See also L. Isaacs, "Demystified Music in the Exploratorium," *Music Educators Journal* 61(April 1975); and "Exploring the Way Music Is Made," *San Francisco Examiner* July 23, 1974.

20. The NEA Art Education Division awarded $20,000, which was matched by $10,000 grants from the California Arts Commission (letter to Frank Oppenheimer from William Kent III, March 7, 1974,) and the Mary A. Crocker Foundation.

21. The initial selection committee included Oppenheimer, Peter Richards (coordinator of the program), Ben Hazard (director of education at the Oakland Art Museum), Ruth Asawa (a San Francisco artist and teacher and the founder and director of the Alvarado Arts Workshop), Gyorgy Kepes (director of the Center for Visual Studies, Massachusetts Institute of Technology), William Wiley (a San Francisco artist), Lydia Vitale (video art curator, De Saisset Art Gallery, University of Santa Clara), Steven Goldstine (director of the Neighborhood Arts Program), Lanier Graham (director of the Institute for Aesthetic Development and former curator at the De Young Museum).

22. Veto power was exercised on one occasion when an artist proposed an anamorphic work that would have occupied too much floor space.

23. That is why occasional exhibits of an artist's sketchbooks or notebooks or even retrospective shows that feature developmental works are so illuminating.

24. Hollis speculated that the famed song of the sirens, whose seduction Odysseus resisted only by having himself lashed to the mast of his ship and stuffing the ears of his crew with beeswax, was also produced by an Aeolian harp, namely the ship itself as its mast and taut ropes were strummed by the wind (interview with artist, Feb. 1980). See also letter from D. Hollis to the Exploratorium, 1979, and Michael Zipkin's review of "Aeolian Harp" in *Odalisque I* 7(Oct. 14-Nov. 3, 1977).

25. Frank Oppenheimer, "Aesthetics and the Right Answer," paper delivered Dec. 29, 1972, AAAS Meeting, Washington, D.C.; published in *The Humanist* March/April, 1979.

Chapter 7. Funding the Museum

1. At a luncheon for civic leaders held at the Palace on November 19, 1968, at which Oppenheimer made his proposal, state senator George Moscone noted that San Francisco has "no museum devoted to physical sciences, the inner world of human biology, and the complex achievements of technology" (David Perlman, *San Francisco Chronicle* Nov. 20, 1968).

2. Interview with John May, March 1980.

3. According to a financial statement of Feb. 10, 1970, a total of $101,280 was raised, and $31,280 of that was in individual donations.

4. Interview with Donald H. McLaughlin, March 1980.

5. Frank Oppenheimer, "Discussion of Budget During Subsequent Years" and financial report, Dec. 1, 1969. See also Exploratorium report "Preliminary Costs Estimates" prepared in October 1968, where Oppenheimer projects an annual operating cost of $650,000 at maturity, figured at pre-inflationary standards.

6. The NSF Office of Public Understanding of Science began accepting proposals in Dec. 1970, but its director, Dr. Alfred H. Rosenthal, turned a deaf ear to Oppenheimer's suggestions regarding the possible connotations of that title. See letter from Frank Oppenheimer, March 9, 1971.

7. Exploratorium application to the Student and Cooperative Program of the Pre-College Education in Science Division, NSF, for support of a high school student program in the Exploratorium shop, April 1971.

8. In 1981 the NSF awarded $329,000 to the Exploratorium for a three-year project, "A Series of Museum Exhibits on Electricity," to enhance public understanding of that complex subject, and it subsequently gave $1 million to the museum's Middle and High School Teacher Training Institutes.

9. Conversation with Nancy Hanks, Washington, D.C., Jan. 1979. See also Nancy Hanks, "The Arts in America," *Museum News* Nov. 1973:45.

10. Hearings before the Select Subcommittee on Education, Committee on Education and Labor, House of Representatives, 93rd Congress, 2nd session, on H.R. 332, held May and June 1974. Congressman John Brademas chaired the sessions on a bill authorizing support for a permanent, federal museum agency. Frank Oppenheimer testified in support of the bill with a prepared statement.

11. Panel organized by the Council on Museum Education, N.Y.

12. Barbara Y. Newsom and Adele Z. Silver, eds. (Berkeley: University of California Press, 1978).

13. Letter from Barbara Newsom to John R. Spencer, NEA, August 2, 1974.

14. An NEA press release of Jan. 12, 1971, announcing the new program, expresses its policy of promoting the transformation of museums from "warehouses of objects into exciting centers of educational experience."

15. See Chapter 6.

16. Interview with Jon Boorstin, Jan. 1980. See also the account by Eric Saarinen, cameraman for the project, in *American Cinematographer* March 1975. Copyright and distribution rights for the seventeen-minute, 35mm color film are jointly held by Jon Boorstin and the Exploratorium.

17. "In the act that establishes the National Endowment for the Humanities, the term *humanities* includes, but is not limited to, the study of the following disciplines: history; philosophy; languages; linguistics; literature; archaeology; jurisprudence; the history, theory and criticism of the arts; ethics; comparative religion; and those aspects of the social sciences that employ historical or philosophical approaches" (Guidelines, National Endowment for the Humanities, Division of Research Programs, 1988).

18. *The Exploratorium* 3(April–May 1979):2. See also Exploratorium grant application to the National Endowment for the Humanities, Nov. 15, 1978, to Feb. 1, 1979, "Albert Einstein in Context: An Exhibition to Interpret the Work of Albert Einstein in Conjunction with the Centennial of his Birth." A theme of the exhibit was Einstein's belief that "a comprehensive and simplifying idea mathematically expressed, could be more trustworthy than the results of individual experiments." The exhibits, though intended to teach some physics, "will also be concerned with an understanding of the historical processes that are involved in the development of physics." Besides showing what Einstein did, they would display the triumphs and the puzzles that confronted him at the turn of the century.

19. This portion of the grant was for the purchase of a set of biographical panels on Einstein that had been created by the American Institute of Physics for centennial display.

20. Bruce R. Wheaton, ed., *The Rise and Fall of the Aether: Einstein in Context* (San Francisco: The Exploratorium, 1981).

21. At the luncheon for civic leaders organized by Ruth Newhall in Nov. 1968, Oppenheimer won statements of support from San Francisco mayor Joseph L. Alioto, state senator George Moscone, several regents of the University of California, members of the Palace of Fine Arts League, and the San Francisco Unified Education District. With the help of their letters of endorsement, the city Recreation and Parks Commission was persuaded to approve the Exploratorium's use of the building at a cost of $1 a year (Feb. 27, 1969; see Chapter 1). See also letter from John May, executive secretary, William R. Hewlett Foundation, to Frank Oppenheimer, March 25, 1975.

22. Exploratorium study by Virginia C. Rubin, "The Exploratorium: Comparative Figures Showing Allocation of San Francisco Hotel Tax," August 1983.

23. Frank Oppenheimer, "Status Report," June 16, 1969, The Palace of Arts and Science Foundation.

24. See note 21.

25. Letter from Frank Oppenheimer to Steven White, Alfred P. Sloan Foundation, May 24, 1969. See also letter from Oppenheimer to Thomas Ford, Alfred P. Sloan Foundation, Feb. 19, 1970.

26. This award represented a vindication of the Exploratorium's exhibit philosophy, for it explicitly acknowledged not only the ongoing exhibit development program but also the museum's policy of looking backward, reflecting, revising, and revamping old exhibits and sometimes replacing them with new ones (conversation with Sally Duensing, principal grant coordinator, March 1987).

27. Letter from Harold Snedcof, Rockefeller Brothers Foundation, to Parmer Fuller III, chairman of the Exploratorium board, April 3, 1974. A letter of "unequivocal commendation on behalf of Dr. Oppenheimer for the educational programs he provides for the youth of the entire Bay Area" was also sent, from the superintendent of the San Francisco Unified School District to Snedcof, May 29, 1973.

28. Though beleaguered by strikes, law suits, and tax protests, the San Francisco School Board voted on June 24, 1974, to appropriate funds for its participation in the Exploratorium SITE program. Small grants were also awarded, by the California-based Cowell Foundation and the David and Lucille Packard Foundation, for the construction of a classroom building inside the Exploratorium.

29. Letter to Frank Oppenheimer from Nancy Dennis, program officer, Ford Foundation, Feb. 13, 1976.

30. Although the Lux Foundation found the explainer aspect of the Exploratorium program "peripheral to (its) vocational emphasis," it was ready to support the shop apprentice program (letter to Frank Oppenheimer from Lawrence I. Kramer, July 15, 1970). The Irvine Foundation, likewise, was more interested in the practical training

that the program offered than in its promise to teach substantive science ("Guidelines for Application," James Irvine Foundation).

31. See Chapter 4.

32. Frank Oppenheimer, application for NEH challenge grant, 1977.

33. See note 10.

34. Lee Kimche, "Science Centers: A Potential for Learning," *Science* 199 (1978):270-273.

35. Interview with Signa Dodge, Feb. 4, 1980.

36. Rubin held positions as secretary of the American Ditchley Foundation, New York, and as development director of the Antioch School of Law, Washington, D.C.

37. Exploratorium study for HEW grant application, by Virginia C. Rubin, "A Program to Stimulate and Facilitate the Development of Exploratorium-like Learning Centers as Adjunctive Resources for Broad Spectrum Science Education in Colleges and Universities and Beyond," Sept. 1, 1977.

38. Robert Semper earned his Ph.D. from Johns Hopkins University in 1973, for research on low-temperature magnetic studies of ultrathin iron films. He also taught and conducted research at St. Olaf College, Minnesota, and at Lawrence Berkeley Laboratories and the University of California at San Francisco.

39. The subsidized residents came for anywhere from several hours to several months to study the museum's operational techniques, and by the fall of 1980, more than sixty educators and museum professionals had taken part in the program.

40. Mary Ellen Munley, *Catalysts for Change* (Washington, D.C.: The Kellogg Projects in Museum Education, 1986).

41. Letter to Frank Oppenheimer from William H. Baldwin, April 12, 1978. Thanks to minor delays in fund-raising, there was time before the museum closed for reconstruction for a visit by the president of the Kresge Foundation, and he was impressed.

42. See Chapter 5. Although this bill authorized identification of the Exploratorium as a science education resource, it did not guarantee funds for the purpose; they had to be reallocated every year.

43. The foundation awarded $250,000 for four years "to improve and continue prototypical educational and cultural mission, and to support, strengthen and build management continuity" (1981).

44. Exploratorium report by Virginia C. Rubin, "Facts and Figures: The Exploratorium, a Museum of Science and Human Perception," August 1981.

45. Karl E. Meyer, *The Art Museum: Power, Money, Ethics* (New York: William Morrow and Co., 1979).

46. Interview with John May, March 1980.

47. Letter to Frank Oppenheimer, cited in *The Exploratorium* 4(Aug.-Sept. 1980):16.

48. 1978 Annual Report of the William and Flora Hewlett Foundation.

49. Board chairman F. Van Kasper announced White's appointment at a press conference on February 9, 1987. White assumed office on April 1, 1987.

50. As this book is being completed, construction of a restaurant is under way, and the museum is considering extensive renovation, including the construction of a parking garage ("Memo: Building Renovation Considerations," May 20, 1988). The disputes over the feasibility and desirability of those improvements are reminiscent of the controversies reported here.

Chapter 8. Conclusion and Prospect

1. For a remarkably insightful appreciation of the political ideology that is embodied in museums and museum exhibits, see Donna Harraway, "Teddy Bear Patriarchy: Taxidermy in the Garden of Eden, New York City, 1908-1936," *Social Text* 4(1984):20-64. Harraway focuses on the New York Museum of Natural History as an ideological case study. I am grateful to Martin Donougho for bringing this article to my attention.

2. Interview with Sheila Grinell, April 1987. See also Sheila Grinell, "Profile. Starting the Exploratorium: A Personal Recollection," *American Scientist* 76(May 1988).

3. Frank Oppenheimer, "Aesthetics and the Right Answer," paper delivered Dec. 29, 1972, at the AAAS Meeting, Washington, D.C.; published in *The Humanist* March-April 1979.

4. See discussion in Chapter 4 on the evolution of this exhibit.

5. In March 1987 the Alfred P. Sloan Foundation awarded $200,000 to the museum to expand and update its exhibits on human perception. The grant also included a provision to make an exhibit of ongoing research. It would allow a group of scientists "working on research in cognition and human perception . . . to take intensive sabbaticals at the Exploratorium in order to work with exhibit development staff and incorporate up-to-the-minute research in the prototypes of new exhibits."

6. Opinions attributed to Sally Duensing are based on several interviews in June 1981, Aug. 1986, and March 1987.

7. Visitor reactions were assessed, of course, during Oppenheimer's lifetime. Two doctoral dissertations based on the observation of audience response to the Exploratorium are "The Ethology of Teaching: a Perspective from the Observation of Families in Science Centers," by Judy Diamond (University of California, 1980), and "Friendship and the Museum Experience: the Interrelationship of Social Ties and Learning," by Lee Draper (University of California, 1984). Exploratorium studies of audience behavior were also made by Jenefer Merrill (1976) and by L. Draper and J. Scola (1980).

8. Nelson H. H. Graburn, "The Museum and the Visitor Experience," in *The Visitor and the Museum,* Linda Draper, ed. (Washington, D.C.: American Association of Museums Education Committee, 1977).

9. Cited in Mary Ellen Munley, *Catalysts for Change* (Washington, D.C.: The Kellogg Projects in Museum Education, 1986).

Index